Praise for

Back from Suicide

"*Back from Suicide* is a must-read for everyone, at this moment of our sad history, when teenage suicide is on the rise. I did not put it down, except to eat and sleep. It is a tour de force—pitch-perfect (Wagnerian though it often is). It is a mother's journey to trace the arc, the soul, and the burn-out of this shooting star. Rimer has brought his greatness to life, over and over again. She is a sleuth, a truth teller, and a superb writer. Patrick shines on, even in the depths of his family's and his mother's grief."

> -**Nancy Cobb**, *In Lieu of Flowers: A Conversation for the Living*

"*Back from Suicide* is stunning. It's about love, which drives a mother's quest to understand the roots of her brilliant son's suicide. I have savored it, struggled with it, and felt it roll around in my mind. Lisette Rimer's seamless prose is a tribute to her son's life and an insightful examination of how little one may know those we hold closest and the despair of depression. I am in awe of what she has undertaken and accomplished."

> -**Nancy Pritchard Weiss**, columnist, *The Villager* newspapers, Co-Poet Laureate, Pomfret, CT

"This book chronicles a mother's poignant search for answers after her high-achieving multi-talented twenty-three-year-old son commits suicide far from home. The quest reveals guilt, anger, pain, and bewilderment but also provides useful information about the evolution of treatment for depression and prevention of suicide."

> -**Steve Kotchko**, retired journalist

"By its embodiment of unflinchingly meticulous self-examination, *Back from Suicide* articulates the extraordinarily courageous and penetrating journey of a parent whose child takes his own life. Expressed in uncomplicated and genuine, candid writing, the book's unique accomplishment is its easily understandable, detailed immersion of the reader in emotion, disbelief, and confusion. Repeated attempts to grasp ways to fathom the profoundly misunderstood disease that is mental depression offer a deeply thorough path towards awareness, knowledge, recognition, and acceptance."

-**Ann Warde**, composer, US-UK Fulbright Scholar

"*Back from Suicide* is suffused with the raw love that only a mother can feel and the emotional honesty of someone who has done the hard, unending work of coping with any parent's worst nightmare. Rimer brings Patrick alive on the page. Parents struggling with the premature death of a child will benefit from her willingness to be vulnerable and honest. The same is true for family members of those who are coming out of the closet and struggling with crippling depression. Anyone contemplating suicide should read her story to understand the pain and hurt it causes the loved ones left behind who forever struggle to make meaning of grief in that endless detour that leads only to exhaustion and never comprehension.

Back from Suicide is a timely reminder of the stories behind the statistics of worsening mental health in America. It packs several gut punches and made me cry. It's a testament to the heart and soul Rimer poured into more than fifteen years of trying to make sense of something so senseless."

-**James Hohmann**, columnist, *Washington Post*

"A humble, courageous account that sets out from the natural desire for answers and leads into richer depths, to locate understanding in the original sense of the word: to stand in the midst of. Rimer shows us that we never arrive at knowing, but as Rilke counsels, we can 'live the questions now,' and we can choose, again and again, to turn toward truth."

-**Linden Crawford**, MFA

"In this ultimately uplifting odyssey, Marie Lisette Rimer depicts her despairing, obsessive struggle to understand the suicide of her wonder child, and in the process comes to know her son in a way she might never have. This book is a rich and informative portrait of Patrick Wood's artistry, intellect, power, and relationships— all of which hid his painful and futile battle with depression. By baring the anatomy of depression, Rimer offers sufferers and their families a path toward healing through understanding."

-**Debbie Danielpour**, professor of screenwriting at Boston University, published in *AGNI*, *Lilith*, *Salamander*, *Natural Bridge*, *International Women Screenwriters*, *The Handbook of Screenwriting Studies*, and *The Journal of Screenwriting*

"*Back from Suicide* is a story of a woman who grappled with the gut-wrenching pain that she and her family experienced after her son, Patrick Wood, whom I knew as a piano student of extraordinary capability, made the tragic decision to end his life a few years after I taught him. It is a story of a no-holds-barred quest for understanding of the grim choice made by this remarkable young man, whose premature death resulted in an unfathomable loss to the world. Her account, based on extensive research and experience, encompasses reflection on death, mental health and suicide in general, and delves into Patrick's intellectual brilliance, musical giftedness, social standing, gayness, depression, family history, and end of life. The author's narrative closes by embracing grief as a 'balance between sorrow and beauty.' It is framed by eloquent words from Patrick's beloved twin sister."

-**Deborah Yardley Beers**, former Associate Chair, Piano Department, Longy School of Music

"Rimer's deeply pained and beautifully written exploration of her son's death from suicide, is at once a celebration of a life, a reckoning with a death, and an impassioned inquiry in how and why the inconceivable could happen."
-BookLife Reviews

Back from Suicide

Back from Suicide

PATRICK DAVID WOOD
OCT. 29, 1982 — JAN. 31, 2006
BORN IN MANCHESTER, CT.
DIED IN BERLIN, GERMANY

UND RUH' IN EINEM STILLEN GEBIET.
ICH LEB' ALLEIN IN MEINEM HIMMEL.
IN MEINEM LIEBEN, IN MEINEM LIED.
F. RÜCKERT

STANFORD
2005

Before and After
The Essential Patrick

Marie Lisette Rimer

ISBN 979-8-9877989-0-4

Credits on illustrations are considered an extension
of the copyright page.

Printed and bound in the United States of America

Published by Hillside Woods
Pomfret Center, Connecticut 06259
www.backfromsuicide.com

All proceeds from the sale of *Back from Suicide* will be donated
to the Patrick D. Wood '01 Memorial Scholarship
Pomfret School, Pomfret, Connecticut.

www.patrickwoodprize.org

Cover design by Libby Wood and Nora Robbins
Cover photograph: Patrick, Stanford graduation, 2005
by Myles Morrison

Book design by Marie Lisette Rimer

The following are gratefully acknowledged for reprinted content:

Excerpts from "The Essential Patrick" by Ryan Wirtz, Stanford in Berlin memorial for Patrick Wood, February 15, 2006. Excerpts from emails and phone calls from Ryan Wirtz, 2006–2018. Reprinted by permission of Ryan Wirtz and Judith Hennessey.

Excerpts from *Night* by Elie Wiesel, translated by Stella Rodway. Copyright 1960 by MacGibbon & Kee, pages 2–3. Copyright renewed 1988 by The Collins Publishing Group. Reprinted by permission of Hill and Wang, a division of Farrar, Straus and Giroux.

Excerpts from "When I first met Patrick," by Stephen Pryce, "Patrick Wood Memorial, a place for your thoughts, photos, stories, or memories of Pat," www.patrickwood.blogspot.com/2006/, May 7, 2006. Reprinted by permission of Stephen Pryce.

Excerpts from *The Sorrows of Young Werther* by Johann Wolfgang von Goethe, translated by Burton Pike, Random House, 2004. Reprinted by permission of Penguin Random House.

Excerpt from "Zeugnis Patrick Wood" by Klaus Bogenberger, September 17, 2004. Reprinted by permission of Klaus Bogenberger.

Excerpt from "Abroad: The Newsletter of the Bing Overseas Studies Program," Reprinted by permission of the H.G. Will Center for Overseas Studies in Berlin.

Excerpts from "There Is No Untrodden Snow" by Kurt Tucholsky (aka Kaspar Hauser), translated by Stephen Pryce, 2005, *The World Stage*, Rowohlt Publisher, Vol. 14, April 7, 1931. Reprinted by permission of Stephen Pryce and Rowohlt Publisher.

Excerpts from "I am Lost to the World" by Friedrich Rückert, translation copyright © by Emily Ezust. Reprinted by permission of Emily Ezust.

Excerpts from letter to Robert Wood and family, February 10, 2006, and "For Patrick" by Karen Kramer, February 15, 2006. Reprinted by permission of Karen Kramer.

Excerpts from *Patrick David Wood: Piano Solo and Trio* CD notes by Ann Warde, remastered by Mark Thayer, Signature Sounds, 2011, and from *Playing for Patrick* CD notes by Ann Warde, remastered by Mark Thayer, Signature Sounds, 2015. Reprinted by permission of Ann Warde.

Excerpt from "Dear family and friends of Pat!" by Tobias Bader, "Patrick Wood Memorial, a place for your thoughts, photos, stories, or memories of Pat" by Tobias Bader, www.patrickwood.blogspot.com/2006/, March 6, 2006. Reprinted by permission of Tobias Bader.

Excerpts from "Longy School of Music Student Progress Report, January 25, 1997," and "Longy School of Music Preparatory Studies Division Student Performance Evaluation Form," school year 1996-1997, by Deborah Yardley Beers. Excerpts from emails to the author by Deborah Yardley Beers, April 27, 2019 and May 3, 2019. Reprinted by permission of Deborah Yardley Beers.

Excerpt from "Longy School of Music Preparatory Studies Theory Evaluation Form," by Howard Frazin, June 5, 1997. Excerpt from an email to the author by Howard Frazin, March 14, 2022. Reprinted by permission of Howard Frazin.

Excerpt from "Pomfret School Progress Report," by Mitch Pinkowski, Spring 2001. Reprinted by permission of Mitch Pinkowski.

Excerpt from an email to the author by Phillip Falk, September 17, 2011. Reprinted by permission of Phillip Falk.

Excerpt from "What Hope for Dead Loved Ones?" copyright owned by the Watch Tower Bible and Tract Society of Pennsylvania, published by Jehovah's Witnesses, 1987. Reprinted by permission of the Watch Tower Bible and Tract Society of Pennsylvania.

Excerpt from "For Patrick" by Brad Davis, February 20, 2006. Reprinted by permission of Brad Davis.

Excerpt from an email to the author by Ben Davidson, November 30, 2021. Reprinted by permission of Ben Davidson.

Excerpt from "Words for Pat's service" by Andrew Nielsen. Excerpts from "Twenty-Three" by Andrew Nielsen (MC Lars), *This Gigantic Robot Kills*, by MC

Lars, Amoeba Records, San Francisco, CA, March 12, 2009, recorded by Horris Records, Redondo Beach, CA, The Oglio Entertainment Group, Inc. 2009. Reprinted by permission of Andrew Nielsen.

Excerpts from emails to the author by Jerome Murphy, March 2, 3, 4, and 10, 2020. Reprinted by permission of Jerome Murphy.

Excerpt from "Recommendation for Patrick Wood," Jerry Cain, February 18, 2004. Reprinted by permission of Jerry Cain.

Excerpt from "It's Time to Tolerate Your Equals So Think Before You Speak" by Sara M_____, the *DiRectory*, published by Rectory School, May 31, 2009. Reprinted by permission of Sara M_____ and Rectory School.

Excerpt from "Gareth Thomas" by Gary Smith, *Sports Illustrated*, May 3, 2010. Reprinted by permission of Authentic Brands Group LLC.

Excerpt from "Amanda Todd and Newtown: What Do They Have in Common?" Jason Yingqing Zhao, the *DiRectory*, published by Rectory School, March 1, 2013. Reprinted by permission of Jason Yingqing Zhao and Rectory School.

Excerpt from "My Story: Struggling, Bullying, Suicide, Self Harm" by Amanda Todd, www.youtube.com/watch?v=vOHXGNx-E7E, September 7, 2012. Reprinted by permission of Carol Todd.

Excerpt from "Recent grad dies in Berlin" by Courtney Weaver, the *Stanford Daily*, February 8, 2006. Reprinted by permission of the *Stanford Daily*.

Excerpts from *Night Falls Fast: Understanding Suicide* by Kay Redfield Jamison, Vintage Books, A Division of Random House, Inc., 1999. Reprinted by permission of Penguin Random House, Inc.

Excerpts from *Against Depression* by Peter D. Kramer, Penguin Books, 2005. Reprinted by permission of Penguin Random House, Inc.

Excerpt from *The Noonday Demon: An Atlas of Depression* by Andrew Solomon, Scribner, 2001. Reprinted by permission of Simon & Schuster, Inc.

Dedicated to Patrick

who achieved everything but life.

He lived his life deliberately, in the spirit of what his friends and I called "The Essential Patrick."

—Ryan Wirtz
"The Essential Patrick," 2006

Note from the Author

This book is about my journey through suicide. I am writing about my own interactions with Patrick and my own reactions to his death. I am not speaking for others who played an enormous role. Bob, Colin, and Libby idolized Patrick, and he knew that. But I do not speak for them. I would not presume to know their inner thoughts, not even those of Bob, who has a right to his own interpretation of Pat's story.

Real names are used throughout except where indicated. Most were contacted and in agreement with publication. Some could not be found or did not respond. Regardless of consent, no one is meant to be implicated in Patrick's death. No one is responsible but Patrick himself.

Contents

Foreword   xxiii
Preface   xxix

The Last Day   1
The News   7
Panic   13
What Happened   21
Who Was He?   53
After Berlin   95
Back to School   107
Two Griefs   121
Afterthoughts   129
The Gravestone   143
Discovery   149
"The Project"   163
Other Deaths   177
Stanford   183
The Notes   197
Reckoning   213
Dr. Hu   233
Christopher Street Day   251
Munich   259
Where Did He Come From?   263
Resurrection   285
The Interment   297
The Long Term   305
Epilogue   313

Appreciation   317
Illustrations   327
Notes   331

Foreword

When we were twenty-three years old, my twin brother Patrick died of carbon monoxide inhalation on a cold and snowy night, alone in his apartment in Berlin. He had placed three cast-iron skillets with charcoal on top of hot pads in his shower. He left a note warning those who would find him of poisonous gases in the bathroom. He laid a towel along the bottom of the bathroom door. The images of this scene live in my body.

I was in my house in Burlington, Vermont, when my mother called to tell me. It was late afternoon Monday, February 6, 2006, sunny, the ground covered in a light layer of snow. I had just graduated from the University of Vermont with a bachelor's degree in studio art. Patrick had earned his bachelor's in mathematics from Stanford with distinction in 2005 and had been accepted to the computer science master's program there. In our twinship, we were standing on two different psychic foundations. I was plotting my move to California—a fantasy I had discussed with Patrick a month before he died. "We could find a place in San Francisco when you go back to get your master's," I told him. I was hoping to begin sharing our adult life together, filled with banter and adventure. I was hoping while Patrick was dying.

The tone in my mother's voice was terrible. "Lib. Are you sitting down?" She was crying, and I remember her voice as solemn, trembling, and it scared me. I walked down the hall into my bedroom and closed the door. "He didn't make it…. Patrick … he didn't make it," she said. I remember feeling a sharp pain below my heart. I recall very little of what either of us said after that.

Patrick and I were close. I adored his sense of humor and revered his talents. We had a silly, sarcastic humor and could spend hours laughing, playing outside, drawing, listening to Tchaikovsky and Radiohead, cooking, playing computer games, and watching movies. In my eyes, Patrick had so many admirable traits: he was gentle, kind, brilliant, studious, hilarious, sensitive, goofy, handsome, and successful. I knew him to have depressive and perfectionist tendencies, and my mother and I collaborated on ways to support him, to boost his self-esteem, alleviate his nerves. We recognized that his mental life entailed a strong and critical inertia. We knew he set a high bar and that his notable achievements never measured up to his expectations. Still, there was creativity, laughter, improvisation, and genuine connection. We were a strong and playful team. I hold these memories dearly.

A few days after Patrick's death, my older brother Colin, my mother and father, and I boarded a plane to Berlin to identify and retrieve Patrick's body. While we were there, the Stanford Center in Berlin, where Patrick had studied in 2004, held a memorial service for him, which marked the contrast of life before and after my twin brother. When we returned home to Connecticut, we held Patrick's funeral at the gothic-style chapel of our alma mater, Pomfret School, where he was valedictorian in 2001. Over four hundred people attended his service. Friends and teachers praised him and played music. Family cried. Bagpipes guided footsteps from the chapel to the base of Pomfret Hill, where we bid our farewells as Patrick transitioned into the essence of what would never be. The ground was frozen, covered in snow. Hereford cows speckled the fields adjoining the cemetery. We were surrounded by life, struck with grief, shock, and guilt.

Losing Patrick altered our family dynamic. Security became obsolete, smiles devolved to sullen stares, and laughter—it disappeared. I moved home to Hillside, the small farm in Connecticut where we both grew up, to be with my mother and father. I needed to learn from my family how to move with grief, make meaning, and honor my twin. In many tearful conversations, my parents shed light on the other suicides in our family, and I began to see Patrick's depression within the greater context of health and family heritage. Like Patrick, the depressive genetic weight carried by our grandparents presented itself with no other viable options to end their suffering. I learned that my mother's mother overdosed on prescription medication and that my father's father drowned himself in a river. My parents began to share untold stories of sadness, resilience, and determination in our lineage. There was an emerging platform of open dialogue and polyphony. We seemed to make sense of loss by turning our attention to family history, by honoring those before us—a group to which Patrick now belonged. We were finding our way, and I began to feel hopeful, driven by primary process thinking once again, planning a future without my other half.

My mother, especially, centered her wonderings in family history. I could witness the catharsis she embodied in making sense of her own character traits and the decisions she made as a mother. She brightened in our conversations about my grandparents, and this process seemed to relieve her of endless circular doubt. It seemed to give precedence for her imperfections. In my own grief, I was looking to her for grounding, and I, too, sensed a revitalization in family roots. I began to feel connected and driven by pride. I fantasized about what I could become in life. She shared with me that her father served as a flight surgeon during the Korean War and became chief resident at UCLA in 1958 as a gastroenterologist. His father, my great-grandfather, was a clinical professor of pediatrics at Bellevue Hospital in New York City and volunteered his medical services to Ellis Island immigrants for twenty years.

In living and posthumous spirit, my family made the new meaning that grief demands. They inspired me to get a master's degree in psychology, to counsel children with depression and anxiety in Hawaii, and assess psychiatric patients at a hospital in the Bay Area. Patrick had been admitted to Stanford Hospital for suicidal ideation while he was a student there. I wanted to understand his experience. I wanted to make up for not being with Pat at the hospital.

A psychoanalysis teacher once told me that there is always more to learn, and that through psychology, we are ever informed. She made me curious about the process of not knowing, of self-analysis. She shed light on why I have watched my mother struggle with understanding for the last sixteen years, ten of which were spent in writing this book. My mother had much to learn. She went through years of therapy. She read books about suicide and depression. She retraced Patrick's life from Connecticut to Palo Alto to Germany. Her discoveries forced her to make sense of the cues, the ambiguities, the signs that didn't add up. She recreated the part of Patrick she had missed.

I traveled much of the same road with her. We combined our discoveries. We connected by sharing stories of Pat. We accepted each other. We described our guilt without fear of reaction. We compared endless stories of suicidal patients and victims. Every one brought us closer to the paradox of suicide, the often glistening surface of a shattered psyche. Every one helped me be with my mind, be free in my thinking, accept myself, and continue to love Patrick.

I miss him dearly, I often dream of him, and I lie awake at night riddled with guilt and regret. Every day, I am generating new experiences with him, finding new meaning through my profession, within conversations and adventures with my mother and my partner, immersing in nature and the arts. Patrick walked with a depression that I had not understood—still do not understand, and I often wonder if his suffering was curable. I only know that I have to keep trying.

Back from Suicide is my mother's attempt to keep trying. It exposes what she feels she did wrong and what she did right. It examines an illness we all underestimated, a mental illness hidden under stunning mental achievements. It goes beyond the surface of depression because it has to. It has to reach the other children isolated because of their differences, teased for their awkwardness, bullied for being gay, and mentally damaged by those assaults. It has to reach the children who can't understand their suffering because that very ability is under attack. It has to reach the other Patricks who are suffering alone, who are unexplainably sad, who don't fit in, who spend hours in their room because they can't risk more disappointment. They sleep too much. It's the only escape. And then it dawns on them: Why not sleep forever? *Back from Suicide* explains the loss of control because it has to. It's the only way to reveal the essential Patrick.

Elizabeth Antoinette Wood
Patrick's twin sister
September 1, 2022

Preface

While one person can never shut out the world entirely, it can always shut out them.

—Patrick Wood
"Wanted or Unwanted," 1999

Living with suicide is an oxymoron. You are living, but it's a half-life. You are not living in the full sense of the word. You are living a distortion. Every decision is undecided. Small matters become big. You can't put one foot in front of the other. Your breath is short. Your sight blurs. Your hearing dims. Your speech falters. You are like the spinning ball of death on your computer screen when it freezes. You stare at the screen, waiting for your software or your document to load. You plod away on the old operating system, the system you know, but it's slow. It can't get through the complex tasks you need, especially after you have been to a memorial service, a funeral, and a burial for your son, and when you look for his last emails, you can't open them. They are nothing but asterisks and blank spaces on the screen. You stare at the messages that have disappeared along with your son. You call a technician, who tells you your email inbox is too full. You will have to buy more storage space for your email account, and then you will have to reopen nine hundred corrupted emails. One by one. Nine hundred times. You break down on the phone. The technician waits for you to stop crying and says he's sorry.

And then there is Pat's email password sent by his friend Ryan and lost in the mass of corrupted emails. And then another password for a website with the last pictures Pat took of his friends, of Berlin, of his final Christmas tree, of treetops in the woods near his home pointing toward clouds in the sky as if he was contemplating his new place in the universe. You freeze. You cannot handle the files you are seeing. Your system crashes, and finally, there is nothing but a blinking question mark on your screen. Where is he? Where did he go? You are frozen in a time when he was here, when you could press the button on the back of your computer screen, the chime would ring, and the happy face would appear.

Instead, you restart your computer. You put the blinking question mark aside and turn back to the eulogies, the bills, the letters, the copies of death certificates, and an email dated two months before he died. You print it to make sure it doesn't disappear along with your failing operating system:

December 19, 2005

Hey Mom,

Can you do me one last favor and ask Dr. Danenhower how long he'd be willing to write the prescription for? Just so I can get an idea if I need to think about planning another visit in the spring or summer :-) Thanks!! Looking forward to seeing you really soon! I'll give you the details about the train trip as soon as I get them figured out (in the next couple of days).

Love, Pat

The cycle of shock, half-life, and crashing repeats itself. You try to break the pattern by studying his apartment, his books, his internships, his psychiatrist's notes. You travel to his cities and talk to his friends. You talk to anyone who knows him or knows suicide. Where does this come from? Where does it go? You don't get answers, but you keep trying. You settle for asking questions. The answers don't make sense. They stare at you—his sadness, his crying, his rejections. They don't add up to suicide. They mostly jump up and smack you after the fact, after the suicide. They clobber you as if they're standing on his grave shouting, "DO YOU GET IT NOW?"

Not really. I get a simplified version: Depression makes you feel so bad that you put a gun to your head, a noose around your neck, or you light charcoal in an airtight bathroom as Pat did. I know that's *what* happened, but I don't know *why*. The answers lie in the grave with Pat, and even his answers might not be enough. The search for answers is more like an endless detour around his death. Resolution comes from exhaustion instead of comprehension. There aren't any answers. Only questions.

In one of our last conversations, I asked Pat about a quote from Elie Wiesel. I was teaching his memoir in my middle school English class. *Night* is about Wiesel's survival through four concentration camps during the Holocaust. In 1944, Wiesel and the Jewish community of his hometown of Sighet, Hungary, are forced into ghettos and transported in suffocating freight trains to Auschwitz concentration camp. Wiesel loses his mother and youngest sister to the Auschwitz gas chambers. His father dies at Buchenwald not long before American troops liberate the camp in 1945. Wiesel barely survives. He becomes a living corpse of his former self. But in the calm before the darkness of his long nightmare, as a young boy, Wiesel is religious. He studies the Talmud and prays in the synagogue of Sighet. A humble caretaker named Moshe the Beadle asks Wiesel why he prays. Wiesel can't answer. He knows that praying is like living and breathing, but he doesn't know why. Moshe explains that questions are the "true dialogue," that "man raises himself toward God by the questions he asks Him.... Man questions God and God answers. But we don't understand His answers. We can't understand them. Because they come from the depths of the soul, and they stay there until death."[1]

I didn't understand Moshe's meaning, and I wanted to explain it to my ninth-grade English class. They would want to know why Wiesel prays if God doesn't answer. I waited for the right moment to ask Pat what Moshe meant as he and I ran errands the day after Christmas in 2005. He was home from Germany and would return the next day. We picked up a prescription for antidepressants from Woody Danenhower, a doctor and neighbor who had treated Pat since he was seven months old. Woody advised him to "take good care of these. It's not a good idea to leave them lying around." Pat nodded and looked down as if he didn't want to think about it, and then we jumped back in the car for the fun part of the day—the annual return of Mom's presents to get something he really wanted. We took back clothes from T.J. Maxx and books in German from the Borders bookstore in Manchester, Connecticut. *The Sorrows of Young Werther* was one of them. I knew nothing about it. I had no idea that centuries ago, readers had dressed like Werther and committed suicide or that the book was banned in Leipzig in 1775. I only knew that Patrick loved classic literature and *The Sorrows* was a short favorite, easy for him to squeeze into his backpack and bring to Berlin. I didn't want to burden him with a thick German book. He needed to socialize in Berlin more than read by himself. But Pat already had a copy, and he didn't want me to pay the added charge of buying the other German books in the US. "They're cheaper in Germany," he said, and he explained the difference between euros and US dollars. "How did you learn to read them?" I asked. "You get the sense of it," he said, "and then it just comes. You absorb it."

In between errands, we yakked about the difference between German and French, and then there was a discussion of calculus, which I tried to understand. Mostly I listened and enjoyed the far-off look on Pat's face as he soared above me in abstractions. He floated on air currents, free from the pull of antidepressants and Dr. Danenhower's advice, and when he came back down to Earth,

I asked him what Moshe meant by settling for questions rather than answers. Pat thought about it for a minute, but the weighty subject of Nazi death camps threatened our mood. We danced on to other things—German authors, programming at Siemens, grad school, clubbing in Berlin. We giggled through stories of friends and schools and jobs.

On the way home, we stopped at a pizza restaurant for dinner, and there was a moment when Pat got serious. He said he needed my advice, which he had never said before, so I knew it was important. "You remember that boy I wanted to be with last summer?" he asked. "But then he reconnected with his roommate? I want to ask him one more time on New Year's Eve. What do you think?" And then Pat looked down and pushed food around his plate.

I said if he really wanted to be with that boy, then give it his best shot. Ask him again, and if it doesn't work, then at least he will have tried his best. He'll know one way or the other for sure.

"But what if he doesn't want to be with me? Then what?" Pat said.

I wanted to blurt out, "Of course he wants to be with you. Everyone wants to be with you." Instead, I waited a moment, and then I leaned over the table. "You have the strength," I answered. "You have the strength for whatever happens."

"I don't know ..." Pat said, and his voice got tense, as if he was already paralyzed with fear.

"You won't know," I said. "You'll know when you're eighty-nine. That's when you'll know." It was the only answer I could think of to give him perspective, to help him understand that disappointment would pass.

He shook his head as if he didn't want to know, and we moved on to other topics—his friends in Berlin, the picnics in the Tiergarten, classes at Humboldt University in the spring. Five weeks later, I would be cleaning out Pat's apartment in Berlin. I would find his copy of *The Sorrows* on his coffee table. It was open to the passage where Werther kills himself. I had given him a book that would convince him to die.

Moshe explains to Wiesel that questions have a power that does not lie in answers—that we pray, not for answers, but for the strength to ask the right questions. We are drawn into an eternity where question and answer become one. Years after Pat's death, Moshe's meaning was clear. Questions were all I had. Suicide? How was that possible? How could he want to die?

I hated big questions. I liked the small—how to teach dependent clauses, how to paint the bathroom, what to cook for dinner. My husband Bob and I were putting three children through college. We were close to paying off the mortgage on our home. That was about as big as I got. I had no idea about "depths of the soul" or why people kill themselves.

It's true there was suicide on both sides of our family. My mother and Bob's father—two of Pat's grandparents—had killed themselves. But that was decades before Pat's death. Those grandparents were not a big part of his life. Colin was one year old when my mother died in 1980. He was six when Bob's father died. Patrick and Libby were three. Bob and I had to keep going after both suicides. Two times. There was too much future at stake with young children, but we were guided by the past.

My mother had blamed her drinking on a strict family upbringing. Bob and I would not make that mistake. We would overpower the Wood and Rimer family adversities. We would give our children the best home possible. We would nurture. There would be no rigid discipline and none of the alcoholism we grew up with. And beyond nurturing, we would be open about the suicides in our family. Our children would know the truth when they asked what happened to two of their grandparents. Knowledge would guide them. It would warn them about the alcohol involved in both deaths. It would make them immune to suicide, and that fantasy, that disregard for the immutable patterns of family lineage, was now front and center.

Patrick's last sign of life was checking his phone at 9:00, Tuesday night, January 31, 2006. That was 3:00, Tuesday afternoon my time. I was in school, probably in the computer room helping students finish stories for the school newspaper. Or I could have been writing lesson plans at the large oval table in my classroom. I could have been grading homework or writing news stories or planning a pizza party for my eighth-grade class. I don't remember exactly because I had no idea that the stories my class was reading would become my stories. I had no idea that I would become Edgar Allan Poe's madman imagining the heartbeat of a dead person in "The Tell-Tale Heart" or that Pat would perish like the family in Ray Bradbury's "There Will Come Soft Rains." Their silhouettes on a wall of their house are all that remain after a nuclear bomb destroys a city in California. Their house burns to a pile of ash much like the charcoal in Pat's apartment.

I had no idea that after the pizza party on Friday and a weekend trip to a tack shop in Massachusetts and a day of school on Monday, the question of why people kill themselves would become my question.

Why?

I asked that question everywhere—from Pomfret, Connecticut, where Pat grew up, to Palo Alto, California, where he went to college, to Berlin, where he studied and worked abroad. I asked Pat's friends. I asked therapists. I asked books on suicide. I asked that question for fifteen years. The more I asked, the more questions I had. Power came, as Moshe said, not from answers but from the strength to ask the right questions. I was drawn into Moshe's eternity where question and answer become one, where they come from the depths of the soul, and they stay there until death.

Marie Lisette Rimer
October 19, 2022

Pat's window, Berlin, 2006.

The Last Day

In those terrible hours on the 6th of February, as darkness descended on Berlin, I reflected on our last few meetings. It is easy to believe that everyone has the right to be left alone to lead their own life but we must surely hold our friends more dear than this. We saw but one aspect of the essential Patrick, we should have dug deeper, intruded upon his privacy, for the pain he was feeling must not be borne alone.

—Stephen Pryce
"Patrick Wood Memorial," 2006

Tuesday, January 31, 2006

Patrick Wood was twenty-three years old as he read a leather-bound book in his apartment in Berlin on the last night of his life. *The Sorrows of Young Werther* was dog-eared on passages in German of Werther's misery. "My passions were never far from madness," Pat underlined. "I weep inconsolably toward a dark future."[2] Beethoven's Fifth Symphony played softly in the background. Gay club magazines and men's journals lay on the left side of a coffee table in front of the futon where he sat. Conservative NRA magazines from his home in Connecticut lay on the right. A poster over the futon showed a trash can lying on a psychiatrist's couch. "*Ich fühl mich so leer* (I feel so empty)," it claimed to the note-taking doctor. "*Das Leben kann soo Scheiße sein!!!... man muss sich nur Mühe geben!* (Life can be sooo shit!!!... You just have to make an effort),"[3] said a sign next to it.

A drying rack in front of the coffee table was draped with shirts, underwear, and socks. A blue Hawaiian surfing t-shirt

1

lay among them. Pat's twin sister, Libby, had given it to him on their birthday three months before. Beyond the drying rack were upholstered chairs. To the right was a small alcove with a built-in couch, which doubled as a bed. To the left were shelves with a TV, CD player, and books in English, French, and German—a guide to Berlin, *Dubliners*, *Siddhartha*, *A Briefer History of Time*, *The Noonday Demon*, *L'Étranger*, *Bonjour Tristesse*, *The Elusive Embrace*, and *Goethes Deutschland*. The last was inscribed in German: "Dear Pat, Many thanks for the wonderful time with me in Berlin! You are one fine 'dude,' stay that way! I wish, for your time in Germany, still more beautiful impressions and experiences. Don't forget me; I know I certainly will not forget. Hugs, Simon."

CDs of Schumann, Tchaikovsky, Brahms, Scriabin, Schubert, Rachmaninoff, and Mozart filled a smaller shelf under the CD player. DVDs of *South Park* and *The Office* were nearby. A small drawer contained a German magazine called *Sergej* with a club-scene collage titled "Beauties im August." Pat was near the top of the page, being kissed on the cheek by a handsome man. He looked calm, in control, in his element. Highlights bounced off his cheekbones. His blond hair was brushed up. His blue eyes stared brightly at the camera. His smile was broad.

In a drawer below, a Stanford newsletter showed him standing in front of a massive mechanical bearing at Siemens Corporation in Berlin. His arms were folded confidently. "Patrick Wood," it said underneath the picture, "Computer Science/Mathematics, at his Krupp Internship with Siemens AG Automation & Drives, Berlin, Summer and Fall 2005."[4]

In a folder labeled "Germany," a letter of reference praised Patrick's programming as an intern at the BMW Traffic and Science Department in Munich. "Very good written and spoken German. Very detailed MATLAB/SIMULINK knowledge. Very well structured and commented software programs.... Considerably surpasses the requirements in expression and portrayal skills, judgement, creativity and intellectual mobility, working speed and productivity, workload, independent and initiative, and team player and frankness."[5] At the end, it offered him a full-time job.

A folder labeled "Academics" contained a Stanford transcript with mostly As. A letter from their computer science department welcomed him to the master's program. Boston University gave him As in piano and chamber music. His GREs showed scores of 760 in verbal and 800 in quantitative.

Underneath the folders, a poem by Kurt Tucholsky read:

> When you climb and, breathing heavily, look
> around to admire your achievement in
> climbing such heights, you, all alone—then
> always you discover traces in the snow.
> Someone has been there before you.[6]

A poem by Friedrich Rückert lay next to it:

> I am lost to the world
> with which I used to waste so much time,
> It has heard nothing from me for so long
> that it may very well believe that I am dead!
>
> It is of no consequence to me
> Whether it thinks me dead;
> I cannot deny it,
> for I really am dead to the world.[7]

Windowed cabinets with wine glasses stood on either side of the shelves. Next to one was a bureau with folded clothes. Heavy curtains were drawn across the windows. Dishes with leftover Ramen soup noodles were piled in the sink of the kitchen. A backpack lay on the counter. Inside were half-empty bottles of Zoloft and Wellbutrin pills. A note card from his father included a picture of our family in Connecticut. Aunts, uncles, cousins, siblings, and parents stood next to Pat in front of a baby grand piano in a formal living room. "Try not to take things too hard as you go along life's road. It was great having you home for the holiday," it said. Next to it were Scriabin music books from a Berlin library.

As Pat sat on his futon reading *The Sorrows*, a text message interrupted. His friend Ryan asked about magazines. "Sorry, i don't have them. I'm almost positive i gave them back to you ..." Pat answered.

Another friend asked if he could go out that night. "Hey! Not to be a big bum," Pat replied, "but i seem to have caught some kind of cold bug at work which pretty much laid me flat today, and i think i need time to recover. Sorry about that ... But if you want to go to london calling on friday, i would be more than down :-) lg, pat."

At 8:00 p.m., Ryan called to ask Pat over for dinner. Pat didn't answer. Instead, he prepared to die. He read the page in *The Sorrows* where Werther makes a decision. "To raise the curtain and step behind it! That is all! But why the hesitation and delay? Because one doesn't know what it looks like there? And one doesn't return? And that is now the characteristic of our mind, to project darkness and confusion where we know nothing definite."[8]

Pat placed the open book face down on his coffee table between the NRA and the gay magazines. He tore a page from a book on Tchaikovsky—a gift from a boyfriend named D_____, who had rejected him. He wrote a note on it and left it on the table. "Tell D_____ I'm sorry. Tell him I will miss him." He wrote another note and taped it on the outside of his bathroom door. "Warning/ Achtung! (Hopefully) lethal levels of CO (carbon monoxide)." He brought a box of Kleenex and a roll of paper towels into the bathroom and pressed pieces of tissue into the drains of his shower and sink. He pushed more bits of paper into the joints of the ceiling and down the corners of the walls until nearly every wall was outlined in white tissue. He blocked tiny holes around the light fixture. He brought the duvet from his bed and placed it on the floor underneath the heated towel rack in front of the shower stall.

He brought a pillow for his head. He brought three frying pans, a pair of tongs, a spatula, and potholders from his kitchen. He pushed the shower curtain aside and put everything in the bottom of the shower stall. He ripped pieces of newspaper and put them in the pans. He poured Holzkohle charcoal on top and placed the rest of the bag on the floor next to the shower. He put a bottle of vodka, a jar of sleeping pills, lighter fluid, and several butane lighters beside the pans. He put a cup on the floor. A shaving razor lay on the edge of the shower stall. A bottle of shampoo and a can of shaving cream sat on the edge of the sink.

He locked his apartment door and left his phone on its charger on his bed around the corner from the bathroom so he wouldn't hear it. He closed the bathroom door and placed a towel across the opening at the bottom. He lit the charcoal. He drank vodka and took sleeping pills. He lay down on his duvet on the floor of the bathroom. His head was against the door. Smoke filled the bathroom as messages continued on his phone.

"What r u doing this weekend? How r u? Call me!" "Hey Pat. Call me asap. I've got big news!"

"Hi Pat! How are you doing? Haven't heard from you in ages. I'm on vacation now, have lots of free time and we can hang out. So when are you free? Love Emils."

The Beethoven CD stopped playing. The apartment was silent. Neighbors in the building slept above, below, and next to Patrick in his smoke-filled bathroom. Outside his window, the night was still. Few people walked in the January cold. The quiet street, lined with dark trees, led to distant boulevards where traffic slowed to midnight indifference.

Pat and Bob, the last Christmas, 2005.

The News

I have learned how powerful the irrational mind can be when it is allowed control over the rest of the consciousness.

—Patrick Wood
"Being Shy," 1999

Monday, February 6, 2006

On a crisp Monday, a month into the winter term of 2006, I was grading essays in my tutoring room at Rectory School. Rectory is a junior boarding school in the northeast corner of Connecticut, surrounded by old houses, wide lawns, and low hills that roll in every direction Since the 1800s, "the Quiet Corner" has been known for its healing springs and large summer homes. Its farms are a rural way station along the Boston-New York corridor, beyond commuting distance to cities and largely forgotten by developers.

Rectory School has filled a need for individual attention and small classes since 1920 and is renowned for one-on-one tutoring from elementary to ninth-grade students. My eighth-grade English class had studied grammar, punctuation, and short-story themes. They were using those elements to write essays. Their first attempts were awkward, their thoughts unsupported, their conclusions repetitive. Today, I could see progress. My eighth graders were proving their points with examples from the stories—Squeaky's run-on sassiness and street slang showing her boldness in "Raymond's Run," for example, or the warm and cold settings of "The Monkey's Paw" paralleling the death of the son.

Sun poured in through the two windows of my second-floor corner office. The radiator banged with steam heat. Trees, manicured lawns, and white-clapboard buildings stretched to the south. The dining hall, the art building, the basketball court, and playing fields met woods and hayfields to the west, which rose toward a golf course at the top of a hill.

I looked down at my papers, crossing out needless words and adding encouragement for strong points. Maybe I would run a few errands after I finished grading. Maybe I would email Patrick. We were planning to see him in Berlin during my spring break in March, but he was unsure if he would still be there. It depended on a last-minute requirement for his application to Humboldt University in Berlin. Pat had said Humboldt rejected him because he didn't copy the back side of his transcript showing how Stanford's grading system worked. He was not hopeful about his prospects and said he might be spending the spring in California. "Wish me luck," he said.[9]

His email sounded confused. Why did he think he was rejected if Humboldt only needed a copy of one page? But I didn't want to tell him that. I wanted to keep the conversation light, as in whatever you do is fine with us. I had tried to find out what he would do the previous week. "Paddy, me lad," I had written, "will we be seeing you in Berlin, or are you having to cross the pond by March 12th? Dare I ask how goes the bureaucratic battle?"

He hadn't answered, probably because he hadn't been to his friend Ryan's apartment to use his computer. He might not have seen my last few emails. I would try again in a few minutes. "Paddy, me lad," I was planning to say, "are you there?"

I was almost finished with twelve essays in fairly good shape when I heard footsteps in the hallway coming toward my door. Carpet muffled the sound, but floorboards creaked underneath. I kept working to finish before anybody could interrupt me with the usual time-consuming conversation about a student's progress or an idea for a lesson plan. The footsteps stopped outside my door. I looked up. It was Bob. He rarely came to visit me at school. I wondered why he had driven over instead of calling. He looked away from me. "What is it?" I asked him. "Is something wrong?" At first, I thought it must be one of the horses. We had had a few incidents—a broken leg, a hoof caught in fencing. I thought one of them must have gotten into serious trouble.

"I can't tell you here," he said. "It's bad. It's really bad." He was speaking in a hoarse whisper, looking down at the floor. "You'd better come outside to the car."

I piled papers and folders into my school bag and followed him to the car parked by the door of the main school building. I got in the passenger seat and looked at him with no clue of what he would say. He looked away from me. "Patrick committed suicide. He killed himself in Berlin. He's dead." His voice broke. I stared at him and waited. "I went out for errands today," he said. "When I got home, there was a message on the answering machine. It said to call the director of housing at Stanford. It was urgent. I called, and that's what he told me. I couldn't tell you on the phone, so I came right over. I didn't know what else to do."

I looked straight ahead through the windshield of the car. I covered my mouth. I couldn't believe it. It wasn't possible. I had talked with Pat. I knew he was sad, but he had to be alive. He had to be breathing. It couldn't be possible.

Bob started the engine and drove the few minutes home. I looked straight ahead, breathing—for me, for Patrick. Back and forth, from one to the other. We pulled into the driveway. I got out of the car, staring into space, and went inside. Bob gave me a phone number that I was supposed to call in Germany. I kept staring, not wanting to know what I would find out, and then I dialed the number on my cell phone. Bob waited.

Ryan Wirtz, Pat's best friend in Berlin, answered. He told me, through sobbing gasps, that he and his partner Steve were in the hallway outside Pat's apartment. They had gone to check on him. He hadn't answered their text messages or phone calls. It wasn't like him. The door was locked. Pat didn't answer when they knocked. They were worried. He hadn't told them he was going away. They kept knocking. No answer. Ryan called the Stanford Center in Berlin, where Pat and Ryan had gone to school. Karen Kramer, the director, and her assistant, Jutta Ley, drove over immediately. When they arrived, they called the police. The police broke the lock on Pat's door and saw a note in German on Pat's bathroom door. It said there were poisonous gases in the bathroom. They found Pat lying dead on the bathroom floor while Ryan, Steve, Jutta, and Karen waited in the hallway outside Pat's apartment. As Ryan and I were talking, Pat was brought out in a body bag. Ryan asked me to wait while the bag was unzipped so he could identify Pat's body. I overheard low voices in German. "It was him," Ryan said to me, sobbing. And then, "They brought him out in a body bag. Oh my God."

I waited, staring, not finding words.

More excruciating phone calls came next. Libby was at the University of Vermont, about four hours north. "Lib," I said, my voice shaking. "He didn't make it." She screamed on the other end of the phone. Her screams became distant, as if she had dropped the phone and was crying somewhere else. I waited, knowing our emails about what to do for Pat were too late. Our worst fears about his sadness had come true. I waited, thinking she would blame me for not going to Berlin to help him. She came back to the phone. We talked about how we should have gone to Berlin, and now it was too late. We hung up with the promise that she would be home that night.

The next phone call was to Colin, Pat and Lib's older brother in Tacoma, Washington, where he worked in construction. He was speechless for a long time. I waited for him to take it in. "I can't believe it," he said. Then he choked and coughed and gasped all at once and said, "I just can't believe it. What happened?"

"I can't believe it either," I said. I told him what I knew so far. We talked about him coming home. We talked calmly about getting him a plane ticket and then all of us going to Germany. Ryan worked for the State Department in Berlin and would help Colin get an expedited passport. It was a less chaotic phone call than the one to Libby—more strategic, like a war room. I hated myself for speaking rationally, in some sort of fake control, as if everything would be okay once we were all assembled at home. Was I really functioning during the worst tragedy of my life? I hated that the answer was yes.

Colin would be on a plane in the next few days. Bob and I stared into space. I wanted to help Patrick. I could not absorb that there was nothing I could do.

The death notice.

Panic

My irrational mind immediately jumps in and begins expanding and multiplying the fears and the things that could go wrong ... until I can think about nothing else.

—Patrick Wood
"Being Shy," 1999

That night, I lay awake in the dark by myself in Colin's room. I knew I wouldn't sleep, and I didn't want to keep Bob awake with my crying. I had to figure this out. Patrick was gone. I had no son in Berlin. Where was he? He had to be somewhere. If I could just get to him. He had to be breathing. Somewhere. I imagined him breathing quietly, waiting for me. I'm coming, Pat. I'm coming, now that it's too late, now that I get it. You can't be by yourself. I'm coming. Tears came in gasps, stopping and starting, releasing and choking. I rolled from one side of the bed to the other. My mind went in circles—disbelief, rejection, denial, questions, acceptance, and back to disbelief. It couldn't be. It isn't going to be. I refuse to believe it. I won't believe it. I'll pretend. I'll imagine. I'll find another son. I'll make another Patrick. I'll fantasize.

Lies worked briefly, but the truth would not go away. It cycled endlessly. There was no Patrick. I raced through what that meant. Number one: I didn't understand him. I didn't read him right. I failed my son. It was my fault. I didn't help him. I didn't save my own son. Number two: No Patrick. Gone. Cut out of life. I didn't get it. I couldn't get it. It was not possible. Murder I could almost get, but suicide? It rolled around my head in an endless cycle. Small thoughts came in place of big questions. No Patrick. His music, his wonder, his promise, his future. All of it gone.

I had to figure this out. Why didn't I see this coming? Why didn't I know he was going to kill himself? He looked sad when I took him to the train station after Christmas a month before. He would see a friend in New York and then fly to Berlin. Why didn't I stop him, take him to a doctor, go to Berlin when his voice tightened on the phone a week before he died?

"How are you?"

"I'm okay, but I've been sick. I haven't been to work this week."

"Oh, that's too bad. Do you have a cold?"

"No, no, it's nothing. I'll be okay."

"How was New Year's Eve?"

"Not good. I went to the club, but he didn't want to connect (voice tight). I can't take it anymore (tight exhale). I can't stop beating my head against a wall."

"Oh my God, Pat, I'm so sorry. Oh, that's so hard. I know how much he meant to you. I'm really sorry, but it's not a predictor of the future."

"What?"

"It's not a predictor of the future," I repeated. It was the best answer I could manage, and then I let him talk to Bob.

I should have said, "Pat, do you need help? Do you want me to come to Berlin?" But I didn't. I was scared to go to Germany, scared to fly, scared of spending the money, scared of what I would find, scared of leaving Bob, scared he would feel left out, scared of getting time off from teaching. How would I say I couldn't come to school because my son didn't sound good? He wasn't sick, really. At least not the kind of sickness I understood. He was turned down by a boyfriend on New Year's Eve. He was rejected and couldn't handle it. Is that a sickness?

Instead of taking action when I heard the misery in his voice, I went back to what I knew, the normalcies of life, the routines. Keep things light. He'll come back to the basics, to family, work, friends. I handed the phone to Bob, feeling out of my depth, wondering why Pat was that sad and hoping I could help him long distance. Bob and Pat had an everything's-okay conversation. Pat sounded fine. Bob detected no problem. Was it me? Was I over-reacting? Under-reacting? It was the last time Bob and I would hear Pat's voice.

I had to figure this out. I hadn't understood him. I had missed every sign. I had glossed over his pain. I had tried reason and logic. "You can do it, Patrick. There is nothing you can't do. You are the person everyone wants to be."

Reason and logic hadn't worked, but I kept using them. I had used them the year before when he called me from the locked unit of Stanford Hospital. It was the beginning of February in the winter quarter of his senior year. "I'm in the hospital," he said. "I tried to … I had thoughts of suicide."

Long pause.

"Mom?"

Shorter pause.

"I don't know what to say," I answered. "Are you okay?"

He said he was all right but had to stay there for five days. He was bored. He had gone to a counseling clinic and had himself committed. "I needed to shock myself," he said. He was frustrated that he had to give up his belt, shoelaces, and any sharp objects before he was admitted, but the nurse was firm.

"Should I come out?"

"I don't know yet," he answered. "Let me think about it." He said he was okay. He had friends to visit him, but the worst part was that there wasn't anything to do. He was sleeping a lot because he couldn't do anything else. Friends were bringing his books, and that would help. He would call me the next day. The hospital let

15

him keep his cell phone. "Meanwhile," he said, "don't worry. I'm not going to do anything."

The next day, we had a long discussion about why he was in the hospital. He didn't give the whole story. He was guarded about my questions. "I was depressed," he said.

"Were you depressed about something in particular? Was it a relationship?"

"Yes."

"Was it rejection?"

"Sort of. I can't keep it in perspective." He said he was overreacting about being rejected by a boy from Munich. He didn't belong in the hospital where they put him under a twenty-four-hour suicide watch. He didn't belong in group therapy sessions with drug addicts and alcoholics, where they made him stay for five days and see a psychiatrist he didn't like.

"Do you want us to come out?"

"No, that's okay. I'll be all right."

And I believed him. Of course, he didn't belong there. He was the most thoughtful person on Earth. Why would he do the unthinkable? I would stay awake as long as it took to understand.

I cycled through my useless encouragement, my dumb responses, my impotent cheerleading. I had a false sense of influence, of control. I thought I could will depression away. I could support, love, listen, send money, email, call, nurture it out of existence. Suicide wasn't possible. He was going to be okay. He knew how to solve everything, do everything, be everything.

I didn't see what *he* saw. I didn't read the signs *his* way. I didn't take off the blinders and step away from the dinner party and the teaching and the chores. I didn't sound the alarm. I was doing the wrong job. I didn't hear the voice calling through the haze, "Mom, I need help. Help me, Mom."

The voice was loud and clear now. It drowned me in a swamp of tears on the pillow. It caught me in the biggest mistake of my life. I hadn't paid attention. I had killed my son in carelessness. I had let him suffer by himself. I pictured myself driving on a dark night, Patrick in the passenger seat I took my eyes off the road to look at him. My headlights locked on a tree. We both stared in terror. I killed both of us in carelessness.

The morning light brought a new stab of pain. I stayed in bed until I had to move. I had to do something. I had to figure out what to do. I called my father in Los Angeles. My voice broke down. I couldn't get the words out of my mouth, and by the time I did, he knew what I was going to say.

Libby drove home from Burlington, Vermont. Colin flew from Tacoma. In the days afterward, our screams, tears, sobs, confusion, disbelief, hugs, and loneliness were interminable. Visitors and phone calls were nonstop. When we needed peace, there was none. When we needed solitude, it was broken. When we needed company, we were alone. Over and over, we replayed what we knew, what we didn't know, what we couldn't know. Each of us repeated our thoughts until we ran out of things to say. Colin couldn't believe it. Libby said she should have gone to Berlin. Bob hadn't known how to help him. I hadn't done enough. I hadn't gone to Stanford when he was in the hospital. I hadn't gone to Berlin when his boyfriend turned him down, and these decisions were like death knells, as if I had lit the charcoal myself.

Condolences magnified the guilt. "We're so sorry. I can't tell you how sorry we are. We can't believe it. How could this be? Did you know he was sad?" Over and over from a stream of friends and family.

I knew one thing. I had to go to Berlin. Now that it was too late, now that I couldn't do anything, I had to make it up to him, find out what happened, what I didn't understand, what I had missed. Bob, Libby, and Colin could come if they wanted, but I had to go. I had to be with Patrick and bring him home. I called my friend Lisa Levesque at Rectory School and told her I wouldn't be in for a long time. She relayed the message to the head of the school, Tom Army, who called to say how sorry he was. I explained that I didn't know when I would be back. Maybe never. I didn't know anything at that point, but he took the worry out of losing my job. No deadlines. No time limits to add to the turmoil. "Take as much time as you need," he said. "Come back when you're ready."

The chaos of pain continued until Bob, Colin, Libby, and I found ourselves in the car on an hour-and-a-half ride to Logan Airport in Boston. We were on our way to an overnight flight to Berlin. Bob's brother John was driving. The rest of us were in no condition. Libby, Colin, and I sat in the back seat and stared straight ahead. I wondered out loud, "Is it something I did? What was it?" Libby didn't answer.

"You didn't do anything, Mom," Colin said. "You were good. It wasn't you." And with these almost embarrassingly kind words, Colin deflated my tension. He gave me the forgiveness I needed. Relief washed over me, but it disappeared with the realization that, whatever I did for my three children, it hadn't been enough for Patrick, and that made me a failure to all of them. I had failed to keep their brother alive.

Berlin postcard, Libby's reflection, 2006.

Libby, Berlin airport, a week after Pat's death, 2006.

What Happened

When I first met Patrick, on the platform at Berlin's Bahnhof Zoo, I was struck by his eager smile and his restless energy; he seemed almost to bounce up and down as he talked.... So many of us were conquered by his natural charm and grace, and it is all the more difficult to accept that we were unable to understand him more fully, to embrace all of the essential Patrick in these last terrible months.

—Stephen Pryce
"Patrick Wood Memorial," 2006

Friday, February 10, 2006

Four days after we learned that Pat had died, Bob, Colin, Libby, and I piled out of the bus from the Berlin airport and trudged the wrong way down Kurfürstendamm, the main boulevard in West Berlin. Bob stopped to get his bearings and turned the map one way, then the other. His face wrinkled in concentration. His black jacket flapped against the February wind. Gray hair poked out of a black cap. His voice was weak from no sleep on an overnight flight. We stood on the wide sidewalk, suitcases resting, handles up. Six lanes of traffic drummed by us. Tall, thin people wearing long coats walked quickly around us. We were lost in Pat's city with no Pat.

"I think the hotel is the other way," Bob said. We trudged in reverse, suitcases rolling loudly on sidewalks and bumping on curbs. Bob's shoulders were hunched, and his head was down as he led us to the hotel. Libby hid behind the lens of her camera, her brown hair pulled back, her slight frame dressed in black. Her shoulders, strong from lacrosse and soccer at the University of Vermont, hung limp as she carried her suitcase. She looked away as I glanced at her. She put the camera to her eye as if it gave her a new way to see, as if it filtered the scene.

Colin was silent. He was tall and in shape from years in the army and his construction job in Tacoma. His blond hair was short. His blue jeans slumped. His sweatshirt was little protection against the cold. He scanned the busy street, eyes wide open on his first trip to Europe. Then he suddenly looked down, as if remembering why we were there. We checked into the Hotel Ku' Damm near Pat's apartment in Charlottenburg. The hotel clerk discreetly avoided my swollen eyes and handed me a welcome bag from Ryan, who worked at the American Embassy in Berlin. It held the tools we would need in a foreign land—a cell phone that worked in Germany, a map with the hotel and Patrick's apartment clearly marked, State Department guides to Berlin and Germany, a guide prepared for President Bush's visit to Berlin in 2002, a list of phone numbers, and a condolence letter from the Stanford University Center in Berlin where Patrick had spent a semester. "We wish that we could welcome you to Berlin under happier conditions," said the letter. "Patrick's friends and mentors at Stanford-in-Berlin express to you our deep sympathy and share your grief."[10] President Bush's guidebook explained that "From Berlin, Hitler's terrible crimes were planned and implemented." But today, "where a wall once ran, the city is being knitted together" and had "a fabulous pulse."[11] A letter from Ryan on embassy stationery explained that the guidebooks were given to visiting delegations.

We found our rooms. Libby asked to be with me. Colin and Bob were in the second room. We were staying three blocks from where Pat had been living only days before—three blocks from where his body had been found. And that proximity made me lie on one of the two double beds in the room and sob. "I miss him so much," I cried, my whole self convulsing, a regurgitation of pain that felt like throwing up. But at the same time, I was relieved to be out of control, to be truly feeling something, letting the pain out in wailing, choking gasps. I slept, fortified with sleeping pills. A few nights without medication had taught me that life after suicide was not possible without chemical support.

Saturday, we found the address of Pat's friends, Steve and Ryan, and rang the bell. Cars lined the dimly lit street with wide sidewalks in front of ornate buildings with balconies. I wrapped my coat against the cold. The buzzer sounded, and the door unlocked. We climbed the carpeted stairs, which creaked warmly. Steve and Ryan stood in an open doorway on the second floor. Steve was tall and slender with brown, close-cropped hair. His eyes made contact, but he stayed quiet. Ryan looked similar with dark-rimmed glasses. He wore an Oxford shirt and light-colored slacks. They were both dressed for business.

We stood in the high-ceilinged foyer of Ryan and Steve's apartment with heavily varnished trim. Ryan asked that we take off our shoes. Berlin was covered with sand because of winter ice, and it strayed into every dwelling. We were escorted past Steve's office, where he worked as a translator and where Pat slept when he stayed overnight. A spacious bathroom had a raised tub in front of an uncurtained window. It was in full view of Hectorstrasse apartments, a reminder of why Pat loved Berlin. People were more laid-back here, he had told me. The formal dining room was opulent for a young man just out of Stanford. "It's for entertaining. It's part of my job," Ryan explained. The apartment was courtesy of the embassy, where Ryan worked as the assistant to Ambassador Timken. Ryan arranged the ambassador's daily schedule and prepared for visiting delegations. He gave them tours of Berlin. He handled the ambassador's communication and had top security clearance. He worked well into many nights to keep up with the job. If Pat talked him into going to a club after work, he would grudgingly agree and then fall asleep amid blaring techno music and gyrating men. "The clubs were filled with so much cigarette smoke that I couldn't breathe," Ryan said. "But Pat said they were also filled with hot guys. He had a lot of fun in Berlin. I think we have to remember that. He may have died here, but he was happy most of the time."

We were seated comfortably in the living room on large sofas and upholstered chairs. The bookcase was full of German and American classics. Ryan's laptop was on the coffee table. Steve moved quietly to the kitchen to prepare drinks and cookies. I waited silently, comfortable in Pat's world with Pat's people.

Ryan looked down and then explained. Pat had met a student in one of the clubs. D_____ had a part-time job as a hipster DJ. Full-time students were rare in Germany, where graduation normally took eight years. There was no rush. Tuition was free, and students received stipends. Pat said that D_____ was smart, not just a partier. They would have long, deep conversations at the clubs, which were mostly on the east German side.

"At first Pat didn't want to be with him," Ryan said, "but then he did. By the time he changed his mind, D_____ had reconnected with his roommate. Pat couldn't accept that. He came over and talked about it a lot. We told him he had to move on, but he couldn't. It became repetitive. He told us he was going to kill himself. We tried to help. We thought we had talked him out of it. We gave him the phone numbers of therapists. We checked his backpack for anything lethal when he came over. We made him promise that he wouldn't kill himself. He was here a lot. He used to come over and use my computer."

Ryan showed us Pat's profile on gayromeo.com. "He put these ads out, and he always found people, but then he would change the ads. It was like he was looking for something, but he wasn't sure what. He would try 'government professional,' 'traditionalist,' or 'somebody who voted for Angela Merkel,' and when that got boring, he went through his hipster DJ phase. He was very popular. Everybody wanted to be with him. I mean, think about it. He was a beautiful American. He spoke perfect German, and he went to school in California. Everybody wanted to date him, and actually, he had a hard time handling that."

Ryan knew the GayRomeo dating website would take down Pat's page when they found out he had died. Ryan printed it to show us a picture of Pat sitting at a picnic table with a glass of beer, Bavarian mountains behind him. He was wearing a tank top, a "wife-beater" he called it, and red shorts from his friend Tobi. He had a slight smile.

Profil Nr. 898464 801 Visits

Ich bin der welt abhanden gekommen (I am lost to the world)

Username	kafkafan
City	Berlin Charlottenburg
Area	Berlin
Last visit	28.Jan.2006
Country	Germany
Search radius	In my Country
Language	English, German

Pat's profile on gayromeo.com.

Stats	23.177 cm 66 kg – 5'10" 145 lbs.
Body and ethnics	Athletic & Caucasian
Hair	Short and Blonde
Body Hair	Little, No Beard
Eyes	Blue
Piercings	No
Tattoos	No
Smoker	No
Sex	Gay
Relationship	I am single
Looking for	Friends, Relationship

Temporaryyyyyyyyyyyyyyyyyyyyyyyyyyyyyyyyyyyyyyyyyyyyyyyyyyyyyyy

The *y* in "temporary" was repeated across the width of the page, as if Pat was drifting away from the present and into the beyond where no friends or relationships would be needed. Underneath the profile, in place of his biography, was a blank space. Patrick had deleted his personal description days before he died. "He did it right here on this couch while he was sitting next to me," Ryan said. He covered his face. I looked down and sobbed with him. Pat had erased his life, and Ryan hadn't seen it coming. None of us had seen that he was disappearing, digitally, verbally, visually. He was making himself smaller, going further and further away. He was deleting his life until it was so small, there would be little left to kill.

Ryan and Steve had spent Pat's last weekend with him because they knew he needed help. They had dinner Friday night. They hung out Saturday. On Sunday, Ryan took him to a lecture on AIDS in Africa at the Jewish Museum on Lindenstrasse. Afterward, they had dinner with State Department friends. When Ryan started talking shop, Pat got bored and said he had to go.

"Are you okay?" Ryan asked.

"Yes, I'm fine," Pat said. They made plans to get together the next weekend, but by then, Pat had already bought the charcoal.

They hugged and said goodbye. That was the last time Ryan saw him. Two days after the AIDS lecture, Pat answered Ryan's text about magazines. He had returned the ones he borrowed. That was the last Ryan heard from him. The rest of the week, Ryan worked the long hours of his job as assistant to Ambassador Timken, but he worried that there were no phone calls, no returned messages from Pat.

The next weekend, still no response. Ryan and Steve went to Pat's apartment, a few blocks from theirs. They looked up at his balcony. The curtains on the glass door and windows were closed. They rang his bell on the outside of the building. No answer. A person walking into the building let them in. They knocked on his door. No answer. They tried again on Sunday. No messages. No response.

Monday, February 6, 2006, they panicked. Ryan called Jutta at the Stanford Center. This was not like Pat, Ryan told her. If he had gone away, he would have let them know. Jutta called Siemens, where Pat worked, and found out he had been absent. That was when she knew something was wrong.

Jutta and Karen drove to Pat's apartment, got no response, and called the police. They waited in the hallway until the police arrived and broke the lock on the apartment door. The police scanned the interior, but when they found the note on the bathroom door warning of toxic gases, they called the fire department. They waited, and when the fire department arrived, Ryan watched from the hallway as the firemen pushed against the bathroom door. They felt resistance, as if something was blocking the door. They pushed more. Thick smoke poured out of the bathroom as they pried the door open. The firemen covered their mouths and fanned the smoke. They told Ryan to get farther away. One of the firemen eased into the bathroom and flung open the window. The smoke cleared out. Patrick's body was lying on his comforter behind the door.

The noise of the firemen drew a neighbor from the next-door apartment. She told Steve, Karen, Jutta, and Ryan to get out. "What are you doing here? You don't belong here," she said. She was angry that something was wrong. The police told her to go back inside her apartment, but she continued ranting in the hallway until the police insisted, and she disappeared, muttering her way inside.

Steve, Karen, Jutta, and Ryan waited for hours while the police searched, dusted for fingerprints, and analyzed objects in the apartment until late that day. It seemed like forever, but they waited, sitting and standing in the hall. The apartment was off-limits.

Bob, Colin, Libby, and I stayed silent as Ryan described the moment he saw Patrick. The firemen brought him out of the apartment on a stretcher. His body was encased in black plastic. They unzipped the body bag to expose his face. "He looked … he looked good," Ryan said. "He looked … well-preserved." Patrick had been lying on the floor of his bathroom for six days.

The police changed the lock on his apartment and put caution tape across the door. No one, not even the owner, was admitted. They carried Patrick down a flight of stairs, put him in an ambulance, and drove away. By then, it was nighttime in Berlin. It had started snowing—new, untrodden snow.

On Ryan's first trip to a therapist, he received a card for his wallet, which he looked at during the days that followed. "Patrick is not coming back," it said. "She said I'm supposed to take it out to try to understand," Ryan explained. "I'm supposed to read it when I'm wondering where he is." Ryan had found out about her through the embassy along with other therapists whose names he had given to Pat—people Pat never called.

Over the next few days, Ryan explained that he had met Patrick in Berlin at a Stanford dinner in 2004 when Pat limped into the restaurant on crutches with an embarrassed grin. He had fallen down the stairs at a club and sprained his ankle. "Pat was finding himself in Berlin," Ryan said. "He was beginning to get comfortable with his identity. It takes a lot longer for gay men. They have to keep it all in. Even at 'liberal' universities like Stanford, they can't come out without facing rejection. You think the whole world is open to you when you graduate from Stanford, but it's not. Stanford was a hard place to be gay."

Ryan and Patrick had shared books and math jokes and long discussions with Steve about the structure of the German language. Pat had diagrams of language in his head. He saw declensions of adjectives and pronouns. He spoke high German with no dialect, no local accent, no slang, no shortcuts. He used older wording and inflections. His punctuation was perfect. He spoke German better than Germans. He read classic authors—Hesse, Goethe, Mann, Kafka—lots of Kafka for irony. World War II literature did not interest him, except for Tucholsky, whose anti-Nazi satire caused his books to be burned in Germany in 1933. Pat and Ryan laughed at math jokes and then joked about math jokes. They got carried away with questions like: If a cat lands on its feet when it's dropped, and toast lands buttered side down, how will the cat land with toast strapped to its back, butter side up? The answer (with Pat shaking in laughter): Opposing forces will cause the cat to hover inches from the ground.

On Sunday, Ryan invited Colin, Libby, Bob, and me for an everything-Patrick tour of Berlin. Libby said no. She wouldn't come with us. I couldn't understand why she didn't want to see Pat's Berlin, but she was firm. She stayed in bed and buried her head in a pillow. Her hidden face made one thing clear to me: There could be no judgments on this trip. There could be no questions asked, no expectations. We would respect each other's decisions to participate or not participate at any given time. All guidelines were off. This was new territory—chaotic territory—where we all had to make our own decisions and live by them. The one rule was that there would be no rules. Libby's one "non-rule" was that she would be alone until she was ready to be with us. She would suffer on her terms. She would make her own decisions about where she would go, when she would join us, whether she would stay in the room or walk the streets of Berlin. She would feel her grief unaffected by others. She felt a burden that she couldn't share. She and Patrick were gay twins, and she felt smothered by the presence of her straight family. She had shared her sexual identity with Pat. Now she was by herself, protecting them both against the confusion and discomfort of her family.

She wandered the streets alone, crying, while we toured with Ryan or grabbed lunch or made phone calls or wrote Pat's obituary or scheduled return flights—Pat's and ours. Sometimes she was with Colin. Sometimes she and Colin were with my father and his wife Anne, who flew to Berlin from Los Angeles. Lib left notes about where she would be. Dinner became our emotional barometer. Sitting in restaurants, she showed us pictures from her walks. Bright neon Berlinale bears advertised the Berlin Film Festival. A ribbed skylight crowned the gigantic Sony Center. Bears and lights and theaters swirled in collages. Store windows, bar mirrors, picture frame glass, and U-Bahn train windows reflected self-portraits. She was seeing herself, her new, twinless self. She was rediscovering who she was.

Colin, Bob, and I joined Ryan in his BMW for the Pat tour, which began with the jagged yellow roofline of the Berlin Philharmonic. Its sweeping peaks pierced the blue sky. SchwuZ, on Mehringdamm, was a friendly, gay hangout where dance parties rotated with other hot spots during the week. Its plain façade belied the swirling lights and thumping music that engorged its lower floors on party nights. Tables, which normally lined its wide sidewalk, were withdrawn. But an island of green growth, even in February, protected them from the cobblestone street. The Schwules gay museum was next door. At Mann-O-Meter, the gay and lesbian center on Bülowstrase, announcements for counseling, activities, and resources were posted on a bulletin board. A "Tree of Remembrance" with dark branches was painted next to them with a photograph of Patrick attached to one of the branches. He was standing in front of Siemens with the words, "Patrick we will miss you always," written on the photo. He joined others, lining the branches, who had recently died of AIDS or suicide.

We drove past the Jewish Museum, where Ryan had taken Pat for an AIDS lecture the last night he saw him. Red banners announced upcoming events. Next was the Rotes Rathaus, Berlin's city hall, where Pat and Ryan had met the openly gay mayor of Berlin at a party for embassy staff. The Holocaust Memorial appeared with its massive gray steles—unadorned sarcophagi separated by gray brick paths. Few wandered among them on that cold day. They spread across prime Berlin real estate near the Tiergarten and the Brandenburg Gate. They rose proudly and triumphantly above Hitler's bunker buried underneath a parking lot for apartment buildings nearby. "They don't want to make its location too obvious," said Ryan. "They don't want to attract the wrong people. There's a small sign in the parking lot, but that's about it. I only know because it's part of embassy training. I have to be able to answer questions from visitors."

The American Embassy was located a few blocks north of Unter den Linden in an ornate building. Ryan pulled up to the concrete barriers in front of the embassy. German police stood beyond the barriers and stared at us. I tried to take a picture, but Ryan warned me: "You'd better not. They'll confiscate your camera." I put it down as they continued staring at the car, which Ryan said they probably recognized and was the only reason they weren't coming over to investigate. While we sat in the car admiring the nineteenth-century architecture, Ryan told us how Pat would meet him at the embassy for lunch. He would show his passport to get past the entrance, guarded by German police, and then again to get past the handsome marines who guarded the inside of the embassy. He would find Ryan in his office and then joke that he was thinking of slipping his phone number inside his passport and giving it to one of the marines. He and Ryan would walk to the restaurant at the top of the Reichstag building, which offered good, cheap food. At the embassy Christmas party, Pat had dazzled State Department colleagues, including Ambassador Timken. Pat glowed with knowledge of German politics, German literature, and German movies. He brought his whole, openly gay self to Berlin, and the elite of Berlin welcomed him.

The Pat tour continued onto a flat, expansive straightaway lined with five- or six-story gray, square concrete buildings. Karl-Marx-Allée was the East German main street, designed for large Communist armies after World War II. We waited at a traffic light where the Berlin Wall used to stand. The light turned green, and traffic spread to absorb the extra lanes bordered by wide sidewalks on which no one was walking. Flat-fronted buildings stood behind the empty walkways with no wasted curves, no frills, no whimsy except for the occasional Berlinale bear. They stood in doorways and lifted their paws like two-fisted menorahs. They lured tenants to the boring East Berlin boxes with cheap rents.

We drove through the queer-friendly Kreuzberg neighborhood with shops, museums, and cafés filled with immigrants and students. Ryan pulled the car next to an earlier apartment that Pat had shared, and I dared to look in the first-floor windows. The apartment was colorful and brightly lit inside. We spoke quietly and admired Pat's choice as an older German couple walked by us on the sidewalk—she with tight gray braids wound on the back of her head. Canes and footsteps marched in unison—clunk, step, clunk, step. They stopped at Ryan's car, which blocked their path across the street. They grumbled in German and looked at us accusingly. The man waved a cane at the car for ruining their cadence and then slowly guided the woman around it. We watched in disbelief, brought up short by German order.

Then came more Pat locales—where he got on the U-Bahn, where he and Ryan hung out in the Tiergarten, where he got his hair cut, where he lived in another apartment near a restaurant called White Trash Fast Food. We passed the Opera House and the Technical University, a mass of glass and steel rebuilt after World War II. Most Stanford students did not speak German well enough to attend, but Pat had wrangled a chemistry class there with a cigar-smoking teacher, who sat in a dark room behind a desk piled with books.

Farther west on the crowded Unter den Linden thoroughfare, Humboldt University was another casualty of World War II, but its wrought-iron gates and classical sculptures had been restored to 1800s grandeur. It drew one of the few laughs of the tour. Pat had submitted his Humboldt application a few months before he died. It required two German language exams, he told me: a multi-page form that Steve, a professional translator, had to decode; and certified college transcripts copied "at the official copying place." Humboldt would not take original transcripts from Stanford. The small, "official application accepting building," as Pat described it, was situated at the end of a winding alley, which even Pat's cab driver had trouble finding. After an extra-long drive, covering the sprawl of Berlin, Pat had called to say the journey, the bureaucracy, the day sounded like a Kafka story about a chair.

"A guy sits on a chair waiting in front of an office," Pat told me, "but the door never opens. The guy stays there, determined to wait it out, to wait for the door to open. He waits his whole life. The door never opens. The guy never gives up hope, but he finally dies. Right afterward, the door opens."

"You're living the Kafka novel," I said.

"I don't feel good about it," he laughed.

First, a lightness and then a sadness rolled over me as I remembered that Pat's application for graduate school at Humboldt had been rejected, or at least that's how he had seen it. Steve had told him it wasn't a rejection. It was more like a delayed acceptance. Humboldt needed the back of the transcript, as well as the front, to know how the grades were calculated. But Humboldt's delay snowballed into rejection in Pat's mind, and I stared at the cream-colored buildings of the campus with a small insight. Pat was not seeing, feeling, or thinking. Or, he was seeing, feeling, and thinking too much. It was everything or nothing. He could not control which, and while he could dazzle the embassy staff or be popular at clubs, he could not handle disappointment, no matter how small. He was on a precipice, where delay grew into dismissal, and dismissal into repudiation—all of him, denied, overpowered. He shrank from the sadnesses he couldn't shut out. First, the rejection by a boyfriend. Then the delayed acceptance. Pat had disappeared under a mountain of perception. Or was it misperception? His favorite poet, Kurt Tucholsky, had warned him: There was no untrodden snow. "When you climb," Tucholsky said, "and, breathing heavily, look around to admire your achievement in climbing such heights, you, all alone—then always you discover traces in the snow."[12] And yet always Pat had climbed, and always there were others before him. Life was snow with footprints everywhere. Humboldt was one more footprint.

Humor and sadness became the arc of the trip. One minute I was laughing about Patrick's joke of giving his phone number to a marine at the embassy. The next, I was sobbing with the depth of his depression, the depth of my helplessness, the depth of my guilt. It was not enough to give him names of therapists and expect him to get there. Something was preventing him from doing that, something I could not fathom. I hadn't realized that he wanted relief more than life and that instead of loving him, I needed to save him. Instead of admiring him from afar, I needed to intervene. Steve and Ryan had missed signs, too—signs that we were sharing with each other. And that epiphany—that shared realization— was tempering the chaos. We were not *all* crazy or criminal or negligent or whatever accusing word crept into our minds. We were on common ground, and that made it firmer ground, which strengthened our footing on the foreign soil of suicide. It widened our perspective. It helped us see a part of Patrick beyond his death.

Berlin increased the positives. Friends and lovers had helped Patrick, dated him, gotten him into backstage parties, introduced him to Blue Man Group, met him at clubs, picnicked with him at the Tiergarten, and invited him to dinner. Pat was popular at gay clubs like Café Moskau, with multi-levels of throbbing music and dancing and packed smoky rooms. Dim reddish lights and fast-moving videos glanced off the walls. Thumping-bass techno enveloped handsome faces, cocked cigarettes, and smiling eyes where classical Patrick became a beat-bumping player, where he met young people and began small journeys with them. Berlin was there for him at the end of his life even if I was not.

No matter what his description on gayromeo.com—studious, intellectual, or partier—Pat found people—good people. I could see for myself. Steve and Ryan were caring friends. The city was safe with few crimes against the gay community. The clubs looked like any other storefronts with big windows, plantings, and Berlinale bears. Berlin wasn't foreign anymore. It deflated my tension. It filled me with a better sense of him—a happy sense, a release, actually. I wasn't the only one who had misread him. Others hadn't walked far enough down his path either.

The next few days were a stabbing series of errands. We needed to get the police to give us the keys to Pat's apartment. We needed to clean it and pack his belongings. The police were sure Pat's death was a suicide. All the evidence supported it, but getting them to hand over the keys was another matter. It meant they would have to close the case officially—a final step their investigation might not be ready to take. A Monday of negotiating through Pat's German friend Jutta gave us our first look.

I stood with Bob, Colin, Ryan, and Steve at Patrick's apartment door. I put the key from Jutta in the lock. It turned. I opened the door and stood in the doorway. Libby needed to be alone, again. She vanished into the city while we faced the scene of Pat's death for the first time. She needed to have her own reaction. Whatever she was doing, with or without us, was what she needed to do. She had lost her twin brother, and, in my mind, her decision to leave was a good one because at least she was making a decision. I could hardly blame her for not wanting to be there. What would Pat's apartment be like? Panic overcame me. Images of a shabby, miserable life flashed briefly. But like the rest of Pat's Berlin, it was lovely. Nothing looked out of place. No one had been in the apartment since the police and the firemen had removed Pat's body, and though they had searched for hours to determine the nature of his death, the apartment looked as if they had never been there and Pat had disappeared without them.

His suit, shirts, and pants hung in the closet to the right of the doorway. Cleaning implements and an ironing board leaned in the corner. His shoes were lined up neatly on the floor. Dishes with traces of soup and muesli cereal lay in the kitchen sink on the left. Pots and glasses lay with them. A small refrigerator was below the counter to the right. Pat's books—in German and French—and his TV and CD player filled a bookcase in the living room. The CD player was still on with Beethoven's Fifth Symphony in the tray. The curtains on a large window were closed. The room was dark. The bathroom door, opposite the kitchen sink, was open. Three cooking pans of burnt charcoal were visible on the shower floor. Pat's comforter was on the floor, his cutoff boxers and socks beside it. The firemen, or probably their EMTs, had removed them before putting his body into a bag. It was as if he had worn only the minimum to make their job easier, to be ready for the morgue.

Ryan and Steve searched the apartment anxiously. The coffee table drew them with the NRA magazines on the right and gay magazines on the left. They bent over the table, shuffling through them, looking for clues. The gay magazines were of male models and the club scene in Berlin. Steve and Ryan explained that some were titled *Siegessäule* for the war monument in the Tiergarten. The name stood for acceptance—even victory—of a once-underground and now openly thriving culture. Bob was surprised at the NRA magazines. Pat had taken them when he had been home for Christmas even though he had no interest in guns. Why? So he could leave them on his coffee table when he died? So he could arrange his gay and conservative worlds as he was about to end both? Were they a message to Bob? To all of us? A mocking middle finger? Or maybe the NRA and gay magazines were the closest Pat would come to a suicide note for his family, a jumble of contradictions, a symbol of irreconcilable differences within his family, within himself. We stood in silence. Bob and Colin stared down at the coffee table and then around the apartment. Colin was wide-eyed, curious, calm. Bob was tired, his eyes strained. Their distance from Patrick was palpable. He had come out about his sexuality to Libby and me but not to them. They had suspected he was gay, but they hadn't known for sure until he died, and that separation was now staring them in the face.

What had we done to cause this death? Bob seemed to be thinking as he looked around the apartment. There was no answer. Everything in the apartment looked normal—better than normal—neat, clean, and welcoming. I picked up the red, leather-bound *Sorrows of Young Werther*, lying face down on the coffee table between the gay and NRA magazines. A string bookmark lay between dog-eared pages. "And I am finished!" Pat had underlined. "It would be better for me if I went away."[13]

The rest of the day was a blank. It made no sense, but I felt an insatiable need to make sense of it anyway, and that need wove through the phone calls and the sputtering attempts to organize the apartment. By evening, Libby had rejoined us, and Jutta arrived to translate the police report. She sat on Pat's daybed in the living room. The rest of us faced her on Pat's futon and chairs. When she came to the description of Patrick's body, she stopped. "You don't want to hear this," she said. She was right. I hated listening to it. But I needed to hear everything, know everything, see everything. I needed the facts to understand. I had two brains—one looking for Patrick and the other knowing where he was—and I needed the graphic images of the police report to bring my two brains together. "He was lying on his side," she continued. "One eye was open." At that point, she looked up at me. The pain was too great for both of us. I couldn't be in the apartment anymore.

I walked outside with Bob, Colin, and Lib. The cold night air revived me. The city hummed as if nothing were out of place. Touristy restaurants with beer steins and waitresses in dirndls glowed through large windows on the busy sidewalk. Ice and sand ground under our shoes. Buses and cabs hummed smoothly on Kurfürstendamm. Berlin was orderly, efficient, and loaded with every version of cheap, good food, which Pat had loved—Turkish,

French, Greek, Indian, Thai. I allowed myself to be curious, interested, like a tourist. The conversation was light, meaningless. Where would we eat dinner? Pat didn't like touristy food, which meant that we wouldn't either, and that meant the beer steins and dirndls were out. We settled for a restaurant with young people who sang and toasted during dinner, as Pat had done only two years before with Stanford students.

It felt completely wrong to be looking at a menu a week after Pat was found. I had no appetite. I couldn't read the menu. I cried through the ordering.

"It's not going to work if you keep …" Bob said.

"It's not going to work if you tell me that," I said.

I needed two things to keep going—sleep and food. My father, a doctor in Los Angeles, had brought the sleep part over the weekend. One Halcion should work, two at the most. He gave them to me in the hotel lobby after he and my stepmother, Anne, flew twelve hours nonstop to meet us in Berlin. He was eighty years old. I turned away from him at first, sobbing toward the full-length glass windows that looked out over the gray street, and then I turned into his chest. The sobs came easily, a gushing torrent, which had been blocked by having to function, function, function. Find a funeral director. No, not the perfunctory one. Get the new one in Danielson. He's more sincere. Write the obituary. Get Pat's résumé. List the awards to make the obituary complete. Remember all the awards. Find them. Be accurate. Be thorough. Pat deserves it. He deserves the best, even though I can barely get out of bed. Make arrangements. Drive to the airport. Wait at the airport. Get on a plane. Find our way. Check in. Speak the language. Find addresses. Learn names—long German names. Get telephone numbers. Meet friends. Talk to police. Make the reservation to fly home with Pat. Be on the same plane. Find Pat. Where's Pat? What's happening to him? He's where? Get off the phone in disbelief. He's been taken to Frankfurt because the undertakers in Berlin could not do him justice. He had been dead too long.

Descend into shock. Get this straight. We have flown all the way over here to be with Pat, and he's not here. Eyes close in disbelief. We can't be with him. He will have to fly home by himself in an approved, sealed, metal container in the baggage compartment of an airplane as required by international rules. We will have to get him a separate reservation, his own one-way ticket. It is double the price of our round-trip tickets, plus several thousand more for the metal container. He is coming home in the baggage compartment.

Chaos and pain poured freely onto my father's chest. German soldiers, checking into the hotel, glanced over and then looked away. This was what life was really like. What it would be like. What it was like. This was real life. Pain, front and center. Berlin knew it well, but sixty years after World War II, it was no longer the normal landscape.

Tuesday, Bob, Libby, Colin, and I returned to Pat's apartment to pack his belongings. We opened the black and white patterned curtains to reveal sliding glass doors and a balcony. Bare, angled tree branches and pale buildings lined the street one story below. Ice and snow dotted the sidewalk. The sun shone brightly through the glass. We sat on chairs in the living room. Colin spied Pat's cell phone plugged in by his daybed and checked it for messages. I lay my head against the back of the futon, trying to take in Pat's visions before he died.

"How are we going to do this?" Bob asked. He wanted to set a date to return, know when Pat would be prepared for transport—yes, transport, the same word used for Jewish prisoners during World War II. Patrick was now cargo like they were. Bob wanted to get back to Connecticut, plan the funeral, get the notices in the paper. People needed to know the date of the funeral. The funeral director needed lead time to get the notice in the papers.

"We can't sit here all day," Bob said.

He was trying to make decisions, but I wasn't ready. I couldn't move. I needed to take in everything as Pat had left it, be in his room, be in his head, follow where he went, find him. This was the heart of the Pat I needed to know—the laundry, the books, the magazines, the receipts, the university catalogs with classes highlighted, the food, the CD player, the size of the books he read in German—the old German he had preferred. It's so much more romantic, he had explained. I could read few of the titles. I wanted to stay there, wait for him to come back, surprise him with dinner, yak about his friends, connect. I used to be good at it. Conversations soared—or rather, he soared—and I silently tried to keep up. He could fly into concepts that I couldn't follow, but oh, watching him fly. Could he have been planning this at Christmas? Is that why he came home? To say goodbye? Bob broke the stillness. "How are we going to start this?"

The silence of contemplation, of no functioning, of freedom to arrive at some truth at the crime scene was over. Bob was waiting for me. I threw out a suggestion, which I instantly regretted—a magnanimous wrong idea that was worse than the wrongness around us. I asked Colin to start in the bathroom. I asked him to clean his brother's death bed. I wanted to do it myself. I wanted to do everything, anything for Pat, but those wants were not possible.

Bob started with clothes. Lib … I wasn't sure about Lib. She floated in and out silently with her camera, finding Pat's last moments through her lens, finding closeness with Pat and distance from us. She found the charcoal in the bottom of the shower. She found Pat's comforter next to it, where he lay as he died. She found shelves in the living room emptied of books and CDs. She found bare walls after posters were taken down, chairs filled with boxes ready to ship home, pill bottles on the kitchen counter, and cleaning spray on the bathroom window sill. She took a self-portrait in the bathroom mirror. She held Pat's camera by her face with her eyes closed. Her brown hair lay in wisps around her face. Her eyelids were in shadow. Her mouth turned down.

I found myself in the kitchen washing Pat's dishes. It was the first thing I could see that he needed. That would be an improvement. The rest would be tearing him down. I stood at the sink and then glanced behind myself into the bathroom. Colin was kneeling over the comforter. He was looking at a small brown stain left by Pat's mouth. Tears fell as he hesitated before folding the comforter to put it into a suitcase. I wanted to tell him something that would help, but all I could do was keep washing dishes. I was burnt inside like the charcoal in the frying pans, which Colin brought into the kitchen and dumped into the garbage so I could wash the pans. His head was down, his eyes hidden.

He made more trips, dumping newspapers left over from lighting the charcoal. He threw out three or four lighters he found lying beside the pans of charcoal. Sixteen years later, those lighters stayed in his mind. They made him realize that Pat had been determined. If one lighter didn't work, he made sure he had extras to keep the charcoal burning. "Everybody remembers something different," Colin told me.

By late afternoon, the bulk of the apartment was packed into extra suitcases brought by my father and Anne. We tied Patrick's socks onto the handles so that we could identify them when we returned to Boston. I went to work in the bathroom to finish what Colin had started. I wanted to make it look as if no one had died there. Suicide would scare prospective renters. They might not sign a lease if they knew a suicide had occurred there, even though everything else was normal. Neighboring apartments might be abandoned and the value of the building depreciated. I wanted the normal part to be as good as it could. I wanted the owner of Pat's apartment to know there was no danger, no lingering smoke, no fear of the apartment being tainted. There would be no residual from the suicide of a gentle man who sought the best way out for himself with the least harm to anyone else during and after his death.

I worked into the night after everybody left—an atonement for my sin. I had not done enough. I should have done more, and a calm came over me as I paid the price. I started with the obvious. I packed Patrick's toiletries in a small box. I cleaned the sink and shower stall and toilet. I took out the Kleenex from the drain in the sink and the drain of the shower stall. There was one Kleenex in each slot of the round metal center of the drain. I thought I was done. I noticed a small brown jar on the window sill. It held the sleeping pills that, along with a partly drunk bottle of vodka on the floor, started the process of Pat's death. They made sure he would kill himself painlessly. The Kleenex made sure that he wouldn't kill anyone else in the apartment building. The bathroom was airtight.

I stood on a chair and took out more Kleenex from cracks where the tops of the walls met the ceiling. My hands smudged the walls. They were covered with a film of ash—actually, darker than ash, like the soot from a long-used fireplace. Every vertical and horizontal surface was coated in the charcoal smoke that had hovered for six days until Pat was found. It smudged as I cleaned. I wiped the wall behind the sink. The smudges stood out. They clung to the walls like toxic paint. I kept washing. Every circle with a paper towel left another circle, a smear of gray on the light walls. I climbed the chair to wash the ceiling, which made it look worse. Each stroke of spray cleaner left darker circles on the white paint. All day, well after Pat's clothes, shoes, linens, books, magazines, CDs, CD player, medications, music, backpack, posters, food, and papers had been packed, I filled garbage bags with soot-covered towels and empty spray bottles. I was determined to restore the walls of the bathroom so that the next occupant would not be scared or sad or put off by the fate of my son. They would see that it was clean because he came from a good family, responsible, who did the right thing, who lived properly. We took care of our obligations. We were good people even if we were not good enough for Pat. Those walls would show that I could do something. I would give my son a good reputation by cleaning his bathroom. It was the place where he took his last breath. It was the closest to him I would feel after his death. It was where he left me, and I needed to wash his walls to be in his mind, think what he thought, see what he saw, smell the smoke, feel the sleep, think about raising the curtain and stepping behind it.

On our last full day in Berlin, The Stanford Center hosted a memorial. Friends, family, Stanford faculty, and colleagues from Siemens filled a central room that had a grand piano at one end. Pat had played it after asking students and faculty if they minded listening to his classical pieces. It now stood silently in front of windows that looked out on the bleak landscape. A CD of Pat's music played in the background—the Schumann, Beethoven, and Prokofiev that he had recorded at Tanglewood five or six years before his death. A photo of Ryan with his arm around Pat, both of them in light blue dress shirts and dark ties, hung behind a podium. Pat's head was tilted casually, comfortably, his eyes contentedly gazing at the camera.

Karen, the director, began the service by saying, "Patrick was many things: The New England farm kid who favored the big city; the American who made Berlin his second home; the brilliant mathematician whose piano playing turned sound into ambrosia.... Patrick played this beloved grand piano more than any other student in the history of the instrument—and many have done so. He played it in 2004, when he started coursework here; and when he returned to Berlin for the Krupp Seminar after his internship with BMW in August that year; and during his internship with Siemens since last summer, coming in on weekends and on evenings, just to play. When the instrument is idle now, it will be with a lonelier silence.... The joy of remembering Pat will always be laced with melancholy, not only because of his death, but also because that specific mix was one of the things that made him who he was—a meld of introspection and wit, honed by that acute alertness that he had about him."[14]

Karen went on about the history of the Stanford Center and its connection to Patrick. Haus Cramer had been built and landscaped by Hermann Muthesius at the dawn of World War I. In the early 1930s, anti-Jewish policies caused financial difficulties for the Cramer family, and the house was seized by the city of Berlin for nonpayment of taxes. The family escaped to the United States three months before the Nazis took over Germany in 1933.

The house survived World War II, but a gas explosion left it in ruins until it was restored in the 1970s and leased to Stanford. In 2000, it was purchased by Stanford and became the only property owned by the university outside the United States.[15] A bench and a Cox Orange apple tree would be placed on a corner of the lawn when the ground thawed, Karen said. Their addition to the 1912 registered historical site would normally have taken longer, but the Monument Protection Agency had rushed the approval partly because the original plans had called for a gazebo on that corner of the property. Now, a bench and a tree would become a place of reflection for Patrick's future peers. The house had been part of Pat's history, and now Pat "will have a space in its history," Karen said.[16]

A Siemens co-worker spoke tearfully in German about going to operas with Patrick. A teacher from Stanford translated. Pat's friend Joe Dröge could barely speak when he got to the podium. He broke down, describing how he had collected some of the soil under the tree in the Tiergarten where he and Pat used to congregate. He put it in a small vial and asked Bob to place it in Pat's coffin.

Ryan's voice was unsteady, and his papers shook as he spoke about "The Essential Patrick." He described the Patrick who didn't do details unless he had to, the Patrick who could be "painfully, yet endearingly, flaky and disorganized—not because his exceptional gifts ever failed him, but because he was absorbed in a world of ideas and notations and music (and yes, even gossip and banter)"; the Patrick who set out to discover Berlin's nightlife at Kino International and fell down a set of stairs; the Patrick who defended his lack of grace as he hobbled on crutches, "charmingly defensive and sensitive"; the Patrick who found purity in being lost in thoughts and ideas, especially German romanticism. Nazi Germany did not interest him. He focused less on the balance of power and more on balancing equality.[17]

Ryan talked about visiting Patrick in Munich when he was working at BMW. They met at the University of Munich, where, in 1943, siblings Hans and Sophie Scholl of the White Rose resistance were arrested for distributing anti-Hitler pamphlets. "Their humanist and intellectual approach to resisting the Third Reich particularly inspired Patrick," Ryan said, "because he was a thinker and identified with those who could think with him." After admiring the memorial, Ryan and Pat walked to the English Garden. They bought blueberries and sat near a stream under a cloudless blue sky. They listened to a Beethoven symphony on Ryan's computer and talked for hours until the sun set. They wondered how they would have responded if Hans Scholl had asked them to join his resistance. "In true Pat fashion," Ryan said, "he said that if he were approached by any German guy as attractive as Hans, he would have done whatever he had asked." I looked down and smiled at Pat's humor.

Ryan's voice gained strength as he described Patrick as:

a gentle man, with a grin and goofy laugh … [who] solved puzzles and proofs, created music like a star and amazed everyone with his brilliance. Yet, he did it all so quietly, without ever wanting recognition, without ever wanting to admit to himself how spectacular the essential Patrick could be…. But Patrick was in pain and his soul fell, burdened under the weight of his illness and the struggle of his own emotions—emotions that, like so many aspects of his life, were superhuman. But his struggle was superhuman also and ultimately defeated him. Patrick was a young person who could not continue to fight, despite his gifts; who could not continue to cry, despite the joy he brought to his world; and could not continue to live, despite his energy and passion. He left the world as he lived in it—deliberately, not impulsively, and after what he felt was a rational, calm introspection. We have no choice now but to accept the fact that he felt the time had come, but I also take comfort in knowing that he left us painlessly and that he also felt that he would finally find peace.[18]

Ryan walked back to his chair with his head down. No one moved until Libby stood up and approached the front of the room. A light shone on her hair as she leaned on the podium, looked down, and took a deep breath. In a shaky voice, she thanked everyone for coming, and then she broke down and went back to her seat. The rest of us sat in silence, wiping our eyes.

At the end of the service, the gathering filed outside onto a snow-covered terrace capped by a barren pergola. The pale limestone of the English-style villa rose behind us. We gazed at a corner of the frozen white landscape where Pat's wooden bench would be placed and the apple tree planted in the spring. A brass plaque on the bench would read:

~A place for Patrick in the city he loved~
Patrick Wood 1982 ~ 2006

The snow crunched under our feet as we trudged back inside for coffee and kuchen in the dining room. Friends gathered around as if to cradle me with Pat stories. Two friends from the embassy told how Pat, advised by Ryan, had shown up unannounced for Thanksgiving dinner. Where else would he spend Thanksgiving in a foreign country? they told me. He blended gracefully with Americans he barely knew. Pat's landlord told how Pat had spoken perfect German, how they had planned a trip to Hamburg, how he would welcome us instead.

Friend Tobias had ridden two hours on a train from northern Germany to attend the memorial. He handed me a sympathy card with soulful eyes. "I didn't know he was so sad," he said. Tobi and I promised to meet again, to retrace the trips he had taken with Pat from Hamburg and Lüneburg in the north to Munich, Bavaria, and Austria in the south. They had stayed with Tobi's family in Missen and hiked from one Alpine hut to another in the foothills of the Bavarian Alps. On Pat's memorial website, Tobi said the two weeks since Pat's death were, "the saddest I have had in my whole life so far. When you grow up, the whole world seems to be kind. There are your parents, taking care of you. There are your friends you are having good times with. Everything seems just to be wonderful, in your little protected world. But, you're getting older. And the older you get, the more terrible things are going to happen. People around you, people you love, are getting illnesses, others might have accidents … and others would die. As this is not difficult enough to handle, Pat left by his *own* decision. Left all of us with nothing but questions. And there is no chance to ever be able to tell him, that he is really loved. Definitely, the world has started to scare me. What will be next …?"[19]

Friend Andrew Tompkins had drunk champagne with Pat on New Year's Eve. They had run in the wrong direction and missed the fireworks at the Brandenburg Gate, but they were both so happy that it didn't matter. They laughed so hard that champagne came out of their noses. Andrew's text messages were some of the last on Pat's phone.

Joe and his partner Tibor talked about meeting Pat at Café Berio in 2004. Pat was reading a guide to Berlin while eating breakfast at 5:00 in the afternoon. Who eats breakfast that late? they wondered, but Pat was so handsome they introduced themselves. They offered to help with directions and became close friends.

Patrick's friends crowded around as if to protect me. They talked about one good time after another until the room became quiet, and a kind lady cleaned off the uneaten kuchen from the tables. We were alone, filled with the richness of Pat's German world, oblivious to time. But the lady cleaning the tables had to go home. The richness ended, and someone drove us back to the Ku' Damm Hotel.

Libby, Pat's apartment, Berlin, 2006.

Colin, Potzdamer Platz, Berlin, 2006.

Libby, Stanford Center memorial, Ryan and Karen to the left, Berlin, 2006.

Bob, Stanford Center memorial, Berlin, 2006.

Libby and Patrick, Stanford graduation, 2005.

Who Was He?

Because Patrick was so different from those around him, it was hard to show him acceptance and understanding in a way that he could believe. The inclination was to step back and admire, but that stepping back was perhaps in itself a disconnecting, as if we were sitting in the audience and clapping enthusiastically, rather than being next to him on stage.

—Ann Warde
Playing for Patrick, 2015

Bob and I were born into families created by shotgun marriages. Both his parents and mine gave birth too young, fought with each other, and got divorced. He and I were not going to make the same mistakes. We were together for eight years, two of them married, before we had children. He was thirty-eight and working as a case manager for the mentally handicapped. I was thirty, with a publicist job for the Connecticut State Legislature on my résumé and a master's in education nearly finished. We had a country home, college degrees, and good jobs when our oldest child Colin was born in 1979. During the next pregnancy three years later, I came home from a visit to my obstetrician with the news that there were two heartbeats. We were having twins. I read everything I could on multiple births. The most important advice was to get help from outside the family—someone who wouldn't get offended when you told them what to do. Don't try twins alone. This was in stone. No mother of twins would repeat a solo performance if she had to do it over again, at least for the first six months. Next, I needed to eat for three. No problem there.

Finally, my passion for horseback riding was out. I taught my horse to ground drive instead. Bob and I added another set of baby supplies to the ones left over from Colin, and toward the end of the nine months, it felt more normal to be having twins than a "singleton." I couldn't fit into many clothes by then. The 1980s pregnancy pants with the stretch panels in front were too tight. I was reduced to frumpy house dresses with no waistband. I could barely fit behind the steering wheel of my car, but I pushed the seat back and stretched my feet to the gas and brake pedals. I was mobile throughout the pregnancy, but one observer in a parking lot wondered how. Not long before I was due, I was coming out of a grocery store, getting ready to lower myself into the driver's seat, when I noticed an elderly man sitting in the car in front of me. He stared at me. His eyes got big, and then he said to the woman next to him, "My God! Look at the size of her!"

I was enormous. At five-feet nine-inches tall, I had expanded from 122 to 179 pounds—a nearly sixty-pound weight gain in nine months. At my last ultrasound, the doctor smeared gel on my beach ball of a stomach to get a clear picture of the babies through the transducer. "We have to charge you double," he said. "We need two tubes of gel."

The ultrasound revealed that the placenta was aging: the babies had to come out. I had spent most of my pregnancy worrying that Patrick and Libby would be premature. Now there was another danger. They were postmature. My water was broken in hopes of inducing contractions. I got nowhere. My uterine muscle was too thin. It was like taking an arm muscle and stretching it across the hospital room. There was too much baby to wrap a muscle around and push out. My last words before being wheeled into the operating room for the Caesarean section were, "Get the knife."

Patrick was pulled out of a six-inch horizontal slit in my lower abdomen October 29, 1982, two minutes ahead of Libby. He was seven pounds, twelve ounces. She was nine pounds, two ounces—

almost seventeen pounds of perfect, intact, miraculous babies. I said, "Thank you, God," to no one in particular. "Give me twenty fingers and twenty toes. I can do the rest."

Then the real work began. Feeding and changing two babies in the hospital was tricky, even with nurses helping. I could not make both babies happy at the same time. One would be crying while I was taking care of the other, and nursing them together did not work. Picture a stringy-haired, large-breasted woman, doubly exposed, sitting in a hospital bed, trying to line up two mouths, a baby in each arm, before somebody got overwrought. Maybe supermoms managed, like my twin-bearing mom friends who were pumping breast milk, storing it in the refrigerator, and then heating it for simultaneous breast and bottle feedings. Not this mom. With help, I could nurse them together, but they couldn't always wait to be positioned, so a nurse begged me to cave in to formula and bottle feed. It kept everybody happier.

At home, I was in survival mode. Bob took time off from work, and his mother stayed with us for the first few weeks. She cooked Thanksgiving dinner when Patrick and Libby were four weeks old. We ate turkey, gravy, cranberry sauce, and mashed potatoes while holding babies and cutting Colin's turkey. When she left, and the leftovers ran out, neighborhood moms from Colin's play group brought dinner every night for the next two weeks. They knocked on the door as it was getting dark and dropped off casseroles or spaghetti or soup dishes that gave us a respite for a small part of the day. I apologized to them at the door for accepting their food while still wearing a nightgown and bathrobe late in the day. The days and nights blended together, and there was no time to dress for one or the other.

The next few months, I tried anything that would get me through the 24/7 care. I hired homemakers to help with cleaning and laundry and high school girls to play with Colin—anybody I could find to help during the day while Bob was at work so I could catch up on sleep and handle the right feedings while he slept. Patrick and Libby slept in two cribs in the same room. Colin had his own room and slept through the night. When one twin would cry, the other would wake up and join in. I would bring them out to the kitchen, one at a time, and put them in infant seats, which held them snugly at a forty-five-degree angle. That usually didn't sit well with Patrick, so I would cradle him in my arm while I got formula mixed and heated. When the bottles were ready, I got one baby started by putting a pillow under the bottle so it would stay in place while I grabbed the second bottle and started the next baby. I would sit in front of the two of them and watch their eyes discover the kitchen. I held both bottles until they were done.

With their bellies full, we moved back to their room and onto the changing table, where I hoped that they wouldn't be cranky while taking turns having diapers changed. Sometimes one baby could not get back to sleep, so I would rock that one and repeat the feeding, and then the other would wake up and need to be fed, and this chain reaction could continue for hours. Sometimes both babies cried themselves to sleep because I knew they were fed, changed, and burped, and I could not rock them both to sleep by myself. There is no longer marathon than the first six months of twins. When multiple-birth moms warn that you will eat standing up, they are not joking. You will rarely have a chance to sit down unless it is to rock a baby.

In the following months, Patrick and Libby sat in their twin high chairs for meals and crawled around the house. Before naps, they would crawl into my lap and rest, one in each arm, as if they were part of me. They would listen to stories or just lie still. On weekends, Bob and I would put them in twin car seats, drive to the grocery store, sit them in a twin stroller, and roll through the aisles to the admiration of other shoppers. We took walks up the country road in front of our house, each of us carrying a baby in a backpack. Colin ran alongside. Sometimes we hired a babysitter for Patrick and Libby and took Colin by himself. We worried about the psychological impact of a family growing suddenly from three to five. But if the increase bothered Colin, he never showed it. He held both babies in the rocking chair with our help.

By then, my stomach had shrunk like a popped balloon. Folds of wrinkles hung over my waistband, but I could wear normal clothing, slightly bigger than before I was pregnant. I would scoop up the folds and shove them under the waistband to contain them, and they gradually flattened out.

Patrick would laugh hard as a baby, even with a bottle in his mouth. He clutched the nipple between his teeth and gums, bottle hanging like a big cigar, and waited for me to look at him. He'd smile, make me smile, start laughing, and get me going with him. He took turns sucking formula and laughing, a pre-verbal dinner conversation that took the form of a deep belly laugh, or a screaming laugh if we really got carried away. I would pick him up and give him a hug until he wiggled to be put down and crawl off to the toys on the floor. He sounded like the happiest baby in the world.

In 1983, after fourteen pickup-truck and horse-trailer loads, we moved into a rambling, 1840 Victorian house about half an hour away in Pomfret, Connecticut. Colin was four, and Patrick and Libby were seven months old. Pomfret is a small, rural town with good schools in the northeast corner of the state. The house had been left to the Catholic Church in town and was empty for eight years before we bought it. It was so run-down, it was assessed for property taxes at minus ten thousand dollars—the cost of tearing it down estimated by the town. It looked like Sleeping Beauty's castle, with overgrown bushes and vines covering the outside. Paint peeled from moldy yellow clapboards. Plywood- and plastic-covered broken windows. A no trespassing sign hung on a bare wooden door. Roofs sagged under a dusting of snow. An l-shaped extension with pantry, woodshed, and three-hole outhouse leaned toward the ground.

On the inside, bats and birds flew over broken plaster on dark wooden floors. A giant bees' nest lodged itself against an upstairs bay window. Green paint peeled around an enameled kitchen sink with a drainboard. Brown water stains and mold from a leaky cistern in the attic covered the ceilings and walls. The cistern held the water supply filled by gravity from a spring up the hill. The float valve had been stuck for years. Water poured over the edges and down through the second-floor bedrooms and the first-floor rooms on its way to the dirt cellar, where it eventually flowed out of a downhill corner.

We patched, painted, and refinished for nine months. The resulting livable rooms had plenty of space for dogs, cats, and kids. The yard, with swings, sandbox, and kiddie pool, opened to acres of fields in every direction of the gently sloping hillside. The top of the hill was crowned by woods and a dirt road. We built a loafing shed for my two horses and fenced in about six acres for pasture, which included a pond. In June or July, when we had dry weather, farmers up the road cut the hay fields. Patrick, Libby, and Colin would gather at the edge of a field and watch tractors with mowing machines and side-delivery rakes toss piles of green stalks in the air. The grass lay in rows until the farmers baled it, and we loaded it onto Bob's pickup and stacked it near the loafing shed.

I handled meals, laundry, and wallpapering as a stay-at-home mom. Bob spent much of the time fencing pastures, building sheds, painting porches, installing fixtures, replacing clapboards, mowing lawns, and reglazing the thirty-seven windows of the house. The first few summers, we saw a lot of the bottoms of his shoes. He was up on ladders as high as three stories to reach the tower, added in the late 1800s to serve as a Catholic chapel. There was no Catholic church in town at the time. The Church required that any chapel within a private home be constructed above the living quarters. That meant building a three-story addition. The Holy Trinity symbol of three circles and a cross decorated the outside of the windows, and on the inside, the faint outline of a crucifix and a font for communion could still be seen on one wall.

Libby was always in motion, crawling furiously between the kitchen, dining room, playroom, and living room. At ten months old, she lurched upright from one piece of furniture to the next, and soon she was independent. Patrick studied her mobility, and within two months, he was doing the same. They learned from each other, and they had mirror-image company at each stage of development. What one did, the other would watch and then attempt. I raced to keep up with their mobility, but they both gained speed and started pulling the house apart. Leather-bound books lay on the floor, their brown spines and gold titles scored with teeth marks. A file cabinet was emptied until the blue carpet in the living room was covered in white paper. Crystal sconces were pulled down by their electric cords and shattered on the floor. I lost my temper at the sight of the broken glass. "I can't do this!" I screamed. Patrick and Libby watched me, big-eyed, until I calmed down and cleaned up the glass.

I first knew that Patrick was different when he taught himself to read at two years old. When I was washing dishes, he would bring me a book and ask me a word. "Mom, Mom, whatsis? Whatsis, Mom?" He would pull on my pants until I turned around from the sink, a little annoyed that he was interrupting me, and read the word to which he was pointing. Off he would go until he found another word he needed to know, and then I would get the pants pulling again. I thought nothing of it until bedtime a few days later when he read the entire *Pat the Bunny* book out loud. He had memorized the words I told him, as well as words from previous bedtime stories. He learned to read at the same time he learned to speak. From then on, he raced through *Goodnight Moon*, *The Very Hungry Caterpillar*, and *The Runaway Bunny*. When I marveled at him, he looked down, smiled, and leaned against me, his blond hair soft as silk. He was irresistible in his joy and humility, and I would kiss the top of his head until he squirmed to get back to reading.

Writing followed—first his name, then letters copied from books, then masses of lined paper with words and sentences. He knelt beside a wooden piano bench and wrote so hard that he covered it with indentations of letters. When Bob came home with a new wooden puzzle, he would practically cry if Bob didn't get it out of the shrink wrap fast enough. He would put it together right away, and Bob would have to get bigger puzzles. He taught himself everything—games, words (forward, backward, jumbled, and palindromes), math, and science. He was autodidactic from the very first moment that he pulled on my pants.

By nursery school, he was reading books to other children. His teacher came for a home visit—usually not a good sign. In Patrick's case, it was to let me know how advanced he was and to ask if I needed resources. I said I knew he was gifted, but I didn't want him treated differently. I didn't want him to be set apart, especially in front of Libby. Social interaction was more important than academics at four years of age. If both of them were happy, that's all I cared about. The nursery school teacher agreed.

To help Patrick and Libby adjust further, Bob and I kept them in nursery school another year. They were more than capable as four-year-olds, but they were on the young end of their class, and it showed in their social development. While other children played confidently, they sat back and watched instead of taking part. A kindergarten teacher warned me that twins could lag months behind single children. They take cues from each other instead of older children, and they don't always catch up in the older grades. Patrick might be holding his panda bear in middle school while other boys were growing beards.

It was about this time that I began wondering if Patrick would grow up to be gay. He was physically slight, angelic, gentle, and affectionate. He didn't blend with other children. He tutored them. He was closer to the adults in his world. He loved to snuggle. He lived in a world of books, and he had an endearing way of talking, as if he was reaching through your frazzled mind and grabbing your heart. He would ask for something in a sweet, bashful tone, smiling hopefully, and dance around the room when he got it. Then he would chirp about stories and puzzles and strategies for board games. He wasn't interested in physical play. He was different from other boys. But how different? And what would I do about that difference? One day the answer became clear.

I picked up Patrick and Libby from nursery school in a brightly lit room of the Pomfret Congregational Church. Legos, stuffed animals, and crayons lay near different stations for building, play-acting, and drawing. Teachers were laughing with parents. I held Patrick's and Libby's hands as we said goodbye to the teachers and walked to the car. I belted them into their car seats and drove home past Pomfret School across from the church. Its stone chapel, playing fields, brick Georgian dormitories with white trim, and mature trees planned by Frederick Law Olmsted lined Route 169 in the middle of Pomfret. Farther north, Rectory School graced the road with white colonial-style dormitories and faculty houses. The Vanilla Bean Café marked the turn onto Route 97 with clapboard houses and woods and fields on either side. It continued to our own yellow Victorian, which we called "Hillside."

At five years old, Patrick and Libby were eager to get out of the car and into the kitchen for lunch. They climbed onto old wooden chairs at the kitchen table as I poured juice and sliced apples. I turned on a daytime talk show as they ate quietly, and I made sandwiches. A young man was being interviewed. He had told his parents he was gay, but the parents implied to the talk show host that being gay was unnatural. They wanted their son to become normal. They wanted him to become straight. They had brought him to a psychologist to be "converted." The young man looked down at the floor as his parents said they were convinced that the conversion had been a success. Being gay was a choice, they indicated. It was a wrong choice, and it could be made right, just like any other choice. The satisfied parents watched as the young man looked at the floor and agreed.

I looked at Patrick, his blond head bent down to his lunch. What would I do if he were gay? Would that be unnatural? Would he need to be converted? And if he did, would it really work as the family on TV promised? I didn't know the answers, but I realized that whatever Patrick was going to be—gay or straight—it would be his life, and he would live it the way he wanted. I would never interfere. I would love him no matter what. He didn't need to be converted. He was perfect the way he was.

Patrick's first-grade teacher knew he was bright. He could take an IQ test, she counseled, but what good would it do? He was already a "once-in-a-lifetime" child. He was sweet, attentive, and willing. Teaching him was almost "effortless."[20] We took her advice and didn't test him. We asked teachers to let him be part of the class as much as possible, and when the class was too slow, we asked them to let him learn at his own rate. Some were doubtful that he could handle independent learning in elementary school, but when he sat in the back of the class quietly reading or working on math, they became believers. The best example was a third-grade parent-teacher conference in which the teacher told Bob and me about Patrick reading out loud with her in class. "He was reading in character voice," she said, "and I said to myself, 'Holy shit! He's reading in character! In third grade!'" Bob and I looked at her, big-eyed, and laughed about it all the way home.

Patrick and Libby were placed in separate classes in elementary school so they could learn at their own pace without comparison. Colin was a little more insulated by being four grades ahead, but he and Libby both grew up in Pat's academic shadow, and Pat grew up in their athletic shadows. He was the bookworm who got straight As. They were the popular athletes, the first to get picked for soccer teams. He was the last.

At home, he was always absorbing information, and I do mean always. His mind was insatiable. We had to coax him to watch TV with us so he would stop reading or planning his next move on a board game, but in the middle of a show, he would jump off the couch and disappear with a puzzle or a book or a magic trick.

Colin took piano lessons from a gentle teacher with an antique upright piano in her lakeside cottage. Libby's long fingers invited the same. Patrick watched the two of them at the keyboard for a few months, and at six years old, asked if he could try, too. The common approach emphasized music by ear. But teacher Ann Warde saw that Patrick "could immediately translate musical notation into the spatial, kinetic motion of his hands and fingers on the keyboard." She said, "His mind knew where his fingers were going as clearly and fluently as an astute reader knows words. So, even if his fingers happened to trip, his knowledge and understanding of what was intended was not interrupted, and rhythmically he could fly steadily on, unimpeded and unquestioning."[21] Ann tolerated his lack of interest in musical scales and encouraged his happy pounding through a large part of the standard piano repertoire. Her goal was to have the most fun possible playing music together. She knew that he needed to feel good about himself, that it was the whole person that mattered, and that his own standards were high enough. She was the foundation by which all future teachers were measured.

Ann and Pat read furiously through Schumann, Brahms, Mozart, whatever they could find. Patrick's chirping, but insistent, voice was happily frustrated by the lack of synchronization between notations and piano keys, laughing, joking, and broadly smiling. Ann described him as devouring "every Dover edition of the classical piano music canon that could be found, absorbing it singlemindedly."[22] They would sit at her black upright piano, he on her old-fashioned piano stool at age seven or eight, his feet dangling halfway to the floor. They would be working on a Beethoven sonata, and he would mark notations on the music that he thought might be an improvement—an improvement on Beethoven....

On shopping trips, we were constantly scouring bookstores for music. Piles of Chopin, Mozart, Schubert, Schumann, Mussorgsky, and Beethoven music books covered the Steinway baby grand piano given to me by my grandmother. Patrick practically stood at the keyboard for hours. He was too small to sit on a piano bench and reach the pedals. He leaned against a Louis XVI-style piano bench upholstered with needle-point violins as he fixated on pages of music. He would interrupt his playing to press the pages against the music stand or bend the spine of the book so that the pages would lie flat as he played.

At nine years old, Pat joined a cellist and a violinist for an elementary school chamber group called the Wildwood Trio. They won first place in the Hartford, Connecticut, Camerata competition with their Haydn Trio in G Major.

At eleven years old, Pat and Ann played a Schubert duet at the Vanilla Bean Café during a Wednesday evening music series. Patrick's red sweater and blond head were barely visible through the crowd of people as he and Ann walked to the piano in the front of the room. His small hands kept up with Ann's large hands note for note, and after the loudest applause of the evening, they had ice cream and whispered intently about the details of their performance that only they knew. The crowd approached their table with congratulations, and Pat and Ann slowly returned to the world of everyone else, including Bob, Libby, Colin, and me, who knew nothing about music. Music was not in Patrick's family. He had no role models at home for the notes that flew out of his hands. Music was his voice alone.

Ann wrote on a CD of Patrick's music that "while the world that everyone else lives in could not always find its way back to him, he seemed to know how to live musically in it and to navigate it." He was "sure of the music's path," she said. "He had no period during which he was unsure of that path, during which he would have needed to laboriously forge the required mental-physical links step by step. He was different from other piano students I taught then because he was able to make this connection as soon as he learned about how musical notation worked, with no trial-and-error period."[23]

Most of Patrick's summers had themes. While Colin and Libby were playing outside or staying overnight at the 4-H camp, Pat preferred to stay inside and learn everything about origami or magic tricks or tavern puzzles or Rubik's Cubes or Wyvern cards or Franz Liszt. He filled boxes with folded paper peacocks and insects and llamas and rhinoceroses. We hung them on a small tree at Christmas. He learned backgammon, solitaire, chess, and The Mill, an ancient board game, from the classic guide to game rules, *According to Hoyle*. He learned bridge from my father's mother and had friends over to play mahjong. We set up ivory and bamboo tiles in a four-sided wall on a card table and learned how to build chows and pungs with Chinese characters.

In sixth grade, Pat attended the Longy School of Music near Harvard in Cambridge, Massachusetts. He slumped in the car, half-asleep, for the hour-and-a-half ride to Saturday classes in music theory, piano four-hands, and chamber music, along with private lessons. I would turn on a classical radio station until he got a little smile on his face and said, "Mom, listen to this," and put a cassette tape of Brahms or Rachmaninoff or Mussorgsky in the tape deck. My Christmas presents from him were tapes of Saint-Saëns or Chopin or Liszt, which we would listen to together. He was my personal guide to the greatest music ever written.

Students at Longy performed in master classes and recitals on a concert grand piano in the Pickman Concert Hall. Patrick refused. He didn't like practicing, and he didn't want to play on the brightly lit stage of a 300-seat auditorium. It was too scary for a sixth grader. Piano teacher Deborah Beers set gentle requirements on the practice, at least at the beginning of their three years together. She didn't want to add to the pressure he already put on himself, but she feared he would regret not performing. In their first months of lessons, as he sat at the piano in her high-ceilinged classroom, she told him that maybe he didn't like performing now, but someday he might ask why she didn't push harder. He might return to her years later and say, "YOU KNEW I was gifted! Why didn't you …?"[24] He stared at her, wide-eyed. Should he trust her? Longy was a giant leap from the small, friendly audiences at the lakeside cottage and the Vanilla Bean Café, but he reluctantly agreed. She eased him into the spotlight by playing piano duets with him on stage. They sat on the piano bench together, Pat closest to the audience playing the treble parts. The second year he was there, their four hands raced up and down the keyboard in the first movement of Schubert's "Grand Duo," the Sonata in C Major for Piano, D. 812.

Deborah never pushed him to take on more than he could handle, but he attracted attention with his talent. He was accepted as a Young Performer, a program for gifted students open only by audition. A Longy School administrator gasped when she heard that Patrick practiced only twenty minutes a day. Two hours would have been more believable. But even at the minimum he gave it: "Teaching Patrick," Deborah said, "was like holding the crown jewels in my bare hands. He played music with emotion so beautiful, it was almost painful to witness."[25]

During the lunch break at Longy, Pat, Libby, Colin, and I would walk to the Cybersmith café in nearby Harvard Square. Pat would relax and play the Myst video game on a computer mounted on a table while he ate a sandwich. Not many families had home computers in the mid-1990s.

The third year at Longy, Pat was in eighth grade. The first movement of the Schumann Piano Concerto made his fingers feel especially clumsy. He read music faster than his fingers could play, and he had little experience performing by memory. He preferred to race through sheets of music instead, but memorization was expected in a performance of a piano concerto in a concert hall. Deborah prepared him with mock concerts so he could work out the flaws before the end-of-semester recital. His memorization improved, but the technical difficulty felt hopeless. He knew how the piece should sound, and he was frustrated that he couldn't play what he saw on the score. He flailed at the keys in practice sessions at home and repeated passages aimlessly. Libby's room was above the piano. She could barely stand the repetition, and she would come to dinner, humming the same phrases that Pat messed up. The night before the performance, he practiced in a savage mood, banging the wrong notes on purpose, and wallowing in anger at dinner. He cursed his fingers' inability to do what his mind wanted.

Deborah was unaware of Patrick's turmoil. He had played the Schumann concerto with confidence in lessons and knew it solidly. He had performed an equally difficult Brahms rhapsody by memory the year before. She felt certain he was ready, and she looked forward to an enjoyable performance.

But the next day at the Longy recital, Pat waited backstage in terror. He waited until the final performance when a second grand piano was rolled next to one already on stage and an adjustable piano bench placed in front of it. He stood up mechanically and traipsed to the front of the stage under the glaring lights. His head was down, his shoulders bent over. He bowed without looking at the audience. As the concerto soloist, he sat at the piano closest to the front of the stage. Deborah sat at the second piano a few feet to his left to play the orchestra part. They placed their hands on the keyboards to begin the fifteen-minute movement. He leaned into his keyboard and began the first energetic notes. A few of them faltered, but he recovered quickly, seamlessly, and gave himself over to the music.

Schumann poured out through Patrick's long fingers sure on the keys, his back and shoulders driving power into his arms and hands forming a stream of notes building and softening, back and forth, until the stream swirled and deepened to a climactic finish. But afterward, in the lobby of the concert hall, Patrick was inconsolable. He didn't answer when I congratulated him. He looked into space, as if he didn't know what to think. My cousin Avery got an embarrassed smile when she told him he had made her day, but he didn't speak. Deborah had to contain her enthusiasm because of his agony. She took him away from admiring teachers and parents in the lobby and tried to convince him that he had achieved much more than a mistake-free performance. He had played with artistry and beauty, and he had skillfully recovered from the few wrong notes. He was focusing on an issue that was almost irrelevant because his mistakes were so inconsequential. Probably no one noticed or cared. They were only seconds out of a polished performance, which was exceptional at any age. But the more she tried to convince him, the more he shrank into misery.

At fourteen years old, Patrick had heard a different performance. He closed his eyes in the car on the way home and pretended to sleep. Bob, Libby, and I said some pleasantries. He ignored us. At home, he locked himself in his room and ripped up his program.

I could hear him sobbing. I knocked on his door several times. He finally gave me a narrow slit through which to speak. I offered that he had prepared his best, and that was all he could expect of himself. He could take heart that he had given it his best effort, which maybe wasn't true, but I was over my head in guiding him, in trying to make him feel better. I had never performed. I had no idea how classical music should sound. All I knew was what Deborah told me. Performers make mistakes sometimes, but she would rather hear minor technical flaws and the musicality Patrick achieved than a performance with the right notes and little else to say for it.

It was not unusual for musicians to doubt their abilities right before a performance. Their minds play games with them, especially if they are self-conscious adolescents who are about to perform a concerto in a concert hall. There is always a deeper level to learning a piece, no matter how well a person knows it, and as a recital approaches, the fear of what they don't know can make them feel as if they know nothing at all, and they temporarily forget what they do know. Once the music starts, the fear can disappear. That's probably what happened to Patrick. His panic beforehand turned into a compelling performance once he started to play.

But no matter how minor or understandable, mistakes were not acceptable to Patrick. He closed his bedroom door and locked it again. The sobbing quieted, but he didn't come out of his room for a long time.

He later wrote in a high school essay titled "Rite of Passage" that his bad habits culminated in that concert—the lack of practice, the failure to prepare, "the unshakeable standards of perfection I constantly set up for myself, hoping I could live up to them but knowing it was impossible." Later still, in an email exchange at Stanford, he wrote:

> In all likelihood (and as everyone at the recital took pains to assure me), I did fine, but in my fevered state nothing would have been good enough. I felt that the world was crashing and

burning around me.... But that experience taught me the very real dangers that can arise from seeking too much perfection and being all too willing to beat myself up over the inevitably disappointing result. I don't think it's an exaggeration to say that I knew that I would have to be more relaxed during the rest of my life, and thankfully, I am, having learned the virtues of moderation and coming to grips with the fact that I'm not perfect and will never be.[26]

The concerto was a turning point in his life-long piano study. From then on, he took Deborah's advice to practice proactively, note the weak spots, pencil in questions, and suggest changes. She asked him to list goals like "improve clarity," "clean up rough spots," and "improve down-up part." Methods to achieve those goals included practicing with each hand separately and practicing at slower speeds and without the piano pedal. Her suggestions helped him isolate problems like smoothing out trills. He practiced "hard, early," he wrote, "so that by the time the performance comes, the dirty work is already out of the way." He invited me into his practice sessions so he could yak about his latest pieces. "Hear that chord, Mom? It's a major chord. Now hear this one. Is it major or minor? Can you tell the difference?" I couldn't tell the difference, but Pat didn't care. He enjoyed trying to teach me.

About the same time that Patrick was controlling his recital nerves, Libby took it upon herself to teach him to be cool in middle school. She helped him make friends and picked out his clothes in the morning. His nerdy-looking sweatpants and glasses disappeared. He learned to be funny while he was leading the quiz bowl team to a championship and earning perfect SSAT scores, which were required for admission to selective secondary schools. By the spring of 1997, he and Libby graduated from Pomfret Community School. He won the Highest Academic Achievement Award along with a full scholarship to Pomfret School, a local private school, which attracted boarders from around the world.

Saturday classes and sports at Pomfret would not allow Patrick to commute the hour and a half to Boston for music lessons. He left Longy as an eighth grader winning the Excellence in Theory Award and becoming one of only four students to earn the Preparatory Studies Junior Certificate in 1997. He was chosen to play a Schubert duet with another young student in the commencement concert, which otherwise included only college-level performers. His Young Performer status the year before was a significant accomplishment—out of reach for many students, who went through twelfth grade at Longy without attaining Pat's level of competence. His music theory teacher, composer Howard Frazin, said that he was a "great solfèger,* analyzer, and counterpoint/harmony composer. Patrick is an inspiring student, incredibly hard working, remarkable ears, and has a formidable intellectual sensibility.... If we can get him to learn to yell at people I think Patrick has the talent and skill to be a conductor."[27] The final exam in music theory included an excerpt from a Haydn string quartet in which Pat had to analyze the harmonies, describe the "phrase structure," and describe how cadence was created. His answers, which included phrases like "from the dominant to the tonic," were elementary to him but foreign to me. They earned him an A on the exam. Years later, Howard wrote to me, "Patrick was one of those students early on in my teaching career that very much upped my game. The inspiration I got from working with Pat so many years ago now has never left me. I was lucky to have had him as a student."[28]

For six semesters at Longy, Patrick walked on stage, smiled at the audience, sat at the piano, leaned forward, hesitated slightly, and launched into piano solos, four-hands, and trio recitals. His

---

*Solfège is the system of attributing the syllables do, re, mi, fa, sol, la, and ti to each note of a musical scale. According to Merriam-Webster, solfège is: "the application of the sol-fa syllables to a musical scale or to a melody: a singing exercise especially using sol-fa syllables, also: practice in sight-reading vocal music using the sol-fa syllables." (Merriam-Webster.com Dictionary, s.v. "solfège," accessed November 1, 2022, www.merriam-webster.com/dictionary/solfège)

first movement of the Mendelssohn Piano Trio no. 1 in D Minor was exceedingly difficult for an eighth-grade pianist. It landed his trio in a Lorin Hollander masterclass, and along with Pat's solo and duet pieces, it was a massive repertoire for a middle schooler. But his performances grew more confident, and in student evaluations, Deborah wrote: "Patrick has always been a brilliant student. He reads easily, learns fast, possesses an uncommon general music knowledge for his age, and plays beautifully in performance situations.... [He] piles up musical ideas easily, so easily, indeed, that I often have a hard time remembering he's only fourteen. [He's come a long way in] preparing for performing as well as accepting whatever happens in performance."[29] Later on, Patrick told me that he learned what to do on stage. It was off stage that was hard for him.

Libby hoped to join Pat at Pomfret School, but she was not accepted until a year later. Pat was scared. He and Libby would have to be in different schools for ninth grade. He would have to begin his first year of high school—called the third form, which made it seem even more foreign—without Lib to smooth the way. He would have to navigate the vulnerable stages of adolescence without his other half to shield him against hundreds of unknown and unpredictable teenagers.

During the first year at Pomfret, Pat struggled with the sports required for all students. He was slow to make friends. He walked out of his way to avoid students he feared. He dropped a tray of dishes with a loud crash in front of a packed dining hall and melted with shame. He blushed with embarrassment when he had to speak in class. He was afraid his voice would change in the middle of a sentence. A serious case of acne didn't help. Red blotches covered his face in spite of trips to a dermatologist. He attacked them in the mornings before school as if he were at war with himself. He was glad to have Lib back when she was accepted to Pomfret School for tenth grade.

Praise persisted throughout Patrick's high school years from organ teachers, piano teachers, tennis teachers, and eventually coaches. At the beginning of the lacrosse season, he could barely cradle a ball in the basket of his lacrosse stick, but he wanted to break out of the classroom and try something he wasn't good at. Libby worked with him until he knew how to cushion the ball and rock it back and forth so it wouldn't fall out of the basket. He and Libby shared their strengths. He helped her with math or grammar or whatever homework she had. She helped him with sports and taught him prep school skills—what to wear, how to put on a tie, how to comb his hair. Cross-country was his first athletic success. He said the beginning of a race was exhilarating. The rest was pure hell, but he could skitter across rutted trails and paved roads for miles. Crew was another win. He could keep the rhythm of the four-man rowing team like the metronome on his piano.

In the classroom, Pat was like a second teacher. Some gifted students would shoot their hands in the air and shout, "I know! I know!" while the rest of the class rolled their eyes. Pat was none of that. He was prepared and humble, and he had a keen sense of timing. He read everything and knew the assignment, but he sat in the back of his classes, keeping his knowledge to himself. Other students would answer questions. A lull would open up in the discussion, and after waiting a polite amount of time for others to chime in, the teacher would call on Pat to summarize all the factors and their importance. Why did the South lose the Civil War? A polite pause, and then: "The North had the manpower. It had the railroads and the industry. They could resupply their troops better than the South," Pat said. The class was silent until the teacher spoke.

"You knew that reading better than anybody," I offered after observing the class.

"Ma," he said with a grin and a fake Boston accent, "I'm not smaaht."

Watching him was like watching a miracle. He raised the level of every class. Teachers stretched metaphors to describe him. His senior year AP English teacher said, "Seldom have I had the opportunity to work with a student as consistently insightful, articulate, and intellectually mature as Pat." His writing "is like a sailboat that catches a headwind and is lifted and propelled directly toward its destination. The clarity and power of Pat's diction is uncommon at the high school level. I remember one timed-essay this spring in which he described the entries of a diarist in Addison's satire as 'obfuscatory.'"[30]

In history, Pat was the "go-to guy."[31] In AP Music Theory, Pat wrote that the Beethoven Piano Sonata in C Major, op. 2, no. 3 possessed a "jubilant spirit and ironic delight." It blatantly exaggerated through a "deliberate thwarting of our expectations" and "tongue-in-cheek wit behind the scenes."[32] Pat explained Beethoven as if the two of them were sitting in a Viennese bar and talking over a couple of beers.

Humor increased Pat's confidence. Popular kids and nerds alike loved his jokes and snickered alongside him in class. At the end of a math class, a teacher might ask if there were any questions. Pat would raise his hand. "Have you heard of rain forest math?" he might offer. The teacher would smile and wait in anticipation. "If four loggers cut down six trees, how would the birds and squirrels like it?" And then the class would laugh and smile with him as they carried their backpacks out into the hall.

Patrick could dazzle wherever he chose, but his strongest performance was at the keyboard. Classmates roared with approval at Ginastera, Schumann, Debussy, Chopin, and Brahms. He made them love old music and Radiohead at the same time. He played the classical greats on the grand pianos of Pomfret School, the University of Connecticut, the University of Hartford, and the Boston University Tanglewood Institute. He won a state-wide piano competition. His Hartt School of Music teacher, Margreet Francis, said he was an "innate musician, sincere, intelligent, and motivated."[33] She prepared him with gentle guidance for premier high school recitals at Tanglewood. He found a balance between his high standards and the uncertainty of a musical performance. Performing became easier than informal socializing because he knew what was expected when he played.

At the Tanglewood Institute for high school musicians in Lenox, Massachusetts, he spread laughter, insights, and sometimes just really good jokes. In a dry music theory class one summer, some students wanted to skip the class. It was, after all, summertime. But Pat's friends would go just to hold their heads with laughter at his elaborate exaggerations. In his piano class, teacher Maria Clodes Jaguaribe would touch the back of his head as he walked to the grand piano to play Beethoven or Prokofiev in front of the class.

Midway through his last summer at Tanglewood in 2001, he called to say that a Mendelssohn trio was coming along "pretty well." That meant "spectacular," and Bob, Libby, and I eagerly made the two-hour trip to the Tanglewood grounds in Lenox. Colin was in the army at Fort Lewis, Washington. On a warm summer evening, we walked past the Koussevitzky Music Shed, where the Boston Symphony played. We bought t-shirts and hats at the gift shop. We wandered through a small display of the history of Tanglewood in a Victorian house until we heard a small hum beyond it. High school students in white shirts, black trousers, and ties carried music scores and milled in front of the Chamber Music Hall. A manicured lawn surrounded it. A green hedge beyond gave way to a sun-setting sky and valley below. The Berkshires rose to the south. An arbor to a formal garden stretched to the west. Lights brightened inside the hall. We filed inside, sitting next to Pat, his thin frame in a black suit resting comfortably against the back of the chair. His eyes focused on the stage. His hands held the score of the Mendelssohn Piano Trio no. 2 in C Minor, op. 66. He would be playing the first movement with a cellist and a violinist. Student groups paraded on stage—one of them playing modern music. Pat said the group looked proud of themselves, but he preferred music with melody. He made me relax in my ignorance of atonal sounds.

For the final performance—top billing in the recital—Patrick's trio walked on stage, standing tall and looking straight at the audience. My heart beat faster. I looked down in fear that Pat would make a mistake from which he would not recover. I focused with my ears. Pat began actively, precisely. The violin and cello joined in. The audience of teachers, parents, and high school performers stared silently while the trio built and crafted the lines, repeating, varying, emphasizing. Pat drove the moods with hints of buildup, holding the audience through every twist and turn of the long movement. Simple, tender sections allowed the music to breathe and contrasted with his virtuosity. He began his ascent by attacking the piano, his whole being leaning into the keyboard as if it were an extension of his mind, his fine features calm, intent. He blended with the strings, underlined their parts, flattered them with arpeggios, led them higher, louder, faster, and then swooped down. Up and down, up and down, then to the cello, back to a river of notes that plunged and swept under the violin until the piano emerged with swaying rhythm.

Pat was the conductor, orchestra, and audience all in one. He led his players and supported them. He was the guide and the follower, the director and the listener, at one with instrument, composer, and audience until he lifted all three above untrodden snow in a throbbing peak. He descended to a quiet interlude, which slowed the drama and grew softer still to a long note that left us waiting in suspense. Then to a thunderous double-octave finish in which he bent over and thrust his hands on the keys in total dominance. We watched from below the stage in reverence.

The audience rose in a standing ovation. They hooted and clapped for the loudest applause of the evening. Pat bowed, looking directly at the audience. He was invincible. He was above mankind as he accepted the adulation, and then he walked off the stage into the evening air in front of the glowing lights of the Chamber Music Hall. Students and teachers gathered around him as he talked casually, jokingly, accepting their compliments and congratulating them as well. I watched him as if I were admiring royalty. This has to stay with him for the rest of his life, I said to myself. I couldn't read a note of music. I had no knowledge of how it should sound. But I knew beauty. Pat showed it to me with the joy he felt that night. Phillip Falk, who played the violin, explained later that the piano part was "so much damn harder than the strings. The violin and cello will often carry a languid musical line," he said, "while the piano is furiously crawling up and down the keys with chords and arpeggios. I pointed out this characteristic a few times when we were playing together, but Pat always relished the challenge."[34]

Toward the end of that summer, my father, Anne, Bob, Libby, and I drove to the Tanglewood Institute to hear Pat play the fourth movement of the Prokofiev Sonata in D Minor. Pat was, once again, top billing as the closing performer. We smiled and congratulated him. We took pictures with his teacher, Maria. He put his arm around her and leaned in with a smile. He walked back to his dormitory to change out of his suit, his head held high as our pride followed him like the sun overhead.

My father, Anne, and I made our way to the Koussevitzky Music Shed where the Boston Symphony would be playing that night. Bob and Libby went to a movie in Pittsfield. My father bought us tickets for the symphony, and we ate at an outdoor café near the music shed. It was a covered stage with seating and a lawn beyond for folding chairs and blankets. Pat met us in front of the shed. The peaceful swells of the symphony were alluring but intellectual. At intermission, Pat said we should go hear the student orchestra instead of the rest of the program. "They're good," he said. My father hesitated. He had bought tickets for the Boston Symphony. He respected Pat's musical opinion, but a student orchestra instead of the BSO? Pat explained that his friends were playing—his BUTI boyz—including the cellist from his chamber music group. He had to be there. "I'll see you afterward," he said, and he pulled his backpack full of music onto his shoulder and walked away from the music shed, his backpack disappearing into the darkness.

My father was grumpy about leaving the BSO, but he knew Pat was right about the students being good. We followed Pat through the darkness, and after a short walk, Seiji Ozawa Hall glowed with yellow light from three floors of windows against the black sky. Inside, wooden balconies framed the golden hue of the interior. The air hummed with high school students in white shirts and black pants and skirts tuning their instruments. They quieted, and the conductor walked on stage. The packed audience applauded. The conductor took his position on the podium and lifted his baton. Violins were tucked on shoulders. Bows rested on strings, and after a pause, the music began in quiet, eerie suspense. Flutes joined in. The sound fluttered to a tom-tom beat. My father stared intently. The mood quieted to the eerie suspense of the beginning and then rose steadily until flowing melody crept in. Violin bows swept back and forth. My father leaned forward. Melodies repeated, expanded, wavered, varied, lightened, built, and drummed like a marching band with the students in the orchestra cheering out loud. A flute calmed the excitement. A pianist struck a downbeat, and the full orchestra paraded, flowed, and then raced to a finale. We stood to applaud. Patrick was right. Walter Piston's *The Incredible Flutist* confirmed his flawless taste. Once again, he lifted me, expanded me, changed me.

Family and prep school adulation, however, concealed an undercurrent. Patrick was sensitive to his differences, and he wanted desperately to blend into the prep school jock scene. He wanted the social ease he envied in Colin and Libby. He wanted connection and appreciation, but instead, his ability set him apart. It became an obstacle to fitting in. It made him temper his sharp mind, avoid awkward encounters, and maybe most damaging, repress his emerging homosexuality. He drew inward and feared outside contact. He wrote in an AP English essay: "Tightness seizes and paralyzes me; irrational fear takes hold; I shrink back in my chair and hope not to be seen." The dining hall became a sea of hostility, a lunch table an agonizing choice, the conversation rough. Rich jocks and confident swagger wilted him. He struggled against "the unpredictability of my own character."[35] His mind felt out of control. On his worst days, he felt the world was out to get him. On his good days, he worried about the next bad day. He covered up both of them with a quiet smile.

He called one night from the computer room at the Pomfret School library and told me in a shaky voice that he thought he was depressed. He had found the symptoms on the Internet and diagnosed himself. I knew he was right. He was always right. But along with being top scholar every year and doing well at sports, I didn't realize how bad he felt. Libby and I had recently seen him in a New England schools cross-country meet. He came in eighth in his division ahead of many gangly sophomores bent over and gasping at the finish line. Of course, Bob and I would take him to a doctor. Of course, we would give him what he needed.

We called his piano teacher at the University of Connecticut and discontinued lessons. Pat was feeling pressure at school, we explained. And off we went to the psychologist as if we were going to the pediatrician—a good conversation, a few tablets, and all would be better. Bob went with Pat on a few visits. He said they went well. Pat usually came out of the office with a little smile on his face. He liked the doctor, whose wife was a pianist. He took a break from piano so part of the pressure was off. He seemed okay at home. There were no more phone calls about sadness. Depression under control, I figured. I didn't need to check with the doctor. But in the following weeks, Pat told the doctor that he might have been depressed all his life. Suddenly, the times he wouldn't play outside, the times he stomped off the school bus in anger, the times he ran to his room because children made fun of him, the times he would sob after a piano performance—those times all made sense now. He was sensitive and shy. But doctors had fixed everything before—his weak knees, his flat arches, his acne, his Lyme disease. They could surely fix his sadness. How hard could it be for someone who could do anything, be anything?

I concentrated on the next stage of Pat's life—the stage he deserved. He would attend the college of his choice. We brought him to MIT, Princeton, Harvard, and Yale, where funny, nerdy tour guides made him long to be one of them. My father and Anne brought Libby and Pat to Stanford, where they saw Chelsea Clinton get out of her limousine and walk into a building.

Pat took the SATs twice so he could get a perfect score. He took them the first time during his junior year and scored 800 in verbal and 760 in math. He took them a second time during his senior year to get an 800 in math as well. "I know I can do it," he said when he asked me to pay for the second test. Weeks later, he opened the College Board envelope when he got home from school. There it was—a 740 in verbal and 800 in math. We looked at each other in awe. "Oh my God, Patrick, you did it," I said. He looked away from me. What did this mean? he seemed to be thinking. We didn't know. All we knew was that he achieved his goal of perfect scores in verbal and math. He had attained perfection. The proof was on the paper in front of him. Anyone else would have been thrilled with the junior year scores of 800 and 760 and left it at that. Not Patrick.

He filled out his college applications himself. I never saw them. He didn't need editing or consulting or any of the help other students used to get in to top schools. A small streak of procrastination caused him to miss the snail-mail deadline for his Harvard application. I had to email my cousin Avery, who lived near Harvard, to print it out and hand-deliver it. I think she slipped it under the door of an office that was closed the day before the deadline. He finished his online Stanford application six minutes before the Pacific Standard Time deadline. But when he got the acceptance, he was the happiest I had ever seen him. My response after he read the "Congratulations!" letter with the hand-written "Bravo!" at the bottom: How could they *not* accept him?

Georgetown and Duke also said yes, but Duke did not give Pat the full-tuition scholarship for top students. I called to ask why. An admissions staffer said they had many qualified candidates. I answered that I wasn't talking about just any qualified candidate. I was talking about a valedictorian with perfect SATs, who won nearly every academic prize at Pomfret School. She repeated that Duke had many qualified candidates, and after two or three more tries to get answers, she hung up on me. Yale sniffed that he hadn't requested early acceptance. Harvard and Princeton asked him to write a letter explaining why he wanted to go there. I suggested it might be a good idea to write it so he could say he got into those schools. Pat said no. He didn't care about the letter. He didn't want to go to those schools. I understood, and besides, I told him, he'd already been to Harvard when he went to Longy for three years. It was so close, we parked at the Harvard Law School and walked the few blocks to his music classes.

He was set on Stanford. He wanted to be in California near my father and Anne—on the opposite side of the country from his parents. He wanted to thrive in an accepting college atmosphere. And most of the time, he did. He performed a Scriabin étude in a Stanford recital and was invited to play with chamber groups. His professor, George Barth, tried to free his playing from the constraints of perfectionism and control, but Patrick was looking for another kind of freedom, the freedom to relax and socialize, which he had delayed for many years and which I completely understood. He stopped performing formally after the first quarter. More practicing would have meant too many lonely hours at a keyboard.

The pressure was off. His grades were stellar. He went to parties. He came out to his friends in his sophomore year. He found a boyfriend, broke up with the boyfriend, and felt relief afterward. He played piano for his German class. Friends would visit him at the math building where he tutored students. He would help them for a few minutes, and then they talked for hours. They joked and laughed so hard they could barely see. They chased each other and climbed over the stuffed chairs in the lounge like a jungle gym.

But the lows of depression mingled with the highs. Pat's college friends could see it, but they didn't know how to help. He stayed up too late doing homework. He didn't know when to stop. Libby and I picked him up from school after his first year. He slept too much. He could hardly pack. He wouldn't look up. He slept in the car on the magnificent coastal drive from Palo Alto to my father's house in Santa Monica. I figured it was because he was facing another summer with his parents. We called it the summer from hell. Libby was coaching at soccer camps. Colin was in the army. None of Pat's friends from Pomfret School were around. They lived too far away. It was just Bob, Pat, and me, trying to figure out what to do with one another. Pat wanted a job where he didn't have to think. A Staples warehouse was happy to have him. He had a small car, which he drove to night shifts in a low white building, which rambled through a field. He drove a forklift to move boxes and fill orders. His boss was nice. The workers were okay. They thought he was a little weird when he went on break by himself, reading a book while they went outside smoking cigarettes. But that didn't bother him. The worst thing about the job was that the warehouse was dusty. "You might as well throw dirt on yourself and get it over with before you walk in," he said.

Pat and I drove to Tanglewood to hear the Brahms violin concerto one Sunday. He searched the audience like a periscope for friends from previous summers. But he didn't know the new students, and the rousing violin solos could not erase the disappointment on his face. Tanglewood wasn't the same as when he had played there the summer before—when others looked up to him, and he felt at ease.

Bob and I took Pat to summer theater, out to dinner, anything we could think of that summer to keep him busy, but it wasn't enough. Pat continued seeing a psychiatrist, but he was in his room much of the time, reading or sleeping. I took my horse on a trail ride one day and came home late afternoon. Bob had not seen Patrick all day. He worried about him being in his room but didn't know what to do. "Why didn't you go up there?" I asked. "He's not capable," I continued vaguely. I didn't know what Patrick wasn't capable of exactly, and I also didn't know what to do. Bob said nothing. I went upstairs. Pat was reading on his bed. I told him he had to get outside. It wasn't good for him to be in his room for so long. I didn't know where he should go, but he needed to get out of the house. Somewhere. He seemed to understand and mechanically went downstairs, got into his car, and drove away. I didn't go on any trail rides after that. The rest of the summer, I planned things to do with Pat—clothes shopping, day trips, music camps which he didn't want to do—anything to keep him going. I felt like a camp director.

Pat and I survived the summer from hell with humor. He slept late and came down for breakfast when he felt like it. He would put his head in the refrigerator looking for food, and I would jab him in the shoulder and then act surprised. "Oh! I'm sorry. I didn't see you there." And he would smile and playfully punch me back. We would sit at the kitchen counter reading or eating in silence, spoons clinking in coffee cups. He might tell me a knock-knock joke or a factoid. "Ma, you know why the sky is blue?" And then he would tell me why as if that were a natural thing to store in my brain, which, he pointed out, "isn't finite, you know." He and Bob had a crossword puzzle race at the kitchen counter one day. Bob was a wordsmith. Pat had won a Will Shortz crossword contest in the *New York Times* when he was in elementary school. Bob copied a puzzle out of the newspaper so they would both have the same one. I said go. In a few minutes, Pat beat Bob by several words.

Pat went back to Stanford early that summer. He was accepted as a teaching assistant in a linguistics course. He would tutor students and get a stipend and a place to live, and that's about all he told me. When it came to details, he was sparse. "Whatcha doing?" I would ask lightly to make conversation. "Stuff," he would answer with a sly smile. And if I pressed him, he would get annoyed, break into a little hum, and look away.

I didn't need details. His instincts were pure enough without me knowing specifics. I took what he gave me—what to read, what to watch on TV, what music to like, what to laugh at. He usually prefaced his recommendations with, "Drop everything you're doing, and" read *The Sword and the Stone*, or watch *Will & Grace*, or listen to Prokofiev's *Violin Concerto no. 1*, or check out *The Onion*.

I drove Pat to the airport in mid-August to start the linguistics program. He was eager to go back to school. He would be better off, I said to myself. Back in his college element. Much better than at home with his parents. And he was, for the time being. He liked the linguistics professor. He was good at tutoring, and he absorbed the structure of language like the air he breathed.

But in the next few years, Pat would teach me that he wasn't better off without his parents. Sadness would follow him with or without us. He would teach me something I never thought possible. He would teach me there was something worse than death. It was the fear of not dying. It was called depression.

Above: Libby with the bottle.
Below: Pat in the wagon, 1984.

Bulletin photo by Randy Flaum

LOOKING THROUGH THE GLASS — **Libby of Pomfret Center spent yester-**
Patrick Wood, 2½, left, and twin sister **day at Putnam Public Library.**

Above: Patrick and the author in front of our 1840 Victorian, Hillside, 1989.
Below: Patrick and Libby, two years old, the *Norwich Bulletin*, 1985.

Libby, Bob, Colin, the author, and Patrick, 1988.

"The Wildwood Trio" with Edward Foster (age 9, cello), Patrick (age 9, piano), and Mari Crabtree (age 11, violin) winning the junior division of the Camerata Ensemble Young Artists Chamber Music Competition in Hartford, Connecticut with the Haydn Piano Trio no. 39 in G Major, 1992.

Lib and Pat, first day of school, 1999.

Libby and Patrick, sailing with my father and Anne off the
coast of California near Santa Monica, early 2000s.

Patrick, Renée Fisher piano competition, Westport, Connecticut, 2001.

PROFILE OF A NEWSMAKER

Teen music man begins college on a high note

In the news: Patrick Wood, 18, of Pomfret Center has just completed his third summer semester at the Boston University Tanglewood Institute for gifted high school musicians. He was the valedictorian at the Pomfret School and will leave for Stanford University in September.

Patrick Wood

A *Norwich Bulletin* article during Pat's senior year in high school, which talked of his awards, his "knack" for the piano, and his dreams of travel and independence, 2001.

Above: My father, David Rimer, and Pat, Hotel Adlon, Berlin, 2004.
Below: Pat, Neuschwanstein Castle, Schwangau, Germany, 2004.

Above: Pat at Siemens when he was featured in a Stanford
Overseas Studies Program newsletter, 2005.
Below: Ryan and Patrick, Krupp Internship luncheon, Essen, Germany, 2004.

Pat's grave. Libby's shadow, Pomfret, Connecticut, 2006.

After Berlin

Instead of seeing Patrick sitting at the kitchen table, we now open our magazines to find his half-finished crosswords. The memories are painful but they are vibrant, and in the realisation of what we have lost lies the joy of all we gained by knowing him. Patrick cut a swathe through our lives and his life, his death will echo with us down the years. For me, Berlin will always be Patrick.

—Stephen Pryce
"Patrick Wood Memorial," 2006

I stayed by myself after we got back from Berlin, or at least I tried. I didn't want Bob to see me crying as I answered hundreds of condolences filled with pictures, stories, and wisdom. Friends, parents of friends, teachers, and family remembered Patrick as the child with fine blond hair who loved origami and music and books, the teenager with the sly smile, the college student who laughed when his bumbling math professors lost their equations on sliding blackboards.

I couldn't keep up with the replies, and when I took a break, it was for more obligations—getting copies of Pat's death certificate from the State Department (required for out-of-country deaths) and patching up school debt. I could hear Bob on the phone to a student loan officer who didn't understand English. "He's passed away," Bob explained, which nullified the debt, but there was a pause. "He's passed away," Bob said louder, his voice starting to break. And finally, one more loud, "He's passed away!" his voice breaking with sobs, followed by hanging up the phone and then more sobs.

I reclaimed German and American bank accounts, paid funeral bills, and went through probate. The probate judge asked me how many children I had when I went to her office at the town hall. "I had three," I sobbed. "Now I have two." I think she started to cry with me. Bob and I had little to say. We had said it all in Berlin. We had wondered aloud. We had broken down. We had questioned. We had absorbed. We had functioned. And we had done it all without blowing up at each other, probably because we were numb. We never knew when the other was functioning or dissolving. It was better to say nothing rather than intrude on the other's thoughts. When I cooked dinner, we were silent. Colin and Libby talked lightly. Four or five of Lib's friends from her University of Vermont lacrosse team stayed with us for several weeks. They brought food, cleaned house, cooked dinner, and walked around the house quietly.

One night after the lacrosse friends left and the food from the neighbors ran out, I was making dinner. Lib and Bob were seated at the kitchen counter. There was a stretch of silence, and then Bob said, "If I could have given my life in place of his, I would have." Libby and I didn't answer. I was ashamed. I had not thought to give my life for Pat. I had not thought he was in a life or death situation or that if I offered to die in place of him, that sacrifice would keep him alive. I hadn't seen it as one or the other, that I had to jump in front of him to catch a bullet. As a matter of fact, I was glad to be alive. When I was at my lowest, the gratitude of being above ground kept me from sinking lower. The fact that Bob was willing to die made me feel guilty that I hadn't thought to make that trade. I was happy to be living.

My half-brother, Tom Rimer, flew across the country from Los Angeles. His blue eyes stared into me as he held my hand and talked in low tones. "There isn't much to say," he started, "but just know that there is nothing you could have done. Pat did this. Not you." He gave me one of his Jehovah's Witnesses pamphlets, which I suspected of trying to convince me that death was a good thing. I didn't want to hear that Pat was better off in heaven or that he wasn't in heaven because he was gay and had committed suicide. According to fundamentalists, he had committed two sins. He had rejected the life God had given him and he had been homosexual. I was ready to back away from evangelical preaching, but no, Tom emphasized: "Death is the enemy." It was not God's plan. It was the price we paid for original sin. Death was as bad as I knew it to be. It was a return to dust, a state of nonexistence. The dead "are conscious of nothing at all," said one of the pamphlets. "When a person dies … his spirit goes out, he goes back to his ground; in that day his thoughts do perish."[36] I realized that this was what Pat wanted. He wanted his mind to stop.

Tom hugged me goodbye and drove away a few hours after he arrived. He flew back to his home in Los Angeles the same day he came to see me—6,000 miles round trip in one day. It was all the time he could spare from his wife Bonnie, who was bedridden from multiple sclerosis. After sixteen hours of travel, he would be up at five in the morning the next day to take care of her and then get to his job as a mechanic for the City of Los Angeles.

At night when Bob went to bed, I stayed up late talking on the phone with family, friends, anyone who would listen. I answered a massive number of emails, and sometimes I gave myself a break. Nature shows on television drew me in and turned off the pain. I drifted with mountains and oceans and deserts with wild animals. Sometimes I stumbled on shows about funerals or sex trafficking or disease. The worse the tragedy, the better the distraction. I watched Asian women forced into prostitution in a San Francisco massage parlor. They were discovered hiding in a secret compartment between the walls of the building. They sat on towels red with blood. I watched a boy dying of cancer from the Chernobyl nuclear explosion. His sister became a prostitute to pay for his medical bills.

I watched parents grieving the death of their young child. His body was covered by a white sheet and lay on a metal table in a funeral home. A funeral director drained the blood from the body to begin the embalming. Red fluid ran through a tube into a bucket on the floor. Chemicals would then be injected to slow down the decomposition. The child had lived longer than expected, but the parents sobbed miserably over the small casket as if he had been taken too soon. I tried to feel lucky that I had a son who was brilliant and beautiful and lived for twenty-three years before his own embalming, but I failed.

Some nights I turned off the TV and sat quietly in the dark. I tried to feel what it was like to be dead.

Pat's body arrived in Boston from Germany, but we did not go to meet him. Regulations required that his body had to be shipped in an airtight metal container and picked up at the airport by the funeral director. All we could have done was watch a metal box be put into the back of a hearse. Instead, we planned Pat's wake at the funeral home and his funeral at Pomfret School. We picked out a dark brown coffin with brass handles and a waterproof vault into which it would be placed. I brought Pat's black suit, a new white shirt, and his Pomfret School tie to the funeral home. Pat would look as if he were about to perform at Tanglewood. We figured out the poems, the music, and whether the grave could be dug in February.

On our way into the funeral home for the calling hours, we saw one of Pat's friends sobbing in the parking lot. He could not come inside. "I can't do it," he said. He covered his face and walked away from us as we stood near the door. I watched him get into his car. I wanted to comfort him, to tell him I felt the same way. I didn't want to go inside either. I wanted to get back in my car and drive away. But I turned toward the door. Bob pulled it open. We walked into the lobby. The funeral director came out and explained to Bob that a representative of the family needed to identify Patrick before burial. Bob offered. I was too scared to see Pat's body. Libby and Colin stayed with me. Bob returned. "It was him," he said. "It was definitely him." His eyes filled with tears as he looked away. He said the funeral director advised that it would be better if the casket was closed. Patrick wasn't presentable enough for viewing, and we might want to remember him as he used to be. Pat's hands would not lie naturally. The hands with which he had played piano concertos were sticking up from where he lay. He had been dead too long before undertakers prepared him—first in Berlin, where they could not do him justice, and then in Frankfurt, where more undertakers tried again. His hands were too stiff to maneuver. They would not lie flat against his body.

Hundreds of people waited hours at the funeral parlor to look at Pat's pictures, read newspaper articles about glowing successes, walk past his coffin, offer condolences, shake hands, give hugs, and try to find words. "It wasn't your fault," said Dr. Danenhower, who had written Pat's last prescription for antidepressants.

"Be careful," said a relative on Bob's side of the family. "This kind of thing can end in divorce." I nodded in agreement. I could see how grief could wreck a marriage. It seared every decision, small or large—what to wear, what to eat, what to say, who to call.

Steve and Ryan flew from Berlin to attend the funeral the next day. The Pomfret School chapel was filled as Chaplain Brad Davis said we were "making the best of an awful situation." It was "a brief, collective stand against losing heart entirely."[37] Music director Ben Davidson sang "Panis Angelicus." His tenor voice pierced the irony of a joke he had shared with Pat five years before: Amidst the smiling faces and cigars of Pomfret School graduation, Ben told Pat that if he ever gave up the piano, he would hunt him down like an animal. He could not have foreseen that Pat would give up his life instead.

Ryan read Tucholsky's "There Is No Untrodden Snow" in English:

> Yet when someone is as alone as you are,
> If they meditate, plan for how they will face death,
> Withdraw themselves from the world, and try to look
> ahead, then he might think he had attained heights upon
> which no man had trodden before.

Yet always there are traces, and always somebody else was there,
And always somebody climbed even higher than you ever could, much higher.[38]

Another friend from Stanford, Lauren Schneider, read it in German. She had left Palo Alto abruptly to attend the funeral. She hoped her professors would understand.

Pat's Schumann Piano Concerto trailed out of the chapel as we followed his coffin into the cold. I almost bumped into it on the way out, but I stopped myself. I didn't want to touch the coffin as I walked behind it. It was nineteen days after Pat's death, and I could not accept that he was in the box in front of me. I could not picture him lifeless in the black suit he wore when he played in recitals. Most of me knew he was in that box, but I would not confirm that knowledge by putting my hand on the coffin. I would not dignify that part of me. I was still hoping he was somewhere else—anywhere. I didn't care where. I didn't care if I never saw him again. I didn't care if he hated me, as long as he was breathing, as long as he was somewhere, anywhere but in that box.

Bob, Colin, Steve, cousin John Matthew, and uncles John and Jim carried the coffin to the hearse, and we rode to the cemetery down the hill from the chapel in black limousines. Wide lawns and old houses lined the road until we turned into the narrow iron gate of South Cemetery in Pomfret. It lay in a rural valley between Pat's middle and high schools. Pat would be buried between two schools where he had been the top scholar. We drove through the gate on the one-lane cemetery road, passing old gravestones splayed forward or backward like rotting pickets. Then to the frozen lawn of the newer section where Pat would lie. The hearse backed in to get Pat's casket close to the gravesite, but Bob said in a low voice, "It wasn't the way it should have been done."

We opened our doors slowly and walked toward the gravesite. Pat's coffin was placed on supports above the rectangular hole. Sacraments from Brad Davis broke the quiet of the headstones and the cow pastures beyond. The coffin was lowered into the grave. Colin and Libby stood on the edge and threw white roses when it reached the bottom. A backhoe stood nearby to cover it up. I looked at Bob to see if we should watch the grave being filled, but he signaled that it would be done later, and we left in the limousines. Libby returned the next day, her camera filtering the scene. Flowers mounded over the fresh dirt. Her shadow fell over them.

The following month, Pat's friend Sheena Chandran organized a memorial in California. It would be the third service we attended— the first in Berlin, the second in Connecticut, and now Palo Alto— three services in two countries within six weeks of Pat's death. Once again, Colin, Libby, Bob, my father, Anne, and I were making hotel reservations, flying on a plane, and trying to look presentable. The California sun blinded me as we made our way to the Elliott Program Center near the Stanford golf course on the western side of the campus. The bright sky sickened me, and I began to understand why Romeo "makes himself an artificial night" at the beginning of *Romeo and Juliet*. He is lovesick for Rosaline before he meets Juliet. He hides in the woods at night, and as the sun rises, he shuts himself in his room and darkens the windows. His humor is "black and portentous."[39] The best I could do was wear sunglasses and look enviously at students riding their bikes or walking around Lake Lagunita. I was jealous that they were alive.

Bob and I brought albums of Pat's childhood pictures and laid them on the table at the back of the room. Friends and faculty wandered amongst folding chairs. Libby's eyes were red as she placed Pat's stuffed panda bear on a chair next to her. Pictures of Pat's days at Stanford were shown on a computer projector—Pat at parties, Pat hugging friends in the dorm. He was laughing or smiling in most of them.

Sheena began the memorial, her dark hair flowing from side to side as she took a deep breath and talked of many good times with Pat—the deep conversations, the jokes during math tutoring. She read a eulogy from rap artist Andrew Nielsen, known as MC

Lars, who was performing in Austin, Texas. Andrew had roomed with Pat their sophomore year and was one of the first people Pat came out to. "I felt that there was always so much more before the giant Pat iceberg," Andrew wrote. "There was turmoil beneath Pat's amicable nature, and I never quite understood why."[40]

Privately, friends told of their attempts to get Pat out of his dorm, where he burrowed into homework or slept too much. Patricia Pei, Alice Kim, Ryan Sands, and Andrew Nielsen were a gang of four who "kidnapped" Pat for movies or dinners or concerts or board games to get him out of the dorm. They played Trivial Pursuit, Pictionary, Taboo, and Boggle, which Pat usually won. Ryan worked at Google and made a heroic effort one day. Google offered free lunches to employees and their guests. Ryan drove from Google in Mountain View, picked up Pat in Palo Alto, drove back to Google, had lunch, returned Pat to Stanford, and drove back to Google. No one at work mentioned that Ryan had been gone for much of the day.

The next day, Sheena and another friend, Kyle Duarte, gave my father, Anne, Bob, and me a Pat-tour of Stanford dorms and academic buildings. We started with Pat's first dorm, Junipero, where a parent had written on a window, "Your whole life is ahead of you, appreciate every moment." Then to Kimball, where Pat roomed with Andrew in a dorm room filled with giant speakers. Pat had to climb over them to get to his bed. He wore headphones to muffle the music while he studied statistics. Andrew recorded Pat's voice for the album *Radio Pet Fencing*. They rode bikes together around campus. They laughed more than they worked during late nights at the *Stanford Daily*, where Pat was a graphic editor. Andrew was a cartoonist at the literary magazine nearby.

Next was a junior-year dorm called 680, which Pat didn't like because his roommate sold drugs. The Hoover Tower pierced the cloudless blue sky as we approached the Sloan Mathematical Center. Bicycles leaned against the columns of its arches. A neon sign in a window said "GIRLS RULE." At the southern end of campus, the white columns of Haus Mitteleuropa, Pat's German-themed dorm, led to a common room with a baby grand piano. Sheena told stories of the "Screw-Your-Roommate" dance where Pat met his first boyfriend. I asked her if he felt okay about being a nerd at Stanford. "Everyone is a nerd here," she said. "No one is cool."

More personal recollections came years later. Jerome Murphy had taken a swimming class with Pat at Stanford and noticed he was struggling and sputtering water Jerome joked that the pool water should be flavored with Kool-Aid since so many students were drinking it. Pat gave him a smile and a laugh, and they kept a light banter throughout the quarter. Pat had an aura about him even when he was gasping for breath. "Nothing too silly would get past him," Jerome said. He was apart but alert, intelligent but humble. He was "luminous" and "physically beautiful."[41] He walked across campus, smiling and talking with friends. He seemed "like someone to catch up to," Jerome said, "(not intellectually, which would have been impossible) but personally and socially."[42]

Jerome didn't know if Pat was gay or straight, but he developed feelings for him. He found the courage to make him a valentine at the LGBT center on campus. With the help of a friend, he found Pat's dorm and slipped the valentine, with his phone number, under the door of his room. He didn't hear from Pat, which meant that Pat was straight or not interested. Either way, Jerome avoided him to prevent embarrassment. It was risky to reveal a gay attraction.

A week or so later, Pat came up to him after a film class. He thanked him for the valentine and said it was really sweet. "It was a typically awkward young-person exchange," Jerome said. "But Pat's bravery and integrity in seeking me out to talk, when I had been trying to duck out unseen to avoid any conflict or awkwardness, always stayed with me."[43]

Sometime later, Jerome saw Pat walking in downtown Palo Alto, holding hands with another young man. They dressed alike in hoodie sweatshirts. It was the early 2000s when it was unusual to see openly affectionate gay couples, especially at Stanford, which had a more conservative, "fratty" atmosphere than other California universities.

During a holiday gathering at the LGBT center, Pat walked in by himself. He said hello to Jerome and seemed at ease—casual and curious about the environment as if he didn't need the support that the center offered. "He seemed like somebody well-advanced in his identity and his thinking about orientation," Jerome said. "You felt not that he was ashamed of being gay, but that he had accepted it and so there just wasn't much need to discuss it. He seemed to have already gone through whatever coming-to-terms stage he would have needed."[44] Jerome, on the other hand, was attending regular meetings at the center to help with the "fear and isolation around coming out." He felt "slightly 'behind,' remedial, in contrast to Pat's seeming ease."[45] But Pat's exterior was maybe more of a lesson in his ability to manage the impressions of others. "He came across as well-adjusted enough," Jerome said, "that I have wondered if it was his cognitive brilliance and resulting ability to manage his external circumstances that kept the depth of his struggle so private."[46]

Pat had "a sort of privacy even as he engaged with the world," Jerome continued, like someone who was always thinking instead of going through the motions.[47] He never flaunted his intelligence, but he used references, maybe as a way of testing. He might throw out a reference "to a philosopher perhaps, etc.—then continuing conversation based on the level at which you could meet him. It was as though he was seeking people he could relate to in a more rarefied way, but was used to not finding them.... There was the sense that you wouldn't want to embarrass yourself by trying to relate to him on a level that was too basic. Not because he wouldn't be nice about it, but it might be the niceness of someone who was getting bored and probably just indulging you until he could get away," and you would be left with "silly entertainments ... to engage him."[48]

Jerome and Patrick never dated, but when the news of Pat's death reached Jerome, he could not "reconcile Pat's brilliant, alert personality, the gentle electricity of his presence, and his seeming social comfort, with the fact of suicide."[49]

Bob and I had packed Pat's belongings when he graduated the year before the memorial, but there were more in a storage cube near Stanford. We presented a copy of Pat's death certificate to the manager of the storage unit. The manager had no key. She tried to cut the lock with a bolt cutter, but after a few attempts, she stopped to rest. Bob took over and broke the lock. Several boxes of Pat's textbooks and his iMac lay inside the darkness. He had left them to complete his master's in computer science. We carted the boxes and computer to the post office and mailed them home.

Bob, Stanford memorial, Palo Alto, California, 2006.

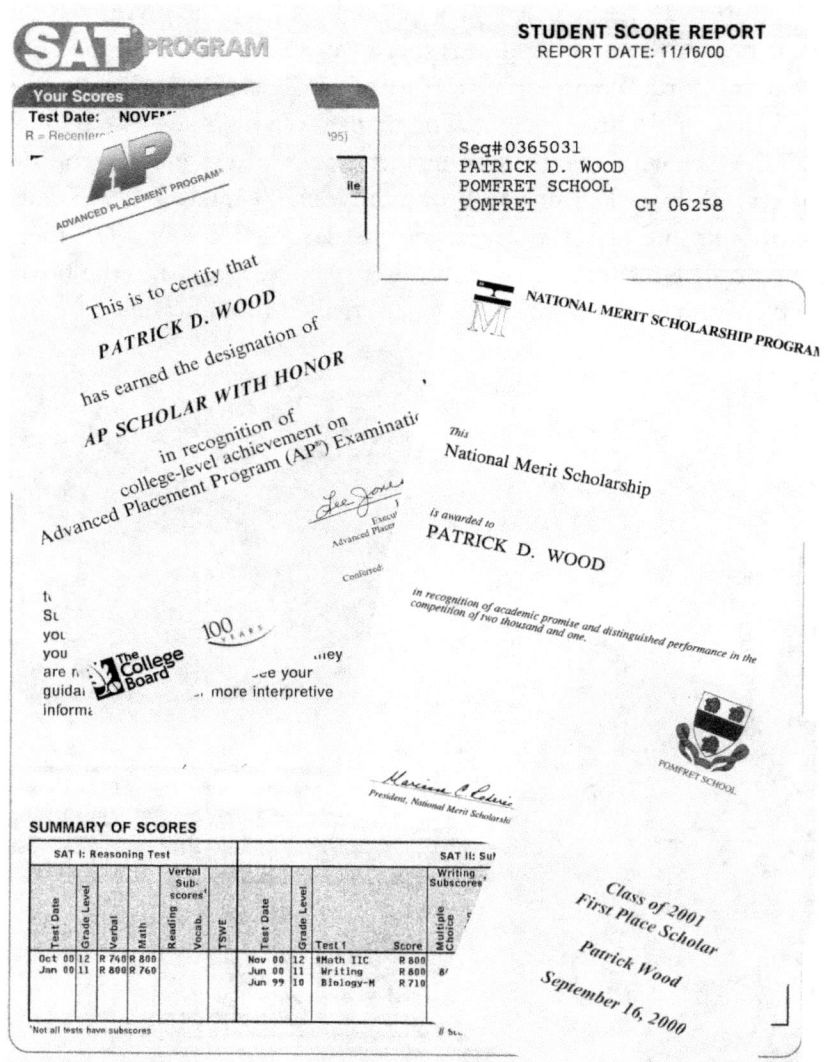

Patrick, 2000–2001. He took his SATs twice so he could
get perfect scores in both verbal and math.

Back to School

A comment is directed my way, followed by scathing laughter, and as I feel the fire rush to my face I wish fiercely that I were somewhere else, safe and warm and comfortable, alone.

—Patrick Wood
"Being Shy," 1999

Back in Pomfret, I arranged Pat's books in his room. *Essential C++* and *Multivariable Calculus* mixed with *Rhinocéros* and the *Complete Preludes* of Rachmaninoff. I poured over Pat's computer files, but after a year of sitting in storage, the hard drive was barely functioning. A spinning ball froze the screen until I brought it to a tech-savvy friend, who loaded the contents onto my computer. He added Patrick as a user so that I could log in as him and see his desktop as he would have seen it. Folders of mostly math and computer science classes revealed undecipherable worksheets. Emails contained requests to apply for jobs. A computer science recommendation said that Pat received the "coveted" A+ in CS107, the third programming course for computer science majors:

> You can only imagine how good a programmer Patrick must be in order to do such stellar work. Because of Patrick's A+, I can attest with confidence that he's an excellent C and C++ programmer and a more than competent Java programmer. In fact, he pulled the highest marks on both the midterm and the

final exam: That alone should be enough proof that he's really fantastic. The bottom line: if I owned my own company, I'd be eager to hire him myself.[50]

In an email exchange with an unnamed admirer, Pat listed sixty-five things he loved, including:

classical music, friends, family, academic rigor, having fun, love, modern science, America, irreverence, beauty, wisdom, modesty, honesty, being able to experience the thrill of discovery, satisfaction in a job well done, quality, my own open-mindedness, hard work, animals (especially my dog Bud), good memories, constantly discovering things I didn't know I could do, working hardest at what I'm not good at, Mexican food, the state of California, the state of Connecticut, France and Frenchness, Germany and Germanness, respect for the military, *The Simpsons*, *South Park*, avoiding making the same mistakes over and over, contemplation, quiet, the environment, people who are fundamentally decent, the existence of absolute truths, logic, people who do the dirty work no one else wants, humor, freedom of speech, libertarianism, the book *The Once and Future King*, British wit, Beethoven's symphonies, Wagner's operas, Radiohead, aspects of life which are unequivocally cool, optimism, modern medicine, knowing how to ride a bike, the fact that you never forget how to ride a bike, facing and conquering fear, incredibly long books that are so good they seem short, good hygiene, lack of intellectual pretension, great conversation, good times, good memories, Western civilization, Buddhism, being away from home right now, sleep, things that warm my heart, knowing what's going on in the culture, people who are indulgent to just the right extent.[51]

Pat described himself as:

the kind of person who would happily spend hours locked in a book store, even if I weren't allowed to buy anything. So I would probably start by making a beeline for the biggest book store in the mall, at which point I would spend a good portion of the night ransacking (figuratively!) the shelves and reading random pages from anything that caught my interest (this would include a lot of culture-oriented magazines, probably more than a few books about Beethoven and Wagner, some books which purported to provide a new angle on some kind of math concepts of interest to me, and maybe a couple of science-fiction or other classics which are high up on my must-read list). It doesn't matter to me whether I can buy something.... I guess you could say I'm good at drooling over things. So I would probably hit some kind of CD/movie store as well and drool over all the recordings and DVDs.[52]

The recipient listed "My favorite things about Pat," including Pat's humility in math classes and his distrust of "people who rely on heavy-handed pretentiousness to make themselves seem important." He admired Pat's belief in explaining concepts with humor and simplicity. He cited Einstein's theory of relativity as Pat's favorite example of "clarity and accessibility." He explained that:

Pat always tries, especially in his math classes to resist the temptation to feel pride at belonging to some sort of exclusive club, at understanding what all those arcane symbols on the board mean to the extent that he would want to deny that kind of understanding to others. That, he maintains, is a trap that's so easy to fall into (and I think he would say that, unfortunately, some professors here have indeed succumbed to that temptation), but it's such a selfish way to go. The minute he has the 'Aha!' of understanding some new concept, he forces himself to avoid the desire to keep it as his own.... He says that being able to share a new idea with others is the best way to test whether you really understand it.[53]

The email confirmed Pat's modesty, his bursting spirit, his thrill in sharing knowledge without vanity.

Between spells of answering emails and combing through Pat's belongings, I walked the fields around our house, sometimes on the phone with my father, sometimes on the phone with other mothers who had lost children, and sometimes just telling myself I was alive. If nothing else, I had my life, and I didn't want to change any more of it. I began to think about returning to school. I had been gone for two months, and if I waited longer, my substitute teacher would want to keep my English class of eighth graders who gobbled up grammar and devoured literature. I didn't know if I was ready to return, but I didn't want to lose them. I needed to tell them what they meant, how they had kept me going when the guilt was intolerable. "Dear Mrs. Rimer," one of them had written, "I have been thinking for the longest time what I should write to you, and I still don't know how to write this. I'm sorry for your loss, and although I know what I say can not change the events that happened, I am really sorry."

My English Department head, Ruth Healy, said I didn't need to let her know if I was ready to come back. All I had to do was drive to the school, get out of my car, and walk to the door of the school building. If I couldn't make it through the door, she would cover my classes, no questions asked. Ruth made it my choice, and that gave me a form of control, which gave me the strength to try.

In the spring of 2006, two months after Pat died, I made it through the door. I walked into my classroom with the giant Harkness table and twelve wide-eyed students. My substitute asked if I was okay. I nodded. I could take over. He packed up his books and his folders of single-spaced lesson plans that he had prepared even though he knew I was coming back. He closed the door behind him, and I looked at my students. They stared at me from around the table. They stayed silent and waited. Some of them were crying. I knew I was in the right place. "Everything relates to him," I said. "The movies he won't see, the books he won't read. Everything. From now on, we're not going to stick to the curriculum," I said. "We're going to talk about what's really on your mind, what really matters. I've learned that's more important than what we're supposed to do." They nodded their heads. A student craned her neck to look out toward the hall. "He's still there," she whispered. "He hasn't gone away." My substitute was listening outside the door to make sure I was functioning. The class and I smiled together. "He's so different," someone said. "We're glad you're back." We smiled together again. I explained that I would be shaky, tearful, and disorganized, but they could ask as many questions as they wanted about Pat, about me, about what happened. When we were ready, we were going to read *Romeo and Juliet*—but not like any other class. We weren't going to stick to the text. Whatever they needed to know about Shakespeare, about tragedy, about life ... that's what we would discuss, no matter how tangential or how long it took. Slowly, the tears disappeared. The questions came, and by the end of the period, we were no longer teacher and students. We were all students learning to grieve with each other and within ourselves.

Sometime later, when we were more relaxed, a student mentioned to someone sitting next to him that *Romeo and Juliet* wasn't believable. How could two people kill themselves over love? Why would we read something so far-fetched? By then I had been to an "Out of the Darkness" walk for suicide survivors. I had joined a large room of bewildered and crying strangers who had lost parents, siblings, friends, and children to suicide. About twenty of us wore white ribbons for the loss of a child—twenty people in one room who had been through that hell. After listening to stories of suicides, we walked outside for five kilometers in the pouring rain. I shared an umbrella with a woman who had lost her teenage niece and her niece's boyfriend. The girl had begged her mother for drug money. The mother refused. She was fed up with giving them money. The girl got angry. She and her boyfriend sat in a car with the motor running in the mother's closed garage in Springfield, Massachusetts. When the ambulance arrived, one was dead. The other died in the hospital soon after. I waited until the class stopped chatting and the student looked at me. "It happens," I said quietly.

Actor Brian Dennehy reinforced the relevance of *Romeo and Juliet* when he spoke to another English class at Rectory School where his son and daughter were students. Dennehy had played Montague, Romeo's father, in the Baz Luhrmann movie. On a spring term day, he towered through the door of the classroom and sat cross-legged in a small chair with a copy of the play in his lap. His eyebrows furrowed as if he were speaking to college-age theater majors. The eighth graders listened silently as Dennehy explained that Shakespeare had lost one of his twin children, Hamnet, in 1596, probably of bubonic plague. He could have been suffering the loss of his son when he wrote the play. He was young enough to know the pain of love and old enough to know disaster, and he heightened those themes with Juliet's character. She looks at Romeo as he climbs down the balcony after the first night of marriage. She sees him as if for the last time:

> Methinks I see thee, now thou art below,
> As one dead in the bottom of a tomb:[54]

I wrote to Dennehy that he had spoken to me like no one else in that room. Only a few months before, I had also lost a twin child. Dennehy was right about Juliet being the brains of the play. At the age of thirteen, she sees the dangers of passion better than Romeo. At the age of fifty-eight, I wished I had her foresight when I saw Pat for the last time. Instead, I left him standing at the New Haven train station on his way back to Berlin, my failure to boost his morale written all over his unsmiling face.

There were a few awkward moments in school. A student's mother addressed my English class about starting a public speaking club. She and her son chose Monty Python's dead parrot routine to demonstrate how creative and fun public speaking could be. A pet shop owner and a customer with a parrot battle over whether the parrot is really dead. Every manner of expressing death is used. The parrot is deceased. It has expired. It has "ceased to be." Finally, the customer slams the parrot on the counter as proof that the parrot is an "ex-parrot."

The class was not laughing. Some were looking at me. I looked down, and when the skit was over, I thanked the mother and wished her good luck. The student sat back down in class. Nothing more was said. A few days later, the student came up to me after class and said his sister had been a good friend of Pat's at Pomfret School. She was devastated when he died. The point was made: Death can be funny, especially to an eighth grader, but to that eighth grader, it wasn't funny anymore.

Students kept me going. I went back to saying words like *cool* and *awesome* more than usual. Teachers listened to my memories of Pat and gave me hugs. They took me aside and opened up about their own suicide losses or their uncles who were gay, or they sobbed with me as we listened to the Gay Men's Chorus of Los Angeles singing "True Colors." Some had known Pat, who had worked at Rectory repairing computers when he was home from Stanford. They helped me fit quietly into the school routine until, one day, I realized I didn't have to be quiet anymore.

The finance director spoke to the student body about losing a gay friend to AIDS. It took years for the friend to reveal that he was gay. He was afraid he would lose his job coaching wrestling and teaching English. He was afraid the school would think he was having affairs with male students. And when he died, his fears turned out to be justified. Within a day of learning he died from AIDS, an administrator asked others at the school if the gay teacher had been fooling around with male students. It was a shameful desecration of a good man's life. The finance director's story helped me understand why Pat had been so careful about coming out. He never knew whom he could trust. Everyone could turn against you when you were gay. There were too many examples.

The finance director opened the way for me to speak publicly. He had outed the pain of homophobic discrimination. In 2009, the word "gay" was a standard insult. It was an acceptable N-word. I was hearing it in the hallways of the school, mostly as a joke, but now I wanted students to know the implications. It was a delicate subject at a middle school. I would be speaking to students as young as fifth grade. But if an administrator could do it, so could I.

"It is not okay to call someone gay or fag or homo," I told the student body in an assembly. "You are hurting people when you do that, and who are these people? They are us. They are our brothers and sisters, parents and children. They are my children. Of my three, two are twins, and both of them are gay, including my son Patrick, who committed suicide three years ago."

I paused. The auditorium was full of teachers and middle schoolers who waited patiently. They stared at me. There was no chatting with neighbors or looking around distractedly like in some assemblies. I went on about how gay put-downs are still accepted and that almost 90 percent of gay and lesbian students were verbally abused in school last year. Almost half of them were physically harassed, and more than half were cyber-bullied. More than two-thirds felt unsafe at school. "Think about that—being scared every day and trying to cover it up," I said. "We went through those times as a family. Patrick was awkward in sports, and kids picked on him. That's life, we told ourselves. We have to endure and grow tougher. What other choice is there? But Patrick did not grow tougher, and he made a fatal decision for himself because of his pain and depression. I'm not saying you are all that vulnerable, but I am saying that words can hurt. And when they are aimed at people with depression, they can kill. Do not underestimate the power of what you say."

I showed three ads from the Gay, Lesbian and Straight Education Network (GLSEN) telling kids it's not okay to say "that's so gay." In one of the ads, comedian Wanda Sykes overhears teenage boys at a restaurant laughing loudly and making fun of a tacky figurine, calling it gay. She asks them not to say that when they mean something is bad because it's an insult. She picks up a pepper shaker on their table and tells them it's like if she thought the pepper shaker was stupid, and she said it was "so sixteen-year-old boy with a cheesy mustache." The boy with the straggly mustache looks into space to absorb the put-down. The screen turns black as Sykes closes the ad, telling us to realize the harm of saying "that's so gay."[55]

Students applauded strongly, but cultural change was slow. One day after my assembly, a student in my English class let "that's so gay" slip out. The class stopped talking. They looked at her and then at me. She turned red. I said nothing. There was no point in embarrassing her further. We continued with the lesson as if it had never happened.

Gradually students opened up about sexual orientation and suicide. They came to my tutoring room after school. They sat down heavily on wooden chairs. They stared out the window and waited until I closed the door, which I wasn't supposed to do. It was not a good idea to close a door that didn't have a window, but I closed it anyway. Students knew Patrick was gay. They knew he was a pianist and brilliant, and they wondered how that could lead to suicide. One student talked about bullying against a gay relative. Another student liked the Wanda Sykes video. He felt better knowing that gay discrimination had been called out in front of the whole middle school.

One student told how he learned he was gay. He had seen a boy taking a shower when he was thirteen years old and had gotten an erection. "That's how I knew," he said, and then he looked down at the floor. The other student in the room and I looked down as well. We were hearing a story he might not have told anyone else. We were learning firsthand that being gay was not a choice. It was something you discovered on your own with no one to guide you. You entered a foreign kind of puberty that you hid so you wouldn't be shunned or beaten up in a mostly boys' school. Your difference isolated you. It came between you and almost every encounter. It drove you underground, made you question your worth, made you doubt yourself at a stage in life when doubt was all around you. The three of us sat quietly to give that burden the respect it deserved.

Another visitor was a shy eighth grader with a disability. Sara M_____ suffered from cerebral palsy and walked on the toe of one leg because it wouldn't flex like the other. She limped in pain made worse by her giant backpack, which she thumped on the floor when she arrived in class. She was too self-conscious to use crutches. She suffered snide comments from students for walking as if her legs were uneven, which they basically were. She felt a kinship with Pat because of a gay cousin in her family and because she was curious and indignant about suffering of any kind. She would rush into my newspaper class and talk about injustice faster than I could understand her. She interviewed students and teachers for an article on gay discrimination. One student answered that "God made Adam and Eve, not Adam and Steve." A teacher pointed out that "the Bible says that men should not be with other men, but it also says that men should not eat shellfish, and men should not loan money with interest. That being said, we're not about to punish bankers or shun people who eat oysters. Why should we hold anything against homosexuals?"[56]

During the last weeks of school one year, a sixth grader, whom I barely knew, knocked on my classroom door and said, "You have to read this."

"What's up?" I asked. It was last period, almost time to go home.

"You just have to read this," he said, looking me in the eye.

I glanced at a page of a *Sports Illustrated* magazine. It pictured a thick-necked, sharp-cheekboned rugby player with a dragon tattoo on his left arm. His right hand covered most of a rugby ball. I flipped the page over to see how long I was in for.

"No, you have to start here," he said, quickly flipping it back.

Okay, this was serious, I said to myself, and out of a little curiosity and a lot of obligation, I did as I was told. The first page mentioned a six-foot three-inch, 225-pound bruiser, who had lost eight teeth, fractured both shoulders, and broken his nose five times. He had been named to the Welsh national rugby team more times than any other man and could drink his teammates under the table. At the bottom of the page was the unfinished sentence that said, "among active players in major professional team sports…" At this point, I looked up at the student, who nodded his head that I could turn the page. I flipped it over to reveal the rest of the sentence. In giant letters, it said that Gareth Thomas was "the only openly gay male athlete."[57] I looked at the student in disbelief. The boy looked back at me. He said I could keep the magazine, and then he disappeared down the hall.

In 2013, Jason Zhao, a ninth-grade Chinese student in my newspaper class, wanted to understand bullying and suicide. He had seen a video of Amanda Todd, a tenth grader in Port Coquitlam, British Columbia, Canada, who was pleading for help. She had been harassed in school and on social media. She had been persuaded to expose her breasts online when she was in eighth grade, and then she was blackmailed to do more of a "show." She refused. Her photo was posted on a pornography site and a link sent to her contacts. She was called a "slut," a "camwhore," a "pornstar," and she was beaten at school.[58]

The blackmailer stalked her online through several schools and changes of address, insisting that she give him three shows. She used alcohol and drugs. She started cutting herself and drank bleach. She went on antidepressants and received counseling but then overdosed and spent two days in the hospital. "Im stuck …" she wrote on flashcards in a nine-minute black and white video in 2012. "Whats left of me now … ncthing stops I have nobody … I need someone." She ended with a color picture of slash marks on an arm with a knife lying next to it. A barely readable tattoo said "Stay strong" with a heart after it.[59] A month later, she hanged herself.

Jason understood her pain but wondered how death could be an answer. He had seen students bullied in China, and he had fought against it. He wanted to fight it again, this time in the student newspaper. "Bullying is an inevitable thing," he wrote, "but what we can do and control is to step up and fight against it in any way, instead of staying back and watching it happen."[60]

Amanda's extortionist, or sextortionist as he became known, was Aydin Coban from the Netherlands. In 2017, he was sentenced to nearly eleven years in prison for blackmailing thirty-four young girls and men. He began stalking Amanda when she was eleven years old.[61] Given his cruelty, Amanda's suicide seemed understandable. At least that's how the media portrayed it. But Jason had a point. Why didn't she fight more? He himself had been bullied as a middle-school student in China. He had stood up to it and won. His head of school suspended the bully, and eventually, he and the bully became friends. Why was suicide the only answer? Not all victims of blackmail killed themselves. Why did some lose hope and others fight back? There was an underlying cause of suicide that Jason wasn't getting, a fundamental reason why some emerged from injustice and others succumbed. Bullying was not the whole reason.

Patrick's balcony, second floor, Berlin, 2006.

Pat and my father, David Rimer, Stanford graduation, 2005.

Two Griefs

I expected the good times I had with Patrick to be joined by many more. I looked forward to evenings spent playing Scrabble, not just old score sheets that bring a catch to your throat.

—Stephen Pryce
"Patrick Wood Memorial," 2006

The summer after going back to school, I learned that my father was dying of cancer. I could not fit another death in my head, nor could I face a cross-country trip, but I had no choice. My father had flown to Berlin to be with me, and I had to fly to Los Angeles to be with him. I sat next to a young girl on my flight to the West Coast. She wore a t-shirt that said, "Yo, it gots to bounce," across her breasts. I started to cry. I had lost a son who loved opera and mathematical equations, and now I was sitting next to someone who broadcasted a sexual body part. She looked at me and then turned to someone on the other side of her. I gulped Ambien and fell asleep. We changed planes in some major city along the way. I wandered around a boarding gate area sobbing. I didn't care who saw me.

I found my father shuffling down the hall of St. John's Hospital in Santa Monica. In 1967, he founded the St. John's Hospital gastrointestinal laboratory and was Chief of Gastroenterology. Now, in 2006, he was like any other patient fighting for his life. I barely recognized him from a few months before at the Stanford memorial in Palo Alto. His hair was white. He used a walker to shuffle up and down the hallway. His skin was red and peeling from chemotherapy. It looked like he was burning from the inside out. He rolled his IV stand beside him, his hospital gown hanging loosely around him. "Hi, Lisel," he greeted me, as if nothing were wrong.

I was losing my father, but on the way to his chemotherapy, brain scans, and radiation treatments, I clung to stories about Pat from Ryan Wirtz. "Patrick wasn't always depressed," Ryan wrote to me. "He would be happy, then he would be sad. During those happy times, he was great, and he was looking forward to the future.... We were all consumed with the struggles that Pat endured and what was 'wrong' with him. We wanted to say, okay, now I get it."

In Ryan's dreams, Patrick came back to Berlin from the Pomfret cemetery and knocked on Ryan's door. He was tired of being stuck in the ground in Connecticut. He had made a big mistake in dying. At first, it was really exciting, particularly with the beautiful policeman who took him away that night in February, but then there were little things that annoyed him—flying back to the United States in a metal box and the old-fashioned dead people in the cemetery. Most of them were standoffish colonists, and Pat had had enough. Being dead was really boring. There was nothing to do, and it was dark all the time in his coffin. He apologized to Ryan for the drama.

What if Ryan hadn't worked so much? What if he had been more assertive in making sure Pat had help? "Patrick knew there were options," Ryan wrote. "He knew that he could reach out. It would have taken two minutes for him to walk to our apartment, but he didn't. Steve called and invited him to dinner at 8:00 p.m. the night he died, but Pat didn't answer. He was still alive because he checked his voicemail at 9:00 p.m. He knew we were there for him, but he still did it, and he wanted to make sure he was successful.

"Patrick was twenty-three years old," Ryan said, "by all accounts an adult.... In my work, he would be old enough to be trusted with state secrets at levels beyond Top Secret affecting US national security. From a legal perspective, our society had given him total domain over how he chose to live and what he did.... Realizing this makes me feel better, sometimes. Other times, it makes me feel worse. It makes me wonder which is worse: knowing that I could have prevented Pat's death and failing, or knowing that it was totally unpreventable, and I was powerless."

On long phone calls, Ryan said that he had wanted to be with Pat early in 2004, when they were students in Berlin. They had roomed together on a trip for interns to the Krupp villa in Essen, Germany. Ryan had put his arms around Pat one night, but Pat said no. "He was just getting comfortable with being gay," Ryan said, "and he needed to explore his sexuality on his own. I understood that, and I was willing to wait for him. I was two years older, and I had gone through the initial stages of being gay. I hoped Pat would get past that stage and that we would eventually be together. I loved him very much. I wanted to marry him someday."

Pat had killed himself because of rejection from a DJ named D____, but the more I learned, the more I realized that Pat was doing much of the rejecting, including Ryan and the very same DJ. D____ had wanted to be with Pat in the summer of 2005, but Pat said no, and then he changed his mind after it was too late, after D____ had reconnected with his roommate. Pat wasn't killing himself over rejection as much as his own indecision and confusion. Rejection was not the whole reason. There was something deeper, something pathological ... something I would not discover until years after his death.

I made four trips to California within twelve months after Pat died. My father's cancer had spread from a lesion on the back of his head the year before. It biopsied negative for cancer twice, and by the time he had it removed anyway, it tested positive and had spread to his lungs. Then it spread to his spine, liver, brain, and stomach. He stopped treatment after a brain scan detected seven tumors, including one too big to radiate and others too small. He was eighty-one years old.

During the first few visits, my father was clear-headed. I brought a tape recorder to preserve his stories—how he was drafted out of Harvard toward the end of World War II, how he was sent to the University of New Hampshire by the army instead of Normandy with his unit, how half of his unit died in the invasion of Europe.

He met my mother after he graduated. They moved to Philadelphia while he was in medical school at the University of Pennsylvania and then to Rochester for an internship at Strong Memorial Hospital. He was drafted again, this time by the air force during the Korean War, and became a flight surgeon while training in Germany. The war ended while he was still in Germany, and he returned to Rochester to complete his internship and then moved to Los Angeles for his residency at UCLA. He received a fellowship in gastroenterology at UCLA and went on to found the gastroenterology lab at St. John's Hospital.

My father divorced my mother during the Korean War when they were both too young, too torn apart, too angry. I was five years old. He felt guilty about leaving me, but as we recorded the conversation in his bedroom so he could rest, I told him I didn't blame him for leaving. I was young enough to adjust, and my mother was caring and loving. He looked down, as if he was relieved to die with one less regret.

During the last few visits, the recordings were shorter. My father would talk about his past and then break off, his face tight with pain. "Lisel, I just can't do it anymore," he would say, and then he would lie down even though lying down didn't help. He was in too much pain to do anything, including remembering his past. The medication, which did not keep up with his pain, dulled his mind. It made him drift to unrelated subjects and then lose thought altogether. It blocked his connections. He would begin a thought, and then his sentences would trail off. "I'm sorry. I can't continue," he would say, and look down. Conversations disappeared. Friends of thirty years, who came to say good-bye, ended up staring at the floor, trying to find words. Final good-byes were often not possible. My father could not give his friends the attention they deserved. Sometimes, I would pick up the conversation for him, but there were awkward silences as he struggled to maintain his dignity.

Colin came down from Tacoma to see him one last time. He did chores for Anne and helped my dad in the shower. Libby came down from San Francisco. She looked away from me much of the time, as if she was in too much pain to connect.

Sometimes I cried for my father. Sometimes I cried for Patrick. Sometimes I couldn't tell which. My father saw me crying on the first anniversary of Pat's death, and even though he was days away from his own demise, he cried with me. He cried for Pat in a long howl as we sat in the living room of his house in Santa Monica. His body shook as he hunched over, and then he cried in another long howl for himself. We looked down in silence until I took that moment, the moment I had not had with Pat, to tell him what he meant to me. "You are a teacher and a life-giver," I told him. He looked at me, nodded his head, and then looked down again.

Sometimes there were moments of clarity. At a dinner one night about a month before my father died, Anne, my aunt Beverly, her daughters Avery and Polly, and I sat at the dining room table, waiting for my father. He walked slowly to the head of the table and stood behind his chair. We looked up at him expectantly. He held on to the back of the chair and said, "We are made up of the people we know, and I would like to thank you for what you have made me." We bowed our heads as if we were saying grace before the meal.

By my last visit, my father could barely eat or walk. He spent much of the day in bed. A hospice doctor came to listen to his lungs, which had been perforated by tumors, allowing fluid to seep in. His lungs had been drained but had to be checked regularly.

My father sat on the edge of his bed as the young doctor put a stethoscope on his chest. My father tried to take the deep breaths he had asked of his own patients. The doctor took the stethoscope off and put it around his neck. He looked at a small bulge on my father's stomach above his waistline. "That's the tumor," he said. My father looked down and then back up with no expression. The tumor looked like it was trying to poke through his stomach. I closed my eyes. This was one more panic. This was Patrick part two, only the opposite version—the slow death versus the sudden, the visible versus the unseen.

When the hospice doctor left, I tried to make my father feel good about being more experienced. "Does he know what he's doing?" I asked. "He's very good," my father answered. "He knows his stuff." It was another death knell.

As my father deteriorated, I tried to see him one last time, but I was too late. He stopped eating about a week after I left. The pain medication was increased to extreme levels. On the morning of February 16, 2007, he became agitated with pain. The hospice nurse and doctor were called. Anne tried to convince them to again increase the medication. She had become the doctor and my father the patient. The pressure was exhausting. All her nursing, tending, listening, and trying was about to be over, and it wasn't going well. My dad was suffering too much, and as much as he and Anne had prepared for that moment, with every conceivable detail decided— the living trusts, the new bank accounts, the cremation, the funeral, the reception after the funeral, including the jazz band he wanted—despite an entire year of confronting every contingency, his unbearable pain during the last twenty-four hours could not be anticipated. It took too many hours of hospice communication to again increase the morphine so that he could die in the peace he wanted. Hospice did not want the morphine instead of the cancer to kill my father.

Almost a year to the day after Pat's death, I was, once again, writing obituaries and organizing photographs and black clothes for funeral gatherings.

My father showed me how to live in pain (make each day the best possible), how to fight cancer (chemo *is* worse than the disease), how to die (don't try to forecast—live in the moment), and hardest of all, how to accept that his deadly melanoma tested negative two times before he had it removed. His answer: Medicine is not 100 percent. It's not a perfect science.

My father showed me how to keep going after tragedy. He made me walk in the woods with him after Pat's funeral in Connecticut. It seemed like a waste of time, but he was right to get me outside, out of my own head. Nature did help. He let me talk about anything, including that I was thinking about suicide. That was the only way to end the pain, and it was the only way I would understand Pat. "YOU BROKE YOUR ASS FOR HIM!" he answered loudly, and the exasperation in his voice made me stop crying. He told me about his own depression and the years it took for medication and therapy to work, how it would have worked for Pat if he had given himself more time.

And then there was the anger he felt. My father was forced into death. He could make no decision about the time or place or how or when. Even the morphine he needed to die in peace was delayed. My father did not have the luxury of making any choices at all, and compared to his lack of choice, Pat's decision to die seemed unthinkable. Pat arranged everything about his death—the time, the place, the how, the when. My father made me realize that Pat had will. He made choices that my father, who spent his life saving patients, could not make.

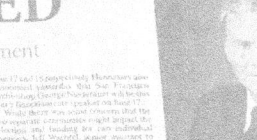

"Recent grad dies in Berlin," front-page article in the
Stanford Daily a few days after Pat's death, 2006.

Afterthoughts

Patrick knew he was not alone when he was alive. He knew that legions of people would reach out to him and he communicated that acceptance in his own Patrick ways.

—Ryan Wirtz
"The Essential Patrick," 2006

Soon after Pat died, 2006

On January 31, a beautiful, nearly perfect person committed suicide. This was not the first time a great and accomplished person had killed himself, but it was the first time this person was my son, and it was the first time I knew this person had every reason to live. There was no terminal illness, no accident, no struggle, no money problems, no lack of family or friends, and no lack of love. There was no reason that I could see.

"He had such a promising future," his psychiatrist said in a shaky voice on the phone when I called after the trip to Berlin. She was finishing her PhD at Stanford. Apparently, she hadn't seen the front-page article in the *Stanford Daily* announcing "Recent grad dies in Berlin." It told of his passion for complexity, his appetite for learning, and his "great ability to draw people into his life."[62] He had drawn her in as well, which made him a brutal defeat for her therapy. He could have been the first patient she had lost.

Initially, she was open and consoling about their "therapeutic relationship."

"Did you know he was capable of this?" I asked.

"It's difficult to predict a person's potential for suicide," she offered. But this was a person who loved people, music, books … life.

"I thought he was going to be okay," she said quietly. Her voice grew small, as if she could no longer speak sensibly of Pat's death, as if she was absorbing her own loss.

August 8, 2006

What was my part? What was Patrick's? The year before he killed himself, Bob and I helped him move out of his Haus Mitt dorm room at Stanford after graduation. Bob carried a box out of his room to load into the rental car. Pat and I were left alone, Pat at his desk, checking last-minute emails. I sat on the bunk bed behind him and asked if he thought Berlin would work out socially.

"Yeah, it will be good," he answered. "I'm giving myself a year."

A year to see if he liked living in another country? Did he mean something else? Fourteen months later, I am spinning his message around my head, the serious tone of his voice, the eye contact as he said it. He turned away from his computer screen to stare at me sitting on the bed. I stared back at him, then down at the floor, confused, hurt. A year for what? And then what? Bob came back to move another load. The conversation changed, and I would never ask those questions.

The signs were there—the breakdown when he checked himself into Stanford Hospital. "I don't belong here. I'm not like these people," he would confide. His email recounting a teary visit to his psychiatrist, his coming out to me on the phone. I thought my response would help him.

"Are you ready?" I said.

"I'm ready," he answered. "I'm gay. Sorry, no grandchildren."

"I don't care about that. I just want you to be happy. If you're okay with it, I'm okay."

"I'm okay with it," he said. "Actually, it's a huge relief. I'm so glad I told you."

And then I said something like, of course, I would never be upset, and I wouldn't tell Dad unless he wanted me to. He said no. He would tell him himself.

There were more signs—his shakiness during graduation, his head on my shoulder on the way to a restaurant in Palo Alto, his need for a relationship. But that's all they were—signs. They weren't direct. Now I hear them. They were attempts to tell me, bring me in, help me see, reach me. They were muffled cries of a drowning person, which I heard vaguely and then dismissed. Now that the person has drowned, the cries seem like shouts. I walked away from a victim screaming for help. I misinterpreted the signs. He was perfect. That's all I could see—the normalcy, the typical, the goodness.

At home, I like to be left alone to figure out what I should be. I hide in a small room on the second floor of our house. It's warm and sunny and crammed with too many clothes, pictures, and condolence letters. I look at myself in the full-length mirror on the back of the door. I am gaunt, sallow, defeated. I sit awkwardly, trying to respond to a large basket of envelopes labeled "condolences to be answered." A smaller basket holds "condolences answered." I wander to other thoughts. Should I be angry? Violence was committed, but how can I be angry when the murderer has given himself capital punishment? Should I be guilty? I *was* guilty. I cringed at what I didn't do. Then I toyed with what I did do. I gave him a Stanford education, for God's sake. Did he really throw that away? Within a year of graduating?

Should I be hurt? What should I be?

I bounce back and forth like the marble in the wooden maze that Pat used to play. I rotate the wooden level of the maze, weave the marble past holes, but I can't get to the finish. My marble drops through the holes. I cannot figure out the maze of suicide.

I add up the plusses and minuses of what I did and didn't do. Bottom line: Nobody was responsible for killing Patrick except Patrick. He's the one who lit the charcoal in the airtight bathroom. New bottom line: It doesn't matter who lit the charcoal. I blame myself every day. And that becomes bottomless.

September 26, 2006

By the fall after Pat's death, I've relearned parts of life. I drive a car, go to the grocery store, cook dinner. I feed the three horses on our farm, but I don't ride them. Riding is frivolous. I won't be doing that anymore. I walk into the barn, eyes down. The horses look at me, their ears up in anticipation. But I am all business—feed, hay, water, muck the stalls. That's it until Bob invites his brother John for a trail ride in the woods near our house. I agree because it is Bob's idea. That gives me an opening to think about something besides Pat.

Bob saddles up a horse for himself and waits for me to lead my horse Beau out of the barn and mount up. I hesitate. I have forgotten how to get on. After a lifetime of riding, after ten years of riding the horse in front of me, Pat's death has erased my memory of a life-long habit. I have forgotten which foot to put in the stirrup. Beau stands still while I rethink what used to be second nature. I figure out that I need the left foot in the stirrup on the left side of the horse to haul myself up. I line up by Beau's shoulder, facing the hind end. I grab mane and reins with my left hand, hold the stirrup with my right hand, put my foot in, move my right hand to the saddle, and bounce off the ground. I spring up lighter than I remember. I have lost twenty-five pounds in the months since Pat died. My legs settle around the sides of the horse. I pick up the reins, but I'm afraid. I don't know what to expect. What if he spooks? What if he takes off? I'm afraid of an animal I have known for years, but Beau walks slowly, steadily, his ears cocked backward toward me. He is listening for what I want him to do. The air is early fall. The sky is bright The flies aren't bad.

We turn up the road. Hooves clop on the pavement. A cloud of shame comes over me. I have done something horribly wrong. I have caused my child to harm himself. I have let him handle problems that were too big, that were unbearable for him. I have done something terribly wrong. I have lost my son.

October 11, 2006

Hindsight or context? How to judge his death? I am reminded of his surroundings (this is my therapist's idea), the normalcy of his voice, the laughter, the hopes, the plans, the jokes. Then I hear his forced breath through clenched teeth. He barely whispers that he can't take it anymore, that he can't stop beating his head against the wall.

It was worrisome, my therapist agreed. But in context, it was couched in normal conversation. At the time, his pain was not glaring. In my mind, it was glaring, and the source of my guilt was that the glare disappeared when his normal tone of voice returned. My therapist said it was possible that I had under-reacted, but I did hear the normal in context, and now I needed to balance the normal and the glaring in hindsight.

My therapist gave perspective with other deaths—the terminally ill children in her care, for example, whose lives were much shorter than Patrick's. She worked with them in group therapy, and in one session, she showed the children a photograph of Patrick. She explained he had recently passed away and asked them to dress a teddy bear to look like him as a keepsake for his mother, meaning me. What would Patrick like to wear? she asked the children. They looked at the photo of Pat's short, blond hair and blue eyes. They said he looked cool, and they dressed the bear in khaki cargo shorts, a tan t-shirt, and sunglasses. By the time my therapist brought the bear to me in my own weekly session, those children had already died. One of them in a hospital had asked her parents to get her something to eat or drink. She waited until they left her bedside to go to the cafeteria. By the time they returned, she had died.

After several sessions, my therapist pierced the guilt one evening when she said, "You should *not* have known."

"How could I not know?" I answered.

"He didn't want you to know," she said. "He didn't tell you, and if he did, what would you have done?"

I admitted I needed to be hit with a two-by-four. I didn't see the red flags. I latched onto the positives and stayed there. He's brilliant. He has great friends. He has job offers. He's in Berlin where he wants to be. He's who he wants to be. He goes to operas with friends from Siemens. He travels to Munich, Stockholm, Paris. He's got a 3.8 GPA. He'll get his master's in computer science next year, and on and on.

I couldn't get past the glitter. I couldn't understand what he was really feeling—despair, pain … literally pain like beating his head against a wall. I didn't doubt his pain, but I didn't get the source of it. His problems were fixable.

He's only twenty-three. He'll meet another boy. Why is his pain that deep?

It wasn't logical. I was logical.

"Depressed people are not logical," the therapist said firmly. I could not have known that he was going to kill himself. I could not have known that gay people are more likely to kill themselves than straight people or that prior suicide attempts predict suicide completion. I did not have enough information. I could not have known what it was like to live a closeted life and hear much of the world condemn me as sick and perverted. I could not have known what it was like to hide teenage crushes so I wouldn't be called a faggot. I did not understand that young gay people delayed relationships and that those delays put off the maturation that straight people take for granted. Pat had not explored romantically until long after his straight friends. He knew little of the rejection that came with passion. He had spent his whole life avoiding it.

On phone calls, my father backed up my therapist. "You're selecting memories," he said. "You only see what led up to it, not the complete picture." My dad was another believer in keeping memories in context. "You did not go to Germany before he died because you based the decision on reasonable information. You thought he would get help. He told you he would get help. He was capable. He thrived in Germany. He spoke the language, rented apartments, got jobs, aced classes, made friends everywhere—dear friends, loving friends. Everywhere.

"His brilliance deceived him," my father said. "He thought he could solve this problem. He solved everything before—every problem set, every computer program. He could not analyze the solution for depression. He was logical, and it is not. Emotions are not solved."

I was briefly convinced after these conversations. Or, let's just say I functioned. I got through summer. I taught again in the fall. The school was familiar, the students and faculty supportive. The literature brought perspective. The ending of *Romeo and Juliet* became more than a play: Patrick was Romeo, killing himself over love.

"The Monkey's Paw" by W. W. Jacobs became much too real. A father uses a mummified monkey's paw to wish for two hundred pounds to pay the mortgage on his house. He loses his son in the process. The money arrives as compensation for the son's mutilation in a machine at his job. A week after the burial, the mother insists that the father make a second wish to bring her son back from the grave. She hears pounding on the door of their house. She rushes to see her son's mangled body when the father uses the third wish to return their son to the grave. She opens the door to a dark, empty road. A cold wind blows up the stairs as she cries in pain. I knew her desperation to see her son in any form.

In Arthur C. Clarke's "Dog Star," an astronomer wonders whether to judge decisions in context or by their consequences. That was no longer a question for me. Decisions in context were forgotten. Suicide buried them.

The Bible from my ninth-grade reading class became a source of solace. Who else could know tragedy better than the mother of Jesus?

There was more solace from the Jewish villagers in Elie Wiesel's *Night*. In 1944, they refuse to believe that Hitler will exterminate them. The Russian army will surely defeat Germany, they tell themselves, and besides, who could do such a thing in the middle of the twentieth century? Kill entire groups of people? Who could be so cruel? They refuse to believe it in spite of reports of Jews murdered in ditches and babies used as targets, in spite of the arrival of the SS in Wiesel's hometown of Sighet, Hungary, in spite of the segregation of Jews into ghettos, in spite of the long lines in the hot sun waiting to get onto trains, and finally on the trains themselves. They ignore their death sentence until a suffocating train ride that lasts for days. They see flames from an Auschwitz crematorium and smell burning flesh as they are beaten to get off the train. The women disappear in a line to the right. A prisoner rages to the men they will die in the flames. They will burn for not knowing their fate. They walk past a ditch of fire and watch a truck dump its load of young children and babies into the ditch—babies who are alive and whose faces disappear into smoke. They realize they will die in numbers impossible to imagine.

I allowed myself to linger on that passage. Good people had found ways to ignore horror, I told myself. Maybe I was a good person, too.

October 12, 2006

I'm not sure what survival is, but I know what it isn't. It is not becoming stronger. It is not moving through. It is not positive in any way. There is no good from it. We do not become closer as a family. We are not more compassionate, not more anything. We are flooded with grief. We can barely breathe. There are no "gifts," and there are no blessings for which to be grateful. We do not become more accepting. I refuse to admit any good came from Pat's death. I will not dignify it with any hint of "peace" or "rest" or "his suffering is over" or "there is no more pain" or "it was his choice," and worst of all, "He's with God now." There are no positives about a kind, funny twenty-three-year-old, who worked hard all his life, gave his parents the greatest glory possible, cared mostly about being loved, fought a disease, and died from it. I'm not angry, but don't tell me there is goodness in death.

For those left behind, there is no surviving. Suicide drags you down a tortuous path. You follow the line of thinking, the trail. The victim leaves clues. You follow them even though others say it's futile. I say leave me alone. He was my son. He had his reasons. His reasons were valid. He was valid. He was everything. He was perfect, and he deserves to be followed. I will follow his thinking even though I don't understand. I don't want to understand. I'm scared to understand. I may never understand. I may have to kill myself to understand.

"Your window of opportunity is closed," says my therapist. "You are not twenty-three. You will not get there that way." She's been around death a long time. She's had patients who killed themselves, who self-mutilated. "It's a form of control," she says. "I can kill myself or not. I can do it today if I want, or I can wait. I can give myself a limit like an anniversary"—in Pat's case, maybe his hospitalization at Stanford almost a year to the day of his death.

"That was his plan all along," my therapist says. "He just didn't give himself enough time to live."

There is no surviving. There is only biding time, and anyone who says you will someday feel joy or happiness had better run after they say it.

October 17, 2006

A mother, whom I didn't know, heard about Pat's death and sent flowers. She had lost a daughter at age ten to disease and a son in his twenties to suicide. Her marriage did not survive. She had one child left out of three. She called to tell me about the deaths of her children, and when it came to the story of her son, she said one thing that stuck. "I didn't do it," she said, with power in her voice. "I didn't kill him." It was the one redeeming quality she had left. She was not the cause of his death.

I tried out the mother's words as if I could talk myself into believing them. It was true. I didn't do it. I didn't kill him. The problem was I knew he had planned to overdose on aspirin. He went to a convenience store on the Stanford campus to buy the aspirin but changed his mind. He checked himself into Stanford Hospital instead. I downplayed his plan because he didn't buy the aspirin. I told myself he didn't actually attempt suicide, so he couldn't really mean it. He must have just been momentarily sad. He couldn't possibly have wanted to … How could *anybody*, least of all Pat, who had everything to live for?

I couldn't see the facts before my eyes. He *shouldn't* be suicidal. Therefore, he *couldn't* be suicidal. I saw him through *my* reasoning, *my* logic, *my* experiences, *my* framework, *my* truths. I insisted on believing what I wanted to believe. I chose.

I saw a loving, gorgeous, brilliant, friendly, and funny young man. Anybody would have been happy with a fraction of his accomplishments. They weren't enough for him. He was vulnerable, lonely, his humor covering his darkness. I knew that, but I thought cheering him on would be enough. "Your biggest fan," I signed my emails. I knew the sad part. I downplayed it. That was my crime.

April 10, 2007

Suicide can happen to the best person on the planet because it *did. That's* the reason. Period. What does that mean about why? It does not mean logic. It does not mean reality. It does not mean a previously written-in-stone formula for success: Be loving, kind, moral, and educated, and you can conquer the world.

Those parameters are gone with depression. Those bets are off. You think you know what you're doing—stable home life, no divorce, stay-at-home mom, thirty-six-acre farm, country town, good schools, doctors for every ailment including depression.

Apparently not.

Pat could explain calculus ("it's elegant"), how to read French ("you just get a sense of it"), how to get perfect SAT scores ("you just read the passage and then answer the questions. It's easy.").

He had the world at his fingertips. He was a math major from Stanford, a person who conquered problem sets, who tutored math for fun, who practically invented logic, who landed the perfect job at Siemens, who was accepted into Stanford's grad school for computer science. Twice. The first time he turned it down. A year in Berlin with an internship at Siemens tempted him away. When he reapplied, the computer science department secretary at Stanford told him he was the only one she knew who had turned down an acceptance. Then they both laughed, overcome by quirky Patrick humor, his whole body thrilling, hysterical. Saying no to Stanford? Are you kidding me? And then getting back in again? The sheer audacity was outrageous—perfect in its madness.

Apparently not.

Day 1,593

It's time to stop the emailing, the chatting, the errands, the idleness, the thinking, the double life. Patrick is dead. What does that mean? It means if I try hard enough, he'll come back in some form, and that possibility—that slim manifestation—is enough to keep trying, to conjure him in some nebulous form.

"What are you doing?" Bob asks.

I don't know. I don't know what I'm doing. Stopping life, being insane, dying before I'm sick?

"My projects," I answer.

I try to explain. I need to publish Pat's CD—the recordings of him at Tanglewood, at Longy. I want the world to hear him play. I need to post articles on his website, write about a scholarship in his name, raise money for it, send money to his schools, email his friends, be with him, be in his world. I'm distant, distracted, not on the team. I'm not a partner. I don't do my share. I'm not here. I'm trying to be with Pat and not succeeding, talking about little things—the weather, the dogs, Libby's cat, what are you doing today? I'm talking in a vacuum or underwater or by remote control. Press one for yes or two for no. I don't want to be normal. I want to be solitary. I don't want to be a partner. Last time I was a partner, Pat died.

I need to be one sinking, hurt, painful, alone person. I need to be the mom I should have been—the mom who should have asked Pat if he needed help and then gone to Berlin and faced up to the fact that he was in serious trouble, the kind of trouble that has nothing to do with Stanford or brilliance or jobs or friends. It has to do with the life of a clinically depressed person. That's how I should have seen him and how I have to see him now. Really see him. I have to do it right this time around. It's too late, but I have to do it anyway. I have to fix a mistake even if I make another mistake, even if it ends in a stream of mistakes, oversights, under-reactions, miscues, misreads. There's no second chance with suicide, but I'm taking it anyway. It's time to understand what I should have understood before—a time I don't want to have, that I should have had and that I have to have now. That's what I'm doing.

Colin, day one, Berlin, 2006.

The installation, South Cemetery, Pomfret, Connecticut, 2007.

The Gravestone

I had dared to dream of a Patrick who would grow old with his friends, whose wrinkled face would betray a lifetime of those laughs and smiles that we would share together and those laughs and smiles that only he could bring. But Patrick had every gift a man could want except more tomorrows than yesterdays.

—Ryan Wirtz
"The Essential Patrick," 2006

Pat's gravesite was bare the summer after his death. Dirt showed through the rectangular mound of sparse grass where he was buried. Bob tried to coax grass to grow, bringing topsoil and water and grass seed in the back of his truck, but that was not enough. The grass was slow to take, and more importantly, he needed to see the gravesite complete with a headstone. I didn't want to face up to it. It was another excruciating obligation. I would be forced to summarize Pat's life on a stone rectangle. But I let myself be driven to a local stonecutter along with Lib, who had moved home from Vermont. She commuted the hour and a half to her graphic artist job in Boston. Colin had returned to his construction job in Tacoma.

I could tell the gravestones were wrong as soon as I got out of the car. The pink and gray polished granite with hearts and angels looked ordinary, for other people. They were not Pat. Pat was not religious. He was not ordinary, and he could not have a stone that was for other people. He needed a classical stone, maybe a German one. Steve and Ryan sent pictures from cemeteries in Berlin.

Some were plain like local stones. Others were ornate steles with sculptures and inscriptions. I drove to Mount Auburn Cemetery in Cambridge, Massachusetts, where Pat had studied piano. I took pictures of ancient stones with vaulted tops and ornate wreaths. One held promise, but where would we find an old-looking stone in 2006? Bob did some research. Rock of Ages near Barre, Vermont, had provided granite for the World War II monument in Washington, D.C. It might be worthy of a stone for Patrick.

Bob, Libby, and I drove in silence to the Rock of Ages Visitors Center. A kind gentleman escorted us to a room with a table. He closed the door, and we started with the basics. The price of the stone would include delivery and installation. The stone would be placed on a foundation deep enough to prevent frost heaves. It was guaranteed not to shift during Connecticut winters. The man asked how big the stone would be, and that brought us to the design. We stumbled through ideas. The man was patient. He offered possibilities. None took hold. Our differences about Patrick, about what was right for him, about not wanting to be there in the first place, drove us apart. We could barely look at each other or speak. It was like picking out another casket. It would never be right.

I went to the car and got my computer. I brought it back with the pictures of Mount Auburn Cemetery gravestones. I took a chance with a picture of a small stone topped by a pediment with a lyre at the peak. Olive branches fanned out from the lyre to the corners of the pediment. The man said the olive branches symbolized wisdom. The lyre was perfect for music. "You could have the peak pretty much as it is here and then the columns on either side," he said. "You could have Patrick's dates between the columns. The Greek style would represent his love of classics. Not many stones have inscriptions anymore, but that's up to you. You could even have Stanford and the year he graduated."

The man began to draw on a large piece of paper. A quiet came over us. But then another hurdle. We wanted an inscription by Friedrich Rückert. It was one of the Rückert-Lieder put to music by Gustav Mahler and loved by Pat. But should it be in German or English? Bob wanted English because people wouldn't be able to read it when they visited the grave. "It's not for other people," Lib said. "It's for Pat. That's who he was. He was more German than American at the end. That's the culture he chose. It should be for him," she finished strongly. Bob was not convinced. I leaned toward the German for Lib and Pat, but I stayed neutral. I didn't want to upset the harmony that we had finally achieved. The man listened as we wound down, unable to agree. We went on to other decisions: Patrick David Wood, Born in Manchester, Connecticut 1982. Died in Berlin, Germany 2006. The stone was as Patrick as we could get it that day. We told the man we would get back to him about the inscription.

The discussion of German or English lay undecided on the silent drive home the next day. It festered until days later when Libby told Bob that if he did the inscription in English, she would wait until he died, and then she would change it to German. When the stone arrived the following year in 2007, it read:

> Und ruh' in einem stillen Gebiet.
> Ich leb' allein in meinem Himmel,
> In meinem Lieben, in meinem Lied.

Bob made small laminated cards for everybody's wallets that gave the translation:

> And I rest in a quiet realm.
> I live alone in my heaven,
> In my love and in my song.[63]

After the stone was installed in the spring, Bob put topsoil and grass seed on the grave. He lugged water in the back of his truck during the dry spells. He joined the Pomfret Cemetery Corporation and helped with maintenance. He cleared brush and raked years' worth of leaves along stone walls. He painted the black wrought-iron gates that led from the state highway at the bottom of Pomfret

Hill into the cemetery. He straightened the colonial-era headstones that were heaved at angles by the frost of Connecticut winters. He helped plan the fencing that separated the cemetery from the cow pasture next door. He opened a gap in the stone wall separating the newer part of the cemetery so that hearses could drive through without backing in like Patrick's hearse had to do. He kept a shovel in his pickup to dig the three-foot-deep holes for cremation urns.

In the spring of 2020, during the coronavirus outbreak, Bob put on a mask and helped dig up a cement vault that easily weighed 300 pounds. He was seventy-nine years old. He dug down through the stony soil until he could get a chain under the vault, which held the ashes of a long-time art teacher at Pomfret School. The teacher's wife had recently died, and she had wanted her husband's ashes buried with her coffin. Paul Nelson, who ran the cemetery, and Bob labored all morning with Paul loosening the soil with a crowbar and Bob digging, then Paul pulling the vault out of the ground with his tractor and Bob guiding the ascent. Paul was eighty-nine. He and Bob lay the vault on the ground beside the gravesite, opened the lid, and retrieved the urn with the ashes. When Bob and I went to visit Patrick that Easter, a freshly dug grave lay nearby with husband and wife reunited.

Ryan came to visit from London in 2014, and on a warm, sunny day, we drove to the cemetery. We parked the car on the dirt road in the newer section. Cows looked at us from the pasture. Colonial houses rose behind them. We walked past gravesites with flowers and ivy to Pat's stone, which had a planter in front with marigolds. Ryan read the inscription in German and then broke down. He cried uncontrollably until we got back into the car. "I loved him so much," he said, and then he apologized for being so emotional. But to me, his crying was a good thing. He was feeling what I felt. He was showing me what those feelings looked like. He was validating my own pain.

Libby and I didn't visit Pat's grave very often. To us, he was more in Berlin and California, but one day, we brought a little California to him. We placed a terracotta planter of succulent plants next to his stone. I wandered to graves of other people I knew, and when I looked back, Libby was lying face down on Pat's grave. Her head was on her folded arms in front of his stone, her length spread over the top of his grave. I thought of Patrick lying silently, unknowingly, in his coffin six feet below her, and then I turned away to let her be with him by herself.

Libby, South Cemetery, Pomfret, Connecticut, 2012.

The plan for Pat's gravestone, Rock of Ages, Graniteville, Vermont.

Discovery

I feel like my own mind is not under my control. When I have been having a really good day and I want my euphoria to last into the next day, my subconscious immediately jumps in and begins laying out doubts. I doubt my happiness because it is so rare.

—Patrick Wood
"Being Shy," 1999

Bob, Libby, and I wandered past the curving glass windows and wooden walls of the Rock of Ages Visitors Center after the initial plans for Pat's stone were complete. Granite wine coasters, rolling pins, and bookends lined the shelves of the gift shop. Black-and-white photos of men standing on giant blocks of granite or sitting on the edges of cavernous quarries covered the walls. Rock of Ages began selling granite in 1885 and earned a reputation for superior stone, which did not crack or discolor. It became the largest producer of cemetery memorials in the United States and Canada and was known for public monuments, including the 9/11 Memorial Glade in New York City.

We toured the brightly lit factory where stonecutters with respirators and safety glasses shaped slabs of granite with hand tools and diamond-tipped grinders. Outside the factory, we boarded a small van to tour the Smith Quarry, from which Pat's stone would be cut. It was the world's largest deep-hole quarry, nearly 600-feet down and lined with gray walls of granite. Stone for columbaria, mausoleums, monuments, and headstones was drilled

149

with pilot holes, cut with diamond wire saws, separated from the walls, and swung by cranes onto bucket loaders, which hauled them out of the quarry on roads between bright blue lakes of water. A chain-link fence separated Bob, Libby, and me from the edge of the vertical drop.

In nearby Hanover, New Hampshire, we wandered on the main street with restaurants and gift shops. Young people Pat's age laughed from open doorways and outdoor tables, enjoying the warm night. The Dartmouth College green and academic buildings lay to the north. A Dartmouth bookstore drew us inside. I went to the psychology section to find books on suicide. There were none. Camping guides, nature books, and New Hampshire travelogues dominated the selections, but on a best-seller table in the middle of the crowded store, a book titled *Against Depression* caught my eye. I gave it my two-page test. If it didn't talk about more than anecdotal stories of people who died by suicide, forget it. I'd read enough of those. They had been helpful. They made me realize that Pat was among many successful and well-loved people who killed themselves.

Kay Jamison's *Night Falls Fast* was one of those books. Jamison detailed suicide histories, methods of death, and the science behind them. She went beyond the anecdotes, and although at first I couldn't concentrate on her scientific explanations, a later reading confirmed her place in the suicide literature canon. She began with her own suicidal depression and the futile hope that it could be controlled rationally. She made a promise with a friend: If either one of them felt suicidal, they would call the other, who would talk them out of it. They both knew suicide well. They had narrowly escaped it. But their delusion of reaching out to each other was confirmed years later when the friend shot himself. Jamison learned respect for "suicide's ability to undermine, overwhelm, outwit, devastate, and destroy."[64]

She touched on the connection between creativity and mood disorders. Suicide is more common amongst highly creative individuals, she said, because they are more likely to suffer from depression and manic depression, also known as bipolar disorder. She cited studies showing that high-achieving composers, businessmen, and scientists (including mathematicians) were five times more likely to kill themselves than the general population.[65] Patrick was outstanding in music and math, two of the areas she named.

Jamison explained further in *Touched with Fire: Manic-Depressive Illness and the Artistic Temperament*, which traced the "fine madness" of great thinkers. Highly accomplished people tend to be overly productive and enthusiastic but also extreme in mood. They live on the edges of life, at the sources of original thinking, where ideas explode and connections ignite. Their thinking is similar to mania with its fluency, rapidity, flexibility, and unique associations. They pour out words of similar meaning or sound. They spew ideas. And if need be, they spew different ideas for multiple solutions. They comb the universe at top speed for far-flung inspiration.

This was Patrick as a child, mired in crossword puzzles, untangling word scrambles, folding origami peacocks, and looking up words so often that the letters on the unabridged dictionary tabs wore off. This was the child who could see patterns in images and numbers in card games faster than Libby and me, even with a ten-second handicap. This was the high school student who was sent home from an SAT preparation class during summer school because he knew all the words in the prep book. This was the college student who preferred rigorous math and computer science and planned to develop "new knowledge in this area" at IBM or Rand Corporation.[66] This was the student abroad who devoured the language and music of German composers in their native land, whose idols were Beethoven and Wagner. This was the intern with a career in software engineering and interface design in a research and development department, who immersed himself in C and C++, Java, artificial intelligence, computer graphics, multi-variable calculus, partial differential equations, probability theory, and complex variables. This was the intern who flooded his bosses at BMW and Siemens with mathematical brainstorming and higher-level coding in MATLAB, a programming language designed for engineers and scientists. Patrick may not have been diagnosed with manic depression, but he lived in a similar universe of infinite possibilities. He walked a moving line between boredom and elation, between madness and genius.

The price he paid was a dual life. Productive thinkers have to search the extremes and return to the world of everyone else, Jamison said. They have to delve into the irrational to find the original and then impose logic. They straddle chaos and reason. They journey, far more than most, between a psychic underworld and the surface of life. Emotions stretch from morbidity to ebullience.

Jamison struck another chord with her discussion of twin studies in *Night Falls Fast*. Nonidentical or fraternal twins, like Patrick and Libby, come from two separate eggs and share only half their genes. They are born at the same time. They share a womb and a special bond, growing through stages of life at the same time. But genetically, nonidentical twins are like siblings born years apart.

Identical twins come from the same egg, which splits in two and distributes the same genes to each egg. Identical twins share all of their genes, and a high correlation of suicide between them would point to genes as an underlying cause. In one study, seventeen out of 129 pairs of identical twins committed suicide compared to only two out of 270 pairs of nonidentical twins.[67] It showed greater correlation of suicide among identical twins. It was strong evidence that genes were significant, and between Bob and me, we had plenty of genetic ammunition in our backgrounds. Neither one of us had been suicidal, but we each had a parent who had killed themself.

I could have stopped there. Maybe genes were the reason Pat killed himself. Maybe they tipped the balance away from nurture and toward nature. But why him and not his brother or sister? I needed more than genetic makeup. I needed to know what makes a person, even a predisposed person, want to die. The book on the best-seller table showed promise. I gave it to Bob. He agreed. This one passed the two-page test.

Peter Kramer began *Against Depression* by discussing the misconception that depression was an acceptable and even desirable state of mind—worse yet, that it was necessary for creative genius. Depression was heroic, a badge of honor, some claimed. It was a miserable slog, but it toughened its victims. It improved their understanding of life. And besides, where would we be without it? What if van Gogh had taken antidepressants? What if he had painted from happiness instead of despair? Would his art show the full range of emotion?

The questions were often asked at Kramer's book signings, and they bothered him. Their clever tone implied that depression was a good thing, that it gave us knowledge, and that we had to endure it to be cured. He described a psychiatrist who withheld medication so that a patient would suffer more and so be motivated to heal. Would we do that for any other disease? Kramer asked. Would we let people suffer through critical stages of cancer or heart disease before treating them? The answer was obvious. Moreover, if we treated depression vigorously, we might have *more* of van Gogh's genius. Deeply depressed artists might live longer instead of dying young like van Gogh at age thirty-seven in 1890.

And then there were the years of lost health, the on-and-off cycle of mood and pain. In fact, by measuring the burden of disease, basically the quality of life, Kramer made the bold statement that depression was "the most devastating disease known to humankind."[68] It might not be as fatal as other diseases, but patients lost days at work, became diabetic, suffered heart disease, and died early. "If it had no effects on schooling and work and marriage and parenting, if it never resulted in suicide, if it caused no daily suffering, if it were as invisible as high blood pressure, depression would still earn its place among a brutal and elite group of chronic illnesses," Kramer said.[69]

The science was in. The damage from depression was as vivid as my father's brain tumors. But the science did not pierce general perception, including mine. Even Andrew Solomon spoke highly of his immobilizing depression in *The Noonday Demon*. "Curiously enough, I love my depression. I do not love experiencing my depression," he said in the last chapter called "Hope." "But I love the depression itself. I love who I am in the wake of it."[70] I could see why Solomon would give depression a constructive spin. He was trying to encourage its victims. And he did. Pat had underlined the last sentence of that quote less than a year before he died.

Kramer disagreed. He had treated depression for over twenty years and seen the devastation, the ruined careers, the savaged lives—some for a little reason, the pile of laundry that became immovable—some for a big reason, the divorce, the professional failure. But reasons were depression's costume. They masked the causes. They did not justify the misery over solvable events. Depression was a disease of perception of reality more than reality itself, Kramer said. Depression was the opposite of reason. It was like looking at a funhouse mirror and believing the distortion even though you knew it was a funhouse mirror.

Some might argue that depression was natural, even necessary for survival. Who would not be saddened by a school shooting or the loss of a loved one? But depression was beyond sadness, Kramer said. It was the loss of emotional regulation. It was a mind that was overwhelmed, that could not concentrate, that obsessed over failure or rejection. It was over-active stress that could not be contained. It was Patrick looking at the website of a man he wanted, hoping against hope, refusing to let go, and wandering around Stanford in a daze. It was a math and computer science major missing classes vital for graduation and then researching how to kill himself at the Meyer Library. Natural did not justify depression. Natural could mean death. It could be our worst enemy.

Depression was also a trap, Kramer said. His description of depression's charm was a mirror image of Patrick—the engaging humor, the articulate introspection. Patrick could confide in me as if he were holding out his hand to bring me closer. But don't be fooled, Kramer warned. The depressed are often self-effacing. They are graceful in conversation. They put others' sensibilities before their own. They charm us, and we are drawn in, but we need to look beyond. Charm hides fragility. It masks vulnerability. It is depression's cover. Patrick's charm could have hidden a fear of failure and a "desperate" need to please others.

Then there was the compulsion I had missed—Pat's perfect SATs and double major in math and computer science, for example. I hadn't seen the obsession they caused, the self-imposed pressure. Nor did I understand that a delayed acceptance to Humboldt University and a boy's rejection would be death knells for Pat's perfectionist tendencies. "Depressives catastrophize the problem at hand," Kramer said.[71] They fixate on the negative. They plummet with despair. They do not recover from disappointment.

If I could sum up Kramer's most important insight, that last sentence would be it. Patrick did not recover from disappointment. He sank lower, harder, irretrievably when expectations were not met. I could hear it in his voice. I could see it when he looked away. While I was praising, he was failing. Minor shortcomings threw him into despair. He was similar to Kramer's outwardly healthy patients decimated by inward, overblown disappointments. Sometimes they were stricken for no reason at all. Depression could come out of nowhere, and that lack of causation helped me understand why Pat would struggle against the "unpredictability" of his own character, as he once described it.

Kramer traced the history of depression research in language that a non-scientific mother could understand. A breakthrough came in 1999 with a study showing defects in depressed brains. Grazyna Rajkowska, skilled in brain disorders such as Alzheimer's, suspected that there was more to the chemical imbalance theory of depression prevalent at the time. The theory claimed that the lack of brain messenger molecules like serotonin and norepinephrine caused depression. Rajkowska went in another direction. She looked at changes in brain anatomy. She collected samples of brain tissue from depressed patients who had died suddenly from various causes, including suicide. With the relatively new technology of computer-aided mapping, she found what looked like brain damage or anatomical pathology. The cells in the prefrontal cortex, which lies behind the forehead, "were weakened, disorganized, disconnected."[72] There were decreases in cortical thickness, cell size, and cell density. Most unique to depression, the glia or "glue," which supports nerve cells or neurons in the brain, was depleted. Glia surrounds neurons, provides nutrients, removes toxins, and generally protects cells "responsible for mood, thought, motion, and diverse functions of the body."[73] They are the "police" of brain cell protection. In Rajkowska's findings, glial cells were misshapen, distorted, or absent altogether. They were failing to support neuron health. "Depression looked strikingly like a disease of vulnerability," Kramer said. It "looked like a lack of armor in a hostile world."[74]

Further studies showed abnormalities in the hippocampus, a part of the brain associated with emotion. It grew smaller in those with depression. The longer the depressive episodes, the smaller the hippocampus. It was more evidence that depression was eroding patients' brains. You could see the damage, Kramer said. When patients were autopsied, you could actually see that their brains had deteriorated as they broke down from stress. Depression had a "physical representation." It was "pictorial." It was "glial cells retreating, and neurons withering." It was a "shrunken hippocampus and disordered prefrontal cortex."[75]

Kramer explained the damage to the hippocampus with the "'stuck switch' problem."[76] The hippocampus regulates stress, he said, which depressives feel keenly. But if stress cannot be controlled, if the "switch" cannot be turned off, the excess stress hormones can kill cells in the hippocampus. Stress can also damage the branches of the cells, called dendrites, which connect and communicate with other cells. The more stress, the more damage to the hippocampus, and the less ability to control stress. In other words, the very cells needed to handle stress are stunted by the stress they are supposed to handle. "Once depressives enter a negative state," Kramer said, "they have unusual difficulty emerging." Their anxiety keeps the stress switch on. Depression becomes chronic, leaving permanent damage behind.[77] With *Against Depression*, Kramer proved the full-fledged standing of depression as disease. Most importantly, he explained to me why a good life could go terribly wrong—not just at the behavioral level but at the smallest level of brain anatomy.

Six months after Patrick's death, I brought Kramer's book to my doctor. He had put me on Ambien for sleep, which worked well, but I was still crying when I went for checkups. I cried on the way to his office. I cried in the waiting room while other patients looked away. I cried in the examining room.

"You should go on an antidepressant," my doctor explained one day during a recheck. "That will help you sleep as well as help your mood."

"I can control my mood," I said. "I can function when I have to. I'm not depressed. I'm grieving. Isn't that normal when you lose a child?"

"You're hurting your brain," he answered. "When you can't stop thinking about the trauma, you're more likely to suffer long-term effects—early-stage dementia, for example, or Alzheimer's. An antidepressant will help repair the damage. Normal grieving or not, you're more at risk. This will do more than the Ambien."

I had Kramer's book in my lap as I was listening. I asked my doctor about the biological evidence of depression—the changes to the hippocampus, the damage to the prefrontal cortex. My doctor looked at me without an answer and then disappeared from the examining room. He returned a few minutes later and handed me a picture of the "Atrophy of the Hippocampus in Depression." It showed two hippocampi—a normal one and one from a depressed patient. The normal one looked robust, with greater definition. The depressed hippocampus looked smaller, like wilted spinach. I stared at them as if I were looking into Pat's brain. I realized I had been guilty of Kramer's criticism. I had not taken depression seriously. I had thought Pat's depression was a personality trait. I had been trying to persuade a terminal disease out of existence as if I could talk to a defective neuron.

The evidence of brain damage caused by depression was indisputable, and yet I wasn't hopeful for future parents helping their depressed children. Depression was difficult to detect. It looked like normal teenage grumpiness. It relied on self-diagnosis, as if patients could magically see into their brains and notice that their hippocampi were getting smaller. Teenagers might know that excessive crying, fear, and inertia were not normal behaviors, but that didn't change how they felt. They had to overcome their leaden hopelessness and maybe even a part of their personality. As Kramer points out with van Gogh, depression can seem necessary for creative genius. But when the cost was too high, young people had to make a case to a doctor for treatment with subjective evidence that could not be verified. It could sound idiotic, be embarrassing, and, in Pat's case, be an admission of imperfection. If young people got past the shame of their inexplicable feelings, talk therapy and medication might help, but it could take weeks for the medications to work, if they did, and if not, months more to test another combination. Along the way, patients might not like the side effects—low sex drive, for example—and stop taking the medication. This was hardly a reliable way to fight what Kramer called the number one debilitating disease around the world. By any measure, the wreckage was staggering. The early onset of depression, the lost quality of life, the absenteeism, the social disruption, and the early deaths from suicide, heart disease, stroke, and diabetes made depression the "major scourge of humankind."[78]

Misunderstanding about depression and suicide was all around—the doubt that depression was a disease, the shallow explanations of suicide in the media. Did Hannah in the teen drama *13 Reasons Why* kill herself because she was bullied and sexually assaulted? Did Lydia in the highly praised novel *Everything I Never Told You* drown herself because her mother pressured her? We don't know because all we're given is a lifetime of Lydia's pushy parents and her sad demise by jumping into the middle of a lake even though she can't swim. A case is made for suicide, but why not look at the part of the case that distinguishes Lydia or Hannah from other high school students with similar or worse problems who do not kill themselves? Not all bullied teenagers or pressured children or rape victims die by suicide. Why?

It's true that most authors of suicide stories are not researching the deaths of their children. They are writing for different purposes. They are writing for stories instead of real answers. They are playing out their own version of suicide. They don't have to go deeply into why people kill themselves. Most readers don't need to know beyond the events that seem plausible. The problem for those of us who do need to know, who are in the real world, suffering real suicide, is that we are desperate. We are desperate to know why, and we will plow through any facsimile of other peoples' suicides to find out why. We are so desperate, we will believe that the drama surrounding suicide—the failure, the rejection, the pressure, fact or fiction—is all we can know, and we can't really understand the whole reason why someone kills themself.

The truth is that the drama is partly right. It triggers the hopelessness of suicide, and it makes a good story. It gets a media conversation going. It makes us aware of the misery of young people. But don't expect to find answers. Drama alone is simplistic and outdated. It assumes that life events by themselves are the cause of suicide instead of pathology. It deceives the many who are looking for real-life answers. We need to get beyond the obvious. We are long past the aware stage. I think Kramer would agree. He would suspect underlying mental health, and he would want evidence beyond the drama to confirm the diagnosis of depression. Ideally, he would want to see the effect on the brain. But instead of looking deeper, we reach for the sensational—the abuse, the bullying—events most people handle without killing themselves. We rationalize depression and suicide when they are not rational. We look for logic instead of anatomical disease. We settle for thirteen excuses why.

We need to insist on more. We need to prevent tragedies like eleven-year-old Carl Walker-Hoover, who hanged himself in 2009 after daily bullying at a Springfield, Massachusetts charter school. And who could blame fifteen-year-old Amanda Todd for hanging herself in 2012 after she was sexually threatened for over a year on social media? But what causes the lack of hope in children that young? Is it bullying? Is it rejection? Is it a predisposition? And if it's all three, which one plays the deciding factor? Even depression may not explain the difference between those who kill themselves and those who don't. The Centers for Disease Control reported in 2018 that 54 percent of those who died by suicide did not have a known mental health condition.[79]

I concentrated on depression with Pat's suicide because it was the most manageable of the factors that contributed. He had suicide in his family. He was gay. He was a perfectionist. He had been rejected. And he was depressed. Of the five, the latter was the most treatable. Pat could have been one of many depressed patients who do not kill themselves.

I tucked the picture of the two hippocampi into my copy of *Against Depression* and drove home. My doctor was right. The antidepressant helped me sleep. I didn't know about any long-term benefit, whether it would delay old-age dementia, but I didn't care. I could sleep. Without it, there was no sleep.

I had never been on antidepressants before. I never had trouble sleeping. I never suffered from depression, even with my mother's drinking and divorces. I thought grief was natural and there was a difference between grief and depression, but I was wrong. After Pat's death, there wasn't any difference. Grief had the same effect on my brain as depression. Grief was one of three "pathways" to depression, which Kramer credited to researcher Kenneth Kendler. The first path is genetic, meaning an internal predisposition to depression. The second is adversity, including childhood abuse and loss. The third path is basically substance abuse.[80] Mine was the second type, a family trauma resulting in adversity. Patrick's death was an external cause of depression. It required the same antidepressant medication as if there were an internal cause, as if I had been born with it. The same disease that killed Patrick was now my own.

Depression poster, Logan Airport on the way to Berlin, 2007.

"The Project"

There was in Patrick the most amazing promise for things to come; in Berlin, he found a place where he could realize it all. He embraced the city and the city embraced him. In this environment, he flourished. By his own admission, Patrick had some of his happiest days here, and, in fact, some of his happiest nights.

—Ryan Wirtz
"The Essential Patrick," 2006

B y the summer of 2007, I had lost my son and my father. School was over, and I could return to the many condolences that should have been answered and the journal entries that should have been written. Instead, I did neither. I shoved the obligations aside so that Libby and I could go back to Berlin. We needed to be with Pat, and we both felt he was there more than anywhere else. We needed to learn what he loved—the schools, the libraries, the cafés, the clubs, the language, the opera house, the philharmonic, and most importantly, the people. We needed to know the people he loved and those who loved him back. We were all curious about each other. Pat's friends wanted to know us, and Libby and I wanted to know them. Were there any clues from his friends, school, or colleagues? Or maybe in the places he frequented—apartments, jobs, restaurants, clubs, sightseeing attractions, friends' apartments? What happened to him that would explain such an irreversible act? Was it more than rejection by the DJ? Was he broke? Was he hurt? Was he failing at work? At school? At anything? Bob stayed home to take care of horses, dogs, cows, and one ancient chicken. Colin was in school in Tacoma. So Libby and I flew out of Boston and were met by Steve at Tegel Airport in Berlin.

Steve stuffed my embarrassingly heavy suitcase into Ryan's BMW and then drove us through the city. He stopped on the side of a street in Prenzlauer Berg. Trucks rolled past us and changed gears in gentle rhythm. Shopkeepers swept sidewalks as he lugged my suitcase out of the car. He guided us to an apartment building with no elevator and then pulled my suitcase up five floors, panting heavily and stopping on the landings. He unlocked the door to an apartment—courtesy of Pat's friend Christian Krüger—with white walls and big windows that opened onto a wide street with bike paths.

Christian showed us the busy neighborhood that night, including places to eat, the Internet café where we could use computers, a small grocery store, the U-Bahn and the S-Bahn stops, and where to get phone cards. He insisted on making the bed for Libby and me even though he was more tired than we were. He had a demanding job with Germany's state department, and university exams were looming. He was still up at midnight, madly cleaning, doing laundry, and preparing to leave for his other apartment across town. He would depart for a week-long trip to Vienna at 7:00 a.m. He wouldn't let us help him as he dashed around. "Don't worry," he said. "I do this all the time. I've already hosted thirty-five guests this year."

I didn't know what to expect when we got to Berlin. We had a few meetings lined up, but I didn't know how they would play out. It was a bad time of year for almost everybody. Karen was away most of the ten days we were there and returned with a bad back and a calendar full of doctors' appointments. Jutta had bronchitis. Tobi's exams were upcoming. Ryan and Steve were undertaking a large move complicated by State Department weight restrictions. The usual constraints of classes and jobs limited Joe's and Tibor's free time. Andrew Tompkins, who had drunk champagne with Pat on New Year's Eve, was moving back to the States to begin his doctorate, and more immediately, he had a major paper overdue. He was researching social movements in Germany, but the actual writing of the paper was "one of those difficult questions."

The next morning, long after Christian was on a plane to Vienna, Lib and I sat at a small kitchen table for breakfast and found a welcome note, guide books, two maps of Berlin (one of which was so detailed that we could find the smallest streets), as many bottles of wine as we could possibly drink, and four bars of chocolate. We felt a sense of comfort that had nothing to do with the sun shining outside or the warm breezes floating through the open and unscreened windows. We were home. Pat's home. The fear of a strange city, a foreign language, and new friends receded. It was time to learn about Pat's world.

Jutta could barely talk for all her coughing, but she had dinner with us and hosted me at her new apartment. Ryan and Steve broke away from their upheaval to have dinner and take us on another Pat tour. Tobi gave us a Pat tour as well in his medieval town of Lüneberg, two and a half hours northwest of Berlin by train. We were transformed by his gentle conversation, marathon listening, and his ancient village, which had survived World War II and where houses and streets sagged from underground salt mining during the Middle Ages.

Toward the end of the trip, Joe and Tibor commandeered us on a Pat Day, known as "The Project." It began with brunch at Berio's, a people-watching café in the Schöneberg section of Berlin. We sat at the same table where they had first met Pat in the spring of 2004. Other restaurants had better buffets, Joe said, but food was not the criteria that day.

Our champagne brunch was followed by a trip to Rheinsberg—about an hour north—where Ryan and Steve had taken Pat for his twenty-third birthday. They saw Frederick the Great's castle and the Kurt Tucholsky Museum housed in one of its wings. Joe, Tibor, Christian, Libby, and I toured the castle and heard of

Frederick's passion for art, his escape from a brutal father, and the decapitation of his probable lover, which Frederick was forced to watch. We wandered the grounds and headed for the Tucholsky exhibit in a smaller wing of the castle. A docent at the front door of the museum handed out strips of paper with the last lines of Tucholsky's "There Is No Untrodden Snow" in German (translated here):

> Yet always there are traces,
> And always somebody else was there,
> And always somebody climbed even higher than you ever could, much higher.
> Let that not discourage you. Ascend, climb, climb.
> Yet there is no peak.
> And there is no untrodden snow.[81]

They were the same lines with which Pat had signed his emails the last few months of his life.

We returned to Berlin for dinner at Pat's favorite Indian restaurant. We sat at the same table which Joe and Tibor had shared with Pat. We ordered Pat's favorite drink, a lassi, which was a frothy milk served sweet or salty. We reminisced about the day and told Pat stories, when along came one of the regulars whom Pat had named Einstein. He showed up as if on cue to re-create a day in the life of Patrick. He had flyaway hair and a shirt pocket full of pens and pads of paper. He laid bulging bags beside his table. He fumbled through some papers in the bags and spoke in German. Joe and Tibor translated that he worked on mathematical formulas, which he hoped would someday quantify social movements in Germany. Einstein didn't remember Pat, but he nodded his head in understanding when I told him of his death. He ate dinner with us and then said a few more pleasantries and gathered his bags. He hung them like sacks of grain off the back of his bicycle and rode into the night. He made the day feel as Patrick as possible, but, actually, the day-in-the-life project was just heating up.

At 1:00 a.m. it was time for clubbing. Café Moskau was a Pat favorite and "mom safe." Red lights silhouetted the sign above a two-story cement box in East Berlin. It opened into a dark lobby with more red and a front desk. Tibor put Joe, Lib, and me on the guest list, and we breezed past the ten-euro charge and the line of stylish men and queens dressed for a late night of dancing. I held on to Libby and followed Joe and Tibor up a dark flight of stairs. The second-level music throbbed with video in the background and men dancing. We eased our way through the crowd past a bar and onto a courtyard with cooler, rooftop air. The lights of East Berlin lit the night sky. Someone gave me a drink. Men chatted and smoked and took little notice of Libby and me. Tibor explained that lesbians were in the minority at these parties, and Lib and I wondered if they had yet to come out as much as men in Berlin. A small group surrounded a striking beauty in high heels sitting on a concrete ledge with legs crossed. She laughed deeply and held a cigarette on the end of her fingers with dark painted fingernails. She wore bright red lipstick and heavy eyelashes. She was known for her shows, which were later, Tibor said—beyond mom endurance.

The twenties-looking crowd was peaceful. They kept to their conversations and didn't look at Libby and me, and that made me feel safe and welcome. They seemed to know that we were there to watch, to learn, to appreciate. I tried not to stare at them, but when I did, no one minded. Joe and Tibor stayed quiet, letting me take in the normalcy of Pat's nightlife, letting me wonder why Pat didn't give himself more time here. After a short while, they asked if Libby and I wanted to see more of the club.

We went downstairs to the "muscle room" where the music was louder and the crowd sweatier. I watched in silence as bodybuilders thumped with pounding beats. It wasn't exactly silence, but the lack of conversation imposed by the noise level gave me a chance to think. It gave me a chance to imagine Pat, to picture him bouncing, yakking, and sparkling. The energy swept us into its path. Libby danced with Joe, whirling through the smoke and colored lights. Muscular young men parted to let Tibor and me join the swirl.

They didn't stare at my flabby clothes or gray hair. They listened when Tibor introduced me. He shouted above the music that I was the mother of a young man they might have seen—a young man no longer here. They smiled in sympathy. Their acceptance of both Pat and me took the pain away.

I felt like I was one of them, that I was with Pat, and I wanted to preserve the feeling forever. I held up a video camera to capture the scene as Tibor and I bounced around. I didn't notice that someone was speaking to me in German until suddenly a man knocked the camera out of my hand. He could tell that I didn't understand him and said, "No more!" and turned away. Tibor explained that photography was forbidden so that everybody could do and be what they wanted without evidence. It was proof that I didn't understand the vulnerability of gay life.

The pilgrimage continued the next day at the Stanford Center to dedicate the apple tree and white wooden bench for Pat. Karen managed to juggle doctors' appointments and limped on crutches to join ten or twelve of us for a few words and a moment of silence. The year and a half since Pat died was humbling, I said in a loud, forced voice. "I feel like someone smashed me in the face for no reason, like I've been stunned and forced into submitting to pain." I hadn't come up with any truth about Pat's death, I said, but maybe Berlin held the answer. It shared Pat's emotions from monumental pain to extraordinary accomplishment. It gave him understanding through literature and music. It shared his evolution from rigid conformity to freedom.

I reminisced with Jutta about Pat's first days in Berlin, how he took a lighter class load so he would have more time for clubbing instead of keyboarding. But before he could begin either one, Jutta explained to him that all students were required to register with the German police. She told Pat where to go and what to do, and he was fine about it. His German was good enough, and there weren't any obvious reasons why he couldn't handle a trip to the police station. But she sensed something different about him. She sensed a levity, not in a funny way, but an airiness, a reverie, a new sense of freedom from which he would have to descend to handle the gritty reality of a police station. She felt like she had to grab his legs and pull him down, and she did by taking him to the police station herself.

At some point during our immersion, Libby and I met Andrew Tompkins at SchwuZ in Kreuzberg, where he had first met Pat. They had spoken German to each other so well that they didn't know they were both American. We talked quietly amongst empty tables until Andrew asked Libby to meet that night when SchwuZ would be livelier. He would show her the table where he last saw Pat. He would show her the chair where Pat had sat so she could see the club as if she were looking through his eyes. I paid the bill as we said goodbye and laughed out loud when I saw the receipt. At the bottom was "Guten sex & bye bye."

Berlin's Schwules (gay) Museum was next to SchwuZ, and that made it mandatory for my gay-life education. A brick wall in front of the museum was lined with bicycles and dumpsters. A sandwich board near the entrance pictured a muscle-bound man in white underwear with the question, "Are you man enough to be a woman!" Inside, black-and-white photos of Grecian-looking men lined the walls. The men reclined seductively, or they wore sailor hats and smiled. Some were dressed in drag. Some displayed their engorged penises proudly. Some enjoyed oral sex. In other museums, they might have been pornographic, but here, they were just plain proud, and they were showing that pride to the world. Go ahead and judge, they said. This is what we're about, and if you don't like it, don't come through the door.

I was happy to come through the door. I was happy that Pat had found a place that shouted his identity with a bullhorn. At Schwules, he could wear it on his sleeve. It was here for all to see, and I hoped that helped him feel as proud as the men in the photographs. Libby commented that there weren't many women in the exhibition, but she didn't seem to care. At least Pat had a place that glorified a part of his life.

A section of the museum showed the history of the gay movement in Berlin. A guidebook explained that gay people had been persecuted since antiquity, based largely on the Bible. In Genesis, God destroys Sodom in retribution for depravity and homosexuality. Sodom became synonymous with the worst of Christian sins. It stoked religious zeal for the beheading and burning of gay people throughout Europe in the Middle Ages. In the second half of the 1700s, the Enlightenment loosened the grip of Christianity. Frederick the Great, the King of Prussia, adopted a lighter tone. He overlooked the death penalty for homosexuality, and he made fun of the church's virulent position. The result was a growing gay subculture in Berlin. Meeting places grew in popularity, including the Tiergarten, where Pat had met regularly with Joe and Tibor for picnics and people-watching. Collections of Greek and Roman sculpture in museums helped to normalize nudity and love of any kind. They dignified same-sex love as a natural part of human nature.

The growing medical profession in the 1800s used pseudo-science to claim that gay people were sexually over-endowed. They were not just criminals. They were declared insane and locked up in asylums. It kept them underground. Those who escaped notice lived quietly by day to avoid angry neighbors and met in Berlin theaters at night. They gathered in the National Theater on Weinbergsweg and the Victoria Theater on Münzstrasse for plays and gossip. They flocked to music halls and specialty theaters to watch female impersonators and muscular acrobats. Men already played female roles in the theater—a custom well-established in Shakespeare's day. It made the crime of dressing as the opposite sex legal on stage, and clubs took full advantage in the form of drag balls and drag comedians in elaborate costumes. The Reichstag answered by passing criminal code 175 in 1870, which punished homosexuality with imprisonment. Gays fought back by establishing the world's first gay self-help organization in 1897. The Wissenschaftlich-humanitäres Komitee (Scientific-Humanitarian Committee) leaped into action with lectures, articles, and pamphlets, including "What

Should the Public Know about the Third Sex?"[82] It provided legal and medical advice. It worked with the police to increase tolerance of gay bars. Arrests still led to lost careers and sometimes suicide, but by 1900, there were twelve gay bars in Berlin. Gays frequented bathhouses, private homes, tobacco shops, and the Tiergarten, a favorite cruising area. Soldiers from the barracks near Tempelhof Field were also available and considered less of a legal risk. They were not as likely to blackmail their liaisons—an increasing fear after the criminal code was passed.

During World War I, gay men enlisted in the military in hopes that they could prove their legitimacy within a male environment. They entertained the troops and prisoners of war by playing female roles. The end of the war in 1917 brought more hope with the fall of the old-order monarchies. Gay and lesbian lifestyles became fashionable. Book stores, hairdressers, and publishers now catered to gay people. Art and literature featured gay themes. The number of gay bars increased to one hundred. Berlin became a major queer capital. Police were increasingly tolerant of artists, actors, writers, and musicians, who emigrated from all over Europe to thrive in the Berlin of the Weimar Republic. It was the calm before the genocide.

In 1933, the German Workers' Socialist Party began terrorizing gay society. Nazis closed gay bars and raided gay libraries. Books were burned. Arrests increased dramatically. By 1935, gay people represented a quarter of those in jails and concentration camps. Same-sex advances could be punished by up to ten years of hard labor. Inmates were tortured and murdered. Gays became *Volksschädlinge*, meaning "social parasites."[83] By 1940, they could be arrested for no crime at all. The Gestapo legalized "preventive custody."[84] It meant gays could be kept in jail or sent to concentration camps without conviction of a crime. They risked death from the mere suspicion of same-sex attraction. The Gestapo hunted gay people throughout Germany like bloodhounds on the scent. They used the pretense of gay crimes to go after political opponents and Catholic priests who would not accept Nazi doctrine. They tortured gay prostitutes into giving up names of clients. Many were sent to camps for supposedly contaminating young Germans. By the end of World War II, every German concentration camp contained prisoners labeled as homosexual. In the Klinkerwerk subcamp of Sachsenhausen, all homosexual prisoners were murdered in 1942.

Gays responded by emigrating to other countries or by trying to blend into the fascist culture. They kept a low profile, bribed officials for leniency, and married sympathetic women called "sand wives" to appear heterosexual.[85] Some supported the Nazi regime. Others traded prison sentences for service in the military and were placed in "punishment battalions."[86] Toward the end of the war, every German man and boy was thrust onto the front lines.

Ingenuity, solidarity, and individual courage during the war resulted in gay survivors afterward. They walked free from concentration camps and reunited in the bombed-out streets of German cities. They reopened bars and clubs. They reawakened with variety theaters, dances, and informal gatherings. Condemnation persisted, but the social upheaval in the United States and around the world in the 1960s brought formal change. By 1969, sex between consenting gay adults became legal in East and West Germany. Ten years later, gays were marching in the first pride parade in Berlin. The AIDS epidemic of the 1980s brought more anti-gay hysteria, but it could not stop the momentum toward full equal rights. From the worst persecution to the greatest acceptance, Pat joined a heritage of gay rights as old as civilization. By 2004, when he began living in Berlin, he could not have been in a more supportive environment for a young gay man.

On the last day in Berlin, Joe, Tibor, Lib, and I drove to Siemens Automation and Drives division where Pat had worked. He had developed a 3D graphic simulation program for rotor dynamics, which he told me on the phone was a "snap." He described it as streamlining a patchwork of code that looked like branches on a tree. His supervisor, Guenther Siegl, was a senior machine dynamics engineer with patents to his name. He knew the graphic simulation would require extensive math and programming. It would surely take two weeks to develop, he thought, but Pat had fun discussing ideas with him. He finished the solution in three days. "We didn't have any student till now who had accomplished such an excellent result in such short time," Dr. Siegl said in an email. But "this was already very unusual and frightened me also a little because it seemed he had set on himself too much pressure at work."[87] A year and a half after Pat died, his program was still in use. Siemens gave him credit as the developer.

Siemens was a multitude of square buildings and straight streets, a city of its own in the northwest part of Berlin. Inside one of the buildings, a security guard at a small counter searched our belongings and gave us guest badges for identification. We were led to a conference room where we met with the director of Pat's division. He had also lost a son, and I looked down at the conference table in shared pain as he said they didn't realize anything was wrong with Pat. He had a good social life for the seven months he worked there. He was out at night with friends, including a Siemens co-worker who took him to the opera. After Pat's death, the director met with colleagues to find out what they could have done, how they could have prevented such a tragedy. But they could arrive at nothing. Pat had shown no indication that he was lonely or depressed—signs that would have prompted them to do more. The director gave us Pat's thick work file and showed us his desk but allowed no pictures because of security.

Outside the building, Joe looked at the file. Pat's responses on a myriad of papers were in perfect German—every word spelled correctly, all punctuation in place. "He writes better than Germans," Joe said, and he shook his head as if wondering if that was a good thing.

We drove to Tegel Airport in silence. I contemplated the broad reach of Pat's life—the bulk of it that I would never understand, the many who loved him in places I would never see. I realized that, as finite as his life was, I would never know all of it.

Above: From the left, Joe Dröge, Tibor Wolf, Tobias Bader, Libby, Steve Pryce, Colin, the author, Bob, Jutta Ley, and Karen Kramer, Patrick's apple tree and bench, Stanford Center, Berlin, 2016.
Below: The author, Tibor, and Lib, Café Moskau, Berlin, 2007.

Lib, the Gay Museum, Berlin, 2007.

Bob digging the hole for Pontchartrain, 2009.

Other Deaths

Patrick could be swept away by Mahler's Sixth Symphony, *or laugh out loud at* Chicken Run. *At such moments he seemed entirely happy, growing into the world, appreciating its art and laughing at its absurdity. Yet the essential Patrick ran far deeper than this.... For Patrick was, in essence, a very serious person and for serious people the world's absurdity can, at times, be hard to take.*

—Stephen Pryce
"Patrick Wood Memorial," 2006

At times Patrick grew distant in the life that went on after him, but each new death, each new hole in the ground, brought him back—the dog he had loved, the cat he had found on the side of the road. And even those he hadn't loved. The horses he didn't care about. The mare whose broken hind leg dangled sickeningly, as if it were hanging by a string. The gelding whose head hung low from colic. Three years after the funerals and memorials, it was time for another hole in the ground—time for a shaggy friend who had taught me how to jump, who had carried kids all over town, who had yahooed through woods and dale with friends who didn't know how to ride and pulled on his mouth to keep from falling off.

Pontchartrain, or Train for short, was a striped-faced bay as big as the lake after which he was named. His hooves were like platters, his back broad enough for a card game. He stationed himself in the paddock next to the barn to watch when I emerged from the house. He nickered loudly when he saw me, in spite of cancer, which had infected his right nostril. It drained in a constant stream of opaque yellow clumps. It smelled rotten when I brought in the feed. I pushed his hopeful head away for fear he would drag his fetid muzzle over my arms and hands, and I would be washing the many layers of clothing needed in the barn in January.

The infection spread to both nostrils, and Train's hairy lips, which once undid metal snaps and opened stall doors, were permanently coated. They looked as if they had been dipped in yellow gruel with blood mixed in. The infection expanded into the many sinus cavities inside his head. Bleeding was almost constant. He was rotting from the inside out. His twenty-nine-year-old teeth became impacted, and the resulting sepsis spread from his teeth to his sinuses to his lungs, and ultimately, to his brain and vital organs. He blew pools of it into the bedding and feed and hay. The cows that we pastured would not eat his tainted leftovers. I snuck medicine into an apple, but he got wise to me and spat out partially chewed bits, covered in blood. Red liquid emptied from his nostrils into his mouth. He was drinking his own blood.

The right side of his face bulged under his eye. The tumor was blocking his airways. He took air in slowly and evenly, but mucus clogged the air space and made him sound like he was breathing through a harmonica—one note on the inhale and another on the exhale, back and forth like the slow wind section of a very small orchestra. And then a loud snort to clear out the blockage. Several breaths later, the notes were back, and the mucus dripped. His stifled breath made me gasp for air.

At one feeding, Train lay on his side in his stall. He stood up and splattered torrents of manure against the wall. It was time to dig the hole. Bob warmed up the backhoe and drove it to the top of the field behind the barn. He chopped through the frost in the ground as I walked Train out of his stall. We walked across the pasture where he had gotten fat on grass, through the frozen stream where he used to drink, and along a rough stone wall. I stopped him next to the hole. A pile of dirt and rocks lay beside it. Bob waited in the backhoe.

Gene, my vet and neighbor, asked if I was ready. I nodded and held on to the lead rope, watching my friend. "No pain," I told him. "No pain." He stood quietly, his ears pointed toward me, his brown eyes locked on me. I watched his eyes as Gene shaved the long winter hair off the underside of his neck for a better look at the jugular vein. I tried to tell Train that he didn't deserve this, that I hated it was happening, and that I didn't deserve the power to do it. Then I hoped that he wouldn't understand any of it, that he wouldn't know why he was standing next to a hole big enough for a septic tank in the middle of a rock-hard field. Gene pricked the vein with a sedative.

Moments later, Train's eyelids closed halfway. His front legs crossed, trying to balance. He leaned back. Gene looked up at me. "Watch he doesn't pull you over," he said. He inserted a catheter while Train leaned on his haunches. He injected 120 milliliters of pentobarbital—one milliliter of barbiturate for every ten pounds of body weight. It pulsed through his heart and then to the outermost layer of the brain, where it began to deaden the pain. It made its way to the cerebrum, where Train lost consciousness, to the cerebellum, where he felt no pain at all, and finally to the brain stem, where his heart and lungs stopped.

Within seconds of the injection, Train dropped—an unsupported twelve-hundred-pound mass, which thundered down next to the hole and then rolled to the side of its crumbling framework. His eyes were open. His body was still until the weight of the barrel forced air out of the lungs in short coughs. The head and neck stretched out as air pushed through the esophagus, flared the nostrils, and gushed out, escaping like long blows. Gene explained that he was trying to breathe but not because he was struggling. His brain stem was taking over, sensing a lack of oxygen, acting involuntarily.

I saw Gene's finger touch Train's eye. "I know it looks gross," he said, "but if you get no reaction there, then he's gone. It's one of the ways to check." Gene pressed his stethoscope behind the horse's elbow, close to his heart. "He's gone," he said with finality.

I stood up, looked at the bulging barrel on its side, and swore I saw it move in exhalation. His flank was rising and falling, or so I thought. "I'll check again," Gene said quickly, and he pressed his hand behind the foreleg to feel for a pulse. Nothing. I felt silly. I didn't know why I saw it move. Then Bob noticed steam rising from his nostrils, warm air escaping and meeting the cold. The now lifeless, subcutaneous tissue was relaxed, its hold released. The gut was settling. Cavities were collapsing upon themselves, the great weight pressing on the ground and gently pushing the last remaining breaths out now that the brain stem was out of commission.

I stood in the cold, waiting for finality to take hold. Gene watched me to see when reality, imagination, and thought came together. I should have known from watching him touch the eye, but I didn't want to know, and Bob and Gene patiently waited until the various tests sank in, and I was ready to watch the horse be rolled into the hole by the backhoe. I looked at Bob. He pushed Train gently with the bucket until he thudded into the hole on his back, his hooves straight up. Bob nudged the hooves toward the middle of the hole, but Train was wedged in a u-shape, his head up and at a right angle to his back, making his hooves difficult to maneuver. Gene jumped into the water at the bottom of the hole and pulled the tail to straighten the barrel and allow the hooves to be pushed over. But Train's head was still torqued, his mouth open, his teeth bared. Gene's boots disappeared under the muddy water as he grabbed the lower jaw and pulled Train's head and neck forward so that they aimed toward the barn at the bottom of the field. They aimed toward his home for the past twenty years. He gave the tail another pull to align it better with the head. I wiped my eyes and closed them in relief.

In the late winter dusk, Gene drove out of the field, and Bob began to fill the hole. He covered the furry tip of Train's ear, and then he shoveled into the dark until the hole was almost filled, and Train would be safe from marauding coyotes.

Bob turned off the backhoe. He would smooth the ground over Train the next day. We walked down the hill together to the barn. I thought of Patrick as a living being in distress, as a brain in desperation. I thought of how he burnt the air with pans of charcoal in an air-tight bathroom, how his heart stopped and his brain stem took over, sensing too little oxygen, how his body was reduced to nothing more than an involuntary alarm system, how his eye opened, and his body strained to breathe. I watched Pat's body try to find air as he lay unconscious. I saw Berlin police listening to Pat's heart, checking his open eye. I envisioned him breathing, his chest gently rising and falling. But I was wrong, just as I was wrong today. I wanted so much for both of them to breathe. I pictured it and made my eyes see it as if the power of my imagination could make it happen, as if I could change the reality before me. I saw what I wanted to see instead of what was there.

I walked down the hill to the barn and thought of the beautiful, graceful, and playful beings who had felt the wind on their faces, given me the best times of my life, and put their heads on my shoulder. They lay in holes in the ground, arranged on the bottom, covered by dirt until their open eyes were closed, and a small mound on the hard ground was all that could be seen.

Patrick, Stanford graduation, 2005.

Stanford

Each day when I wake up holds pitfalls for me that most people never even consider. My struggle against shyness, then, is also a frustrating struggle against the unpredictability of my own character.

—Patrick Wood
"Being Shy" 1999

Suicide is the hardest death to comprehend (this is my therapist talking). It's the hardest to grieve and the hardest to accept. I was a good example (this is me talking). I was so far over my head, I barely understood the vocabulary of the books I was reading. I struggled through *Darkness Visible, My Son . . . My Son . . .*, *The Suicidal Mind*, *Night Falls Fast*, and a ton of other miserable stories. They got me partway, especially *Night Falls Fast* with Kay Jamison's focus on high achievers who descend unexpectedly. Her good friend, with a thousand patents to his name, puts a gun to his head. A twenty-three-year-old Air Force Academy graduate, the same age as Patrick, shoots himself. One of Pat's favorite writers, Virginia Woolf, drowns herself. According to Jamison, most suicides or serious attempts are strongly tied to mental illness—primarily, depression and manic-depression.

Jamison and others taught me that some of the best people on the planet kill themselves, many by carbon monoxide poisoning like Pat. Some leave notes. Most do not. There are triggers—job losses or breakups. There are contributing factors like the struggle of being gay in a straight world. But I wasn't getting *why*. Why were manageable events causing unmanageable reactions? The answer: There were no answers. Each suicide had its own reasons why. *Why* was not available in the literature because nobody really knew why, but that didn't stop me from hoping that they did.

Against Depression by Peter Kramer came the closest. Although Kramer barely mentioned suicide, he knew depression. He knew its distortion and its destruction. He knew the depressed side of Patrick even though he never met him. He showed me who Patrick really was.

Kramer went beyond the case studies, personal accounts, and anecdotes about people who killed themselves. He decried the cultural tolerance for depression. He railed against its seduction as a creative or attractive state of mind. Mood disorder was a disease, plain and simple. It was anatomical. It wasn't Patrick talking himself into dying. It was a damaged brain giving him unreliable information, seeing hopelessness where hope was abundant. It was my father's brain tumors without OxyContin for pain. And if I needed more convincing, Kramer delivered: Depressed patients were defenseless against adversity. "Trivial" matters threw them into a "living hell.… Depression in the brain looks eerily like depression in the person. It is fragility, brittleness, lack of resilience, a failure to heal."[88] He was describing Patrick after the rejection from the DJ in Berlin, after the request from Humboldt University. Each setback, large or small, buried him like shovelfuls of dirt.

In the spring of 2009, armed with hard science I could barely understand, I brought Kramer's book to Stanford in Palo Alto and met with Pat's doctors. A lawyer delivered Libby and me to a small conference room with two of Pat's psychiatrists and another doctor. The lawyer closed the door as she left, and Libby and I walked in slowly. I put my backpack with Kramer's book beside a chair. I looked down and said, "I'm not here to blame anyone. There is enough blame to go around. But I would like to think that we're on the cusp of breakthroughs with depression and suicide, and I would hope that Stanford would use its vast resources to that end."

"Well, we're not exactly on the cusp," said the head of Pat's psychiatric ward at Stanford Hospital.

Wrong again. My thin grasp evaporated. The Stanford doctors would not be explaining suicide that day, but I wasn't finished. By that time, the deadliest school shooting in the history of the United States had occurred when Seung-Hui Cho killed thirty-two people at Virginia Tech and then put a bullet in his own head. Seung-Hui had a history of depression and aggressive behavior. He was convicted of stalking in 2005 and required to get counseling. Virginia Tech professors saw danger signs in his behavior and his writing. One teacher removed him from her class, but the university played over the danger he posed.

In the aftermath of the shooting, talk-show hosts and psychiatrists on TV fumbled with the warning signs of murder-suicides. The questions I had asked myself were now constantly on the news. Why didn't anyone see it coming? Why didn't the school do more? How should they handle depressed students on campus? It was almost entertaining to watch the TV pundits struggle. "Let's see you try to figure this out," I said to myself as I watched them point fingers and bloviate in perfect hindsight. But it was also comforting that I wasn't alone in searching for answers.

I shuddered to connect Patrick and Seung-Hui in any way. Patrick was the opposite of Seung-Hui. He turned his destruction inward where Seung-Hui turned his outward. There was a massive difference between suicide and murder-suicide. But there were also a few similarities. Seung-Hui and Patrick were both twenty-three years old. They both had depression. They both, at various points, refused to seek the help they needed. They killed themselves a little more than a year apart, and their actions raised the fundamental question of how to predict suicide. Kay Jamison pointed out more similarities in *Night Falls Fast*. Both suicide and aggressive behavior could be precipitated by low serotonin levels in the brain. Pat was on medication to restore those levels, but he had reduced the amount to make his supply last until he came home from Germany for a refill.

Not long after the shooting, Stanford President Hennessy promised to review the school's emergency response and mental health policies in an article in the *Stanford Daily*. He asked students to be cognizant of others in distress. I replied to Dr. Hennessy in a letter to the editor that Pat's friends were vigilant, but it was the very nature of his disease that caused Pat's decision-making—and Seung-Hui's—to be under attack. "They are making flawed decisions because the very same mechanism used to make these decisions is malfunctioning." I went on about parents and schools being ill-equipped to detect the severity of the disease, and therefore, the likelihood of a completed suicide. We were asking Patrick and Seung-Hui to diagnose themselves when they were least able. I wasn't making excuses for them. I was under no illusions about who was responsible for killing themselves and others. But the issue of responsibility was getting buried. I was blaming myself for someone I did not kill, and the media was blaming Virginia Tech.

The implications for a university were complex. How much do they reach out, especially if the patient does not seek treatment? How do they know the severity of the depression? "If we are relying on averagely intelligent people to pick up the cues," I continued in my letter:

> we will never succeed. I know because I am one of those failures. I will hate myself forever for what I did not know about depression, for what I missed, for what I did not do for my son, but I also know that there are a lot of people saying the same thing about Cho. They are all blaming themselves, just as I am, because what passes for non-threatening behavior before suicide becomes pockmarked with danger signs afterward. I should have done a lot of things, and so should they who knew Cho. But we don't because we don't know they are necessary. We don't know they mean life or death, and we will not know until we have reliable detection.

I ended with a weak plea that the school initiate follow-up because depressed students will not always seek treatment. "Depression robs functioning until there is very little on which to rely. How do we know when that functioning is gone? We don't, and that is why it is up to us to know more. It is simply in our own best interest to detect and treat more actively and accurately. If I have come away with anything from the loss of my beautiful son, it is this: Depression will kill anybody, but the burden is on us to know whom."[89]

President Hennessey responded in a condolence letter that even the most capable students could be victims of suicide. One reader of my letter in the *Stanford Daily* remembered Pat's "gentle smile and quick wit" from her comic rhetoric class. She hoped that "anyone reading this realizes that suicide is a lonely and terrible solution—there are people who will grieve and miss you with a deep ache." Another reader asked why the paper had given me space. He accused me of "nannying" and said Stanford had no responsibility for a student who had graduated and moved to Germany. "At some point, you just have to let go, lady. Get a grip. Stop projecting your woulda-coulda-shoulda parental replays to compensate for everything you didn't do, just to make yourself feel better." Another countered not to let go of my search for meaning. "Even if some miss the point (as evidenced by a few of the responses), to me and to others your words are precious. No man is an island."[90]

I wrote back that I shared all views at different times in my life. Even my accuser had a point. "Before Pat died," I said, "I agreed completely that schools cannot be traipsing all over the globe to protect students from themselves, that we could not make students live if they didn't want to. As a matter of fact, it is probably that kind of thinking that put me in this situation today." I went on to say:

Now that he's gone, I can only say from experience that the nature of the disease demands more from us. There is no better proof than Pat that depression is a terminal disease and that it operates outside the realm of logic. How do we know when a student has crossed that line? We don't, and so it stands to reason that we should take a conservative approach. As my doctor has told me many times since Pat's death, depression is like cancer, only worse in the sense that it attacks the very decision-making ability that students need to seek help. If you can't depend on the students, and the parents are three thousand miles away and getting the "I'm OK" side of the story, who is left?

It is only the professionals who know that depression does not "heal" after the first "episode." Even on medication, it takes longer to recover with each setback. Severely depressed patients do not "learn" from past failures. They get worse. They become more vulnerable. They are chronically ill, and even if they sought hospitalization once, as Pat did, they may be less likely to do it again because they will think they are beyond hope. My therapist tells me we can assume one thing about suicide: The person is in so much pain that death is a mandate. It's not like they went to a psychological shopping mall and unexplainably picked that choice. I have learned that it is a severe, agonizing, psychological torture, which constricts them internally but allows enough external composure to carry out their plan. Pick up any book on the subject and then think about it as I have done every day for fifteen months. If the school is sincere in improving its psychological services, follow-up after hospitalization is essential. Nobody else is equipped to do it, and the consequences may be fatal.[91]

I was not removing myself or Pat from blame. My letter was not about finding fault. It was simply stating a fact: Schools must be proactive even if they begin with the small step of cracking open the confidentiality that prevents parents and campuses like Stanford-in-Berlin from better communication.

I brought those same thoughts to the Stanford doctors. If we were relying on parents and friends to pick up on the clues, we would never identify suicidal patients. We were dealing with a physical ailment for which there was no indicator other than the patient's self-diagnosis, which he could easily hide. We were relying on a layman's interpretation and opinion. Most importantly, we were assuming that the patient wanted to live, that he had the same instinct to survive as the therapist.

Pat's outpatient psychiatrist listened quietly and said the assessment for suicide was inexact. There was no other way of determining the diagnosis and no way to know Pat's trajectory. "We have to rely on what they tell us," she said. I asked if she knew when her patient's plans were different from her own, when the patient was planning death while she was planning life. Again, she said that objective assessments are not possible. They are dependent on the patient. I asked if she would change anything next time, if she gained anything from Pat's experience. Lib suggested that Pat's psychiatrist could not be expected to read between the lines. She could not know what Pat was planning, but I continued to press the question of whether she would be more guarded with future suicidal patients, if she would be more inclined to keep her distance from the patient's responses and not take them at face value, if anything had changed her perception of how suicidal patients operate, if anything had changed her approach to therapy.

Policies hadn't changed, she said, but, more individually, those working with Patrick had learned the value of continuing treatment, and they would have emphasized that more. Pat had been required to continue treatment as a condition of remaining at Stanford, but beyond graduation, the school could not make anyone stay in treatment.

I hoped Pat's psychiatrist would be more revealing of her personal reaction to Pat's death. He had liked her, and her notes indicated a good rapport. She probed his thinking deeper than I ever did. She might have understood him better than I did. But we had both failed to keep Pat alive, and I was trying to share that with her and find a way forward. What can we do better as a therapist and as a mother? Pat's death had influenced the policies of the Stanford Center in Berlin. Where they had once prohibited communication of any personal student issues between Palo Alto and Berlin, they were now reconsidering. In fact, all of Stanford's study abroad programs were leaving the door open. Siemens had examined their ability to detect mental illness because of Patrick. They, like us, were trying to learn, to improve, to gain insight, to prevent another Patrick or Seung-Hui from happening again.

I suggested that the psychiatrist and I were both mistaken to expect a severely depressed patient to initiate his own treatment in a foreign country, that the very mechanism by which the patient makes decisions was debilitated. I poured out more about distancing ourselves in order to intervene rather than encourage. Where was the empirical evidence for detection, severity, treatment? Where was the barometer? Why were we treating a biological disease by talking about it? All three doctors looked at me as if to say, "Welcome to the problem." The head of the psychiatric ward looked down and spoke quietly. "We're working on it," she said. "We're working on it."

I realized I was hoping for too much. The ability to predict suicide was nearly impossible when patients were honest, and when they weren't, it was more impossible. In Pat's last phone call to his psychiatrist, less than two months before he died, he told her he was bored at his job at Siemens, but he denied being depressed and said he was doing well. She had no way of knowing anything other than what he said on an international call between Berlin and California, and now she might have felt that I was blaming her. In my crystal-clear hindsight, she might have felt I was asking her to admit she could have done better. Worse yet, I was asking when she was grieving on a personal and professional level.

I ran out of questions. The doctors said they were sorry. They handed over a pile of psychiatric notes and watched while Libby and I muddled through bundles of pages. Signed forms and legal language were about all I could digest with two psychiatrists and a medical ethicist watching. It was pointless to ask the most important questions: Why didn't Pat go to a doctor in Berlin? Why didn't he check himself into a hospital? How would they know why? They were thousands of miles away. I fumbled with the mass of paperwork like a small child learning to read.

Libby stayed silent much of the time. Her eyes were big and teary. She looked away from me. The silence continued after we left the conference room. We walked past mission style buildings on the campus under a cloudy sky, in our own worlds. I stared at the sidewalk until a sign for Stanford's LGBT center led us to a small, converted firehouse with a rainbow flag flying. We wandered inside amongst students who asked if we needed help. We grabbed brochures for gay support groups. Stanford was reaching out to Pat even though he wasn't there.

We left for the bookstore, but Lib was agitated. Finally, she said she couldn't understand why I hadn't asked the doctors about the effect of being gay on suicide. "You should have let Pat talk about suicide," she said. "You should have looked to the gay issue. Are you not proud of me, your lesbian daughter? Didn't you think I would be interested in that?"

"Not all gays kill themselves," I said. "Depression killed him, not being gay."

"You don't know that! You don't know what it's like!" she shouted.

"How should I? How am I supposed to know!?"

I walked behind her, but suddenly I couldn't walk anymore. I slammed Pat's psychiatric folder on the sidewalk. Lab reports and input records spilled across the cement. I picked them up and screamed, "Don't you ever accuse me of that! Don't you ever say I don't support you!" A young man on his cell phone ran past us to get away from the explosion.

"People can hear you," Lib said.

"I don't give a shit! You got me going, so now let's have it."

"You could have introduced me as your gay daughter during the meeting," Lib said. "Don't you think having two gay children is significant? Don't you think you should have mentioned that?"

"I don't go around introducing people as gay or straight. It's none of their business. That's for you to say. How would it sound if I said, 'Hi, I'm Pat's straight mother.' I don't introduce people that way. That's for you to say."

"How am I going to do that? Am I just going to throw that out in the middle of your depression questions?" Lib walked faster. I tried to keep up, but she said, "See you later," and disappeared into the bookstore.

She was right. I didn't know what any of it was like. I didn't know depression. I didn't know about being gay. I only knew that Pat had an illness, and not just a psychological illness—a neurological one, as Kramer had taught me. But while I was focusing on images of shriveled brain cells, Lib was looking at a different picture. She was looking at depression from the point of view of being gay— the repressed identity, the failed relationships, the isolation. She had shared those hardships with her twin. They were gay siblings growing up with two straight parents and a straight brother. They were apart from the rest of us, and they hid themselves from a straight family and straight friends. Now she was bearing the brunt of that conflict by herself in a much bigger struggle than I realized. She didn't blame me for Pat's death, but she blamed me for a misplaced emphasis on his ability. Bob and I had been blinded by Pat's genius, and that blindness sidetracked us from the real issue. Pat was not a genius as much as he was a gay twin brother in desperate need of help.

Libby and I made copies of the psychiatrists' notes to read them in private, but then we put them aside. We ate dinners with her partner, Linden, in Santa Cruz. We hiked to the beach with pounding surf. We found out that Pat's roommate, Andrew Nielsen, would be performing a song he wrote for Pat. "Twenty-Three" described Pat's depression, the pain of coming out, and the misery he left behind for his friends. Andrew would not grow old with Pat because he would always be twenty-three. It was "a serious subject for the normally satirical 'laptop rapper,'" said one reviewer. Another claimed that its soulful lament sank it deeper into your heart. On the YouTube website of the video, a comment read, "It really sucks how many people can relate to this song."

We drove north to San Francisco, where Andrew would be performing, past the golden vastness of coastal Route 1, the treeless hills, the sparkling water on beaches and boulders. Windsurfers mingled sails with sky. Fields of yellow mustard mounded into hills to the east. We wormed through commuter traffic in Daly City and then took the fastest streets to save time—Portola to Market to 17th Street in the Castro, with rainbow flags flying, and then to the Haight.

Rattles drowned out conversations in Linden's rusty Volvo. At a stoplight, Lib jumped out to silence one rattle, and by the time she got back in, it was worse. Steering fluid leaked. The radio was broken. The car shuddered when the transmission clunked from first to second gear. It lost momentum, thudded as if we had hit the car in front of us, and then jumped forward. A downshift with an accompanying smaller clunk nursed it up San Francisco hills.

We leveled out on Haight Street and back-and-forthed into a parallel spot close to Amoeba Music. Its neon bowling alley marquee advertised records, posters, and videos. A green and blue mural with stars and balls topped the storefront. The inside was divided by signs for CDs and LPs. Posters covered the walls. A beefy, dreadlocked bouncer gestured at my backpack as if I were going to fill it with CDs. Libby lifted it off my shoulder and gave it to him. She held my hand as we walked past aisles of new and used vinyl records, which spread out from a nave of creaky floorboards. Drums and bass from the back of the building grew louder. Libby guided me to a gathering of Andrew's fans, where she and Linden blended with their dark skinny jeans, Chuck Taylor high tops, and worn t-shirts. The crowd sang, jumped, and waved to Andrew's rhythms. Beats pounded. Heads bobbed. Feet tapped. Andrew bounced. Hand up. Hand down. Words, words, words. Video backed up audible snatches—"Mr. Raven" in nerd rap, "Ahab" with children in fish costumes on the screen behind Andrew.

The music quieted. "This next song is dedicated to my friend Pat Wood. Pat suffered from depression and took his own life, and I really miss him. I want everybody to understand depression better—for Pat." Photos of Pat in fourth, sixth, and eighth grade came up on the screen, followed by pictures at Stanford with Andrew. Then a sharp-toned beat:

Down the hall, there's a kid that I know.
He's kind of quirky, so I say hello.
He's so sarcastic, but he's always right,
Working on those problem sets late into the night.

Mad magazines sit piled by his bed,
A million brilliant thoughts going all through his head.
We bike to class in the autumn rain.
He tells me that he's fine but I know he's in pain.

Pat I miss you dude. It's so hard to say goodbye.
In Europe last winter you were tired of the lie.
Monoxide in the bathroom, but the door was locked.
We were always there for you. You could have called and talked.

I felt guilty and alone and so sick when I discovered
You did it in Berlin. You'd just talked to your mother.
I guess it was too much, depression disillusion.
Maybe suicide's an answer, but it wasn't the solution.

And I wish that you hadn't done it,
Could have won it and moved on from it.[92]

The hipster crowd was silent. Some swayed slowly. I stood behind them, out of place with my gray hair and preppy khakis. Andrew, known as MC Lars, introduced me as Pat's mom, and the crowd turned toward me as if to meet what was left of Patrick's life. When the volume died down, Andrew signed posters of his album *This Gigantic Robot Kills* with Pat's song. "Keep Pat Wood's memory alive!" he scrawled over cartoon figures of a robot with a chainsaw. "Be happy and be yourself. Listen to your friends with an open heart. Your friend, MC Lars."

Friends from Stanford told Pat stories to Libby. "Your brother was so quiet," one of them remembered, "and then he would come out with something hilarious. He would wait for a pause in the conversation, and then he would say something out of the blue like, 'So,... speaking of penises.' And the jokes would pile on from there."

Andrew's backup singer, DJ, said, "He was so smart, but you would never know it by talking to him. He was just one of us."

Mike Love had become friends with Pat at Stanford through their shared interest in German and math. Pat came out to him and Andrew one night when they were driving around, looking for food. They tried to convince him that it was great he was coming out. Now he could tell them which one of them was "hotter," but Pat refused to make that call.[93]

I brought up some memories of Pat about German grammar— the three genders of nouns being harder than French with only two genders. Pat could be wrong 66 percent of the time if he guessed which article matched a noun. He joked that it took him ten minutes to put a sentence together because "they keep putting in the wrong places all the words!"[94]

Mike responded with a litany of German grammar that was out of my depth. He saw my blank expression and asked, "Why did Pat die?" I told him I was working on the answer. I didn't know how I would explain it. But I would tell him and all the other friends who wanted to know, or I would die trying.

Pat, Stanford, 2002.

The Notes

On my worst days, I felt as though the whole world was out to get me.... I sat meekly, buffeted by the rough conversations going on around me.

—Patrick Wood
"Being Shy," 1999

Years later, Pat's medical records showed how much I had missed, not just in the meeting with his doctors but throughout his life. When I say later, I mean much later. It took me eight years to look at them. I had traveled three thousand miles to get Pat's inner thoughts from a Stanford psychiatrist, and then I was too scared to read them. I was busy searching for answers from Peter Kramer and Ryan and Berlin and my father and my therapist and my family. They were confirming. They didn't blame me.

Pat's therapy—not so much. I would learn what I should have known before he died. I would learn truths that I suspected but didn't pursue. I would be exposed for the short-sighted, superficial person that I was. I would no longer be able to plead innocent and wonder why. This was why.

On a winter day, ready for answers, I opened the thick yellow envelope that the doctors had handed me. Three bundles were titled Inpatient Psych Records, Outpatient Records, and Lab Reports. The inpatient records were from Stanford Hospital when Pat had checked himself in the year before he died. Admitting papers said he was "upset, tearful, crying" and suicidal but had not made an attempt. He was "reluctant to discuss his problem other than stating he was upset over a lost romance." He felt restless, with blurred vision, tremors, slowed reflexes, nausea, diarrhea, and heartburn. He couldn't concentrate, skipped classes, wandered around campus in a daze, had no energy, slept too much, and planned to overdose on aspirin. Other ways of killing himself were "too painful." He was stressed from three difficult math classes and the fact that he hadn't told his family he was gay, except for Libby.

A doctor described him as a "thin young man with blond hair and a distinctive nose, cooperative with an instantly likable manner." His speech was "fluent, articulate." His mood was "anxious, dysphoric, a little embarrassed but cooperative." His thought processes were linear and logical, but he was obsessed with a man he had met in Germany. His diagnosis was major depressive disorder recurrent, nonpsychotic mental disorder (meaning he hadn't lost touch with reality), and suicidal ideation. He was put on a 5150 mandatory hold, required by the State of California as a danger to himself.* He was given seventy-five milligrams of Wellbutrin and placed in the locked unit where he was observed every half hour through the night.

Pat described himself as quiet, rarely going out with friends, a "loner," who "sets high goals for himself and never quite makes it." He was pleasant but kept a low profile on the unit. His goals were to "get better, clear my thoughts, and stop obsessing." He

---

*According to Section 5150 of California state law, persons considered a danger to themselves, a danger to others, or gravely disabled can be placed on an involuntary psychiatric hold for seventy-two hours by police or mental health professionals "for assessment, evaluation, and crisis intervention." Libby, for example, was certified to evaluate and place patients on a 5150 hold when she handled admissions at the Santa Cruz Behavioral Health Center Crisis Stabilization Program, the UCSF Benioff Children's Hospital Emergency Department in Oakland, and the Community Hospital of the Monterey Peninsula. She writes about her experiences in the "Dr. Hu" chapter.

agreed to a contract for no self-harm. In a group therapy session, he identified the "cognitive distortion": "If I can't be with the one I love, then life is not worth living." His homework was to come up with new "thoughts to pursue," but he didn't like the group— mostly drug addicts and alcoholics, he told me—"definitely some weird people there. I'm not crazy like they are." By the second day, he said he was fine. He denied suicidal ideation. He kept to himself, watched TV, and talked with doctors "who didn't seem to go beyond the surface." Friends brought him books and clothes.

An academic advisor decided he would not be required to take a medical leave of absence because he had gone to the hospital instead of attempting suicide. The advisor converted two classes to pass/fail and reduced his double major from computer science and math to a single major in math. It meant that he would be allowed to graduate with his class that spring, but he was crushed that he was falling short of a double major.

By the third day, he was "depressed, but improving." He agreed to stay over the weekend so he wouldn't be released without classes to structure his time, but by the fourth day, he couldn't wait to leave. He denied the risk of self-harm. His mood was stable, and he was worried about making up the work he had missed, especially with midterms looming. On the fifth and last day, his discharge summary said he was "in no apparent distress, well groomed and well nourished, sleepy, with uncombed hair." His cooperation was good, as was his eye contact, speech, mood, judgment, and thought processes. He was "goal-directed," and he denied suicidal or homicidal ideation.

Peter Kramer warns that talking to depressed patients is like talking to a charming body double—"an occupying government … while the legitimate ruler was in exile."[95] That's probably who was talking to the psychiatrists. An impostor told them what they wanted to hear so he could get out of the hospital.

Pat's downfall began with a man he had met in Munich when he worked for BMW. The man was confident, masculine, and self-assured. He worked for a German television station and was dressed in lederhosen. He, Pat, and friend Tobias drank beer one night in Odeonsplatz, and that was it—one meeting with no follow-up, no date, no phone call. But Pat could not stop thinking about him. He contacted the man through the GayRomeo site, but the man was "busy." Pat spent the following fall thinking about how attractive the man was and how he could return to Germany to be with him. The man possessed "all the qualities I wish I had." Months after he knew his Munich crush was not to be, he was still emailing him and then disintegrating from disappointment. He made excuses for why the man did not return his advances. He couldn't recognize "no as no." He became frustrated and humiliated. He had no interests. His idealized vision of college, of talking about the meaning of life until 1:00 or 2:00 in the morning, of finding someone special, didn't happen. Shame was constant. Psychotherapy didn't work. Medicine diminished libido.

In Pat's own words in an email to me:

> I remember reading *Huckleberry Finn* as a kid and laughing at the scene where Tom and Huck have to rescue Jim from some building.... There are no guards around, so Huck suggests walking through the open door, but Tom won't have any of it; it's got to be a tunnel dug under the wall, a real, proper rescue. Tom always does everything the hard way.

> It doesn't seem so funny now, since that's exactly the way I am, too. I should have known I was ripe for disappointment when I fell in love for the first time over the summer, having spent up to that point a grand total of one month of my 22 years of existence in any kind of romantic connection with someone else. But I went ahead and poured the other 21 years and 11 month's worth of repressed desires into one person, who rejected me without, at first, my fully realizing it. I spent the fall of this year in heady denial and the winter in increasing restlessness and unease, as I began to realize that I had staked

my entire happiness on being able to go to Germany again and somehow consummate this craving I couldn't get rid of. Finally, shortly before spring break, something snapped, and the next few days were a sharp downward spiral that caught me completely by surprise. I stumbled around campus in a terrified daze, oblivious to anything but the confusion and pain racing through my head. But I remember the weather being particularly beautiful (pardon the hokiness) on the day I went to the Meyer Library to look up "suicide methods" on Google, then to TresEx [Tresidder Express convenience store at the student union] to see if I could buy enough aspirin there to give myself a lethal dose. Instead, I ended up in the Stanford Hospital for a week, during which I couldn't leave and spent most of my time lying on my bed or pacing up and down the hallway, still shocked by how suddenly I had lost so much control.

I'd never been a big fan of the concepts of "real life" or "other people," preferring to stay locked up inside my head and seriously believing I could spend the rest of my life that way, or that if I worked hard enough to make myself perfect in every way, glamour and excitement would naturally follow, at which point I would be ready to embrace life in the real world and would make the transition without a hitch. When that's been your m.o. for your entire life, it's hard to change it in a day, a week, a month, so I have no idea how long that will take or how successful it will be. But I've got the rest of my life to try, and I know what the alternative is now. And hey, after writing this I feel better already :-).[96]

I found out later there was a name for Pat's infatuations. In the mid-1960s, psychology professor Dorothy Tennov was meeting with a student who collapsed in tears as she struggled to ask for an extension on an assignment. The student's fiancé had broken off their engagement, and she could not recover from the rejection.

Other students mentioned the same devastation. They dropped out of classes, lost concentration, cried for days, and hoped endlessly to reunite with a romantic interest. Tennov realized that unrequited love was shared by many but not acknowledged for the danger it posed. It was, in her opinion, the cause of much depression leading to suicide.

She began her study of obsessive love, which she called "limerence" for the simple reason that the word sounded good. It meant an incurable need for emotional commitment and included intrusive thinking, a desperate need for reciprocation, a paralyzing fear of rejection, extreme mood swings, heightened sensitivity, chest pains, lack of concentration, idealized character traits, and constant fantasizing. Limerence explained Patrick's obsession with a man he hardly knew. It was an unreasonable passion, an intense desire, which turned into torment when Pat's romantic feelings were not returned. Neither the man from Munich nor D_____ in Pat's suicide note indicated that they wanted a relationship, but Pat could not let go. He felt an insatiable longing for an unobtainable outcome, which no one understood. Pat realized that the only one who would listen was Werther in *The Sorrows*. Werther knew desire and chaos and solution. He was a partner in misery. He was the therapy Pat wanted.

Tennov could not explain why attractions took control, but she knew limerence was more common in adolescents and that pent-up readiness was part of the reason. For young gay people, that readiness is delayed. Gays cannot express their attraction until they are out of the closet or able to handle the rejection sure to come from the far greater numbers of straight people. A 2017 Gallup Poll estimated the gay population of the United States at 4.5 percent.[97] That means gays face rejection almost all the time. The odds are against them, their chances of reciprocation much less. They can rarely predict the response to their advances. No wonder they take refuge in fantasy, which Tennov says relieves the ache of longing. It forms "a bridge between your ordinary life and that intensely desired ecstatic moment."[98]

One such fantasy is a death scene where an admirer imagines that he is fatally wounded. News of his impending death brings the one he admires to confess his love. That may have crossed Pat's mind as he researched methods of suicide at the Meyer Library at Stanford. A lingering glance from the man in Munich might have given him hope. And that hope might have fueled his own fantasy of more meetings—a dinner in the same crowded Munich square where he first met the man, for example, where booths sell sausage and beer, where men and women in lederhosen and dirndls dance to brassy rhythms on a stage in front of the Feldherrnhalle, where Pat wears a close-fitting t-shirt and blue jeans, where the man is dark-haired and muscular, where he leans across the table and looks into Pat's eyes as the men on the stage leap into the air and land with a loud thud.

And when that scene plays out, why not imagine a scene where the man must come to him? Why not imagine the time, the place, the accident that forces Pat to lie on his death bed, and the man must declare his love before Pat's last breath? And if that doesn't work, why not control his last breath instead? Maybe Pat's death was a limerence suicide. Maybe all Werther suicides were caused by limerence.

The next revelation in the notes made me put down the inpatient pile. Pat said he had "never been that close" to his parents. It hurt like a gut punch to an already bloated case of guilt, but then I realized that he couldn't feel close because he hadn't come out to us. He didn't date in high school. He stayed home or went out with Libby and her friends. He waited until his first year at Stanford, away from his parents, to come out to his friends in his dorm. He couldn't share his real life. He had to guard his words every time he called or emailed. He had to transform himself from the gay college student to the straight, studious son. He couldn't confide in us about the perils of being gay or the darkness of being depressed or the added complication of being a perfectionist because he couldn't have a real conversation—the kind that takes weeks or months or maybe years to develop, that goes deeper than the conversations I thought were deep enough.

One conversation was over the weekend in the hospital. Pat was allowed to keep his phone. He was relaxed, killing time until his release on Monday. We yakked about being bored in the hospital and getting his course load reduced so he could graduate that spring. It meant that he could only major in math instead of math and computer science. He was angry with himself. He could have double majored if he hadn't missed so many classes. But the immediate crisis of not graduating with his class was over. We drifted into family suicide. I went deeper into my mother's alcoholism and Bob's father. Knowledge is power, I figured, and knowledge to a math major at Stanford is more than power. It is a shield. Pat had heard those stories before, but they seemed worth repeating as a way to warn him that his grandparents' depression might be part of him, that his depression might have come more from his family than him. He listened quietly without comment. He had never met my mother and barely knew Bob's father. Their deaths were long ago.

The rest of the notes got worse. Pat was released from the hospital with a list of men's support groups, gay support groups, and therapists. Within a month, he was suicidal. "If I can't be perfect, I don't want to live," he wrote in a journal. Anything and everything assaulted him. He had no defenses. On his good days, he felt "confident, easy-going, and demonstrative. I've started being happy," he said. But then he worried when that would end. He worried when the next disappointment would overwhelm him.

During spring break, Pat and Ryan went to Spain for a week of "self-pampering." Pat used money from the return of a laptop I had given him the previous Christmas. "It's not a good idea for me to have a computer right now," he had told me. I realized he needed Spanish sunshine more than screen time.

Later that spring, he was full of plans for the summer—maybe applying for an internship with Nokia in Helsinki ("they'd be such a cool company to work for!"), maybe staying on campus and collaborating with computer science professors on research, maybe taking a class required for his master's and becoming a teaching assistant. He felt as if his meds were kicking in. "The change was actually more dramatic than I expected. It's hard to tell what exactly brings on a good mood, of course, but I have a good feeling (no pun intended) about these past few days."[99]

I wrote back about my own experiences with rejection. "Time does help," I told him, "and a psychiatrist in college really saved me. But what would throw me out of control is if anything happened to you. I get terrified just thinking about the fact that you really considered . . . I can't even write it. I just hope to God that you run for help every time." I signed the email, "Your biggest fan, as always."

I deposited money in his checking account and talked more about suicide in his family. I thought it would help him understand that his sadness wasn't him so much as a family trait, that it would help him to know the source. He wrote a thank you and said the last few days had been "shaky, but I have hope that the medicine will let me at least get out of this hole and start working on making sure I stay out."[100]

We made plans for his graduation, the luncheon for the graduating class at 11:30 on Saturday, June 11, 2005, the president's reception at 3:30, the "Night Before" party at the alumni center, Steve Jobs at 9:30 in the stadium on Sunday morning, and diploma ceremonies at 12:30. We would help him move out of his dorm on Monday. About a month later, he wrote that he was "feeling pretty bleak, unable to concentrate or get myself interested in anything":

—basically going through the motions and nothing more. I'd have dinner with my friends and sit there in this panicky, anxious state and not hear a single word they said. It was the worst I'd felt since leaving the hospital, and I had a tearful meeting with my psychiatrist last Monday.... We decided to try Zoloft again, since it had seemed to work in the past. Since then I've been feeling better, although that could just be a residual sense of having taken some kind of concrete step in (hopefully) the right direction.[101]

He firmed up his plans for Siemens in Berlin but wrote, "By all rights I should be flying high right now, but for some reason I'm not."[102] I answered that I felt miserable to hear he was still feeling low. His passions would come to the surface even if it took a few dead ends. "That's mom jargon for you deserve a break. I love you. I wish I could spare you this pain."

He went back to his psychiatrist and told me he felt better. They were trying something different. He was working on finding the right combination of medicine, which might take a while. And "even though I won't have much flexibility to experiment over the summer, I think being in Europe will cheer me up regardless … something about the place just appeals to me, and I think it will be important for me to end up somewhere where I can be happy."[103]

On May 22, 2005, Pat came out to me on the phone. He followed up with an email about the relief of sharing that part of his life:

Thanks for being so amazingly supportive and understanding today. I think you made coming out to you about as easy as it could ever be. I know you've gone through this once before, but I just want you to know that I don't expect you to accept this change as though it really didn't change anything or make you unhappy or disappointed in any way, let alone to embrace it wholeheartedly. Not that I don't think you can't, although of course it's completely up to you and you've been wonderful so far; I just want to avoid falling into the trap of thinking that this is all about me and my issues, so if I ever forget that, you can always point to this email to remind me what I promised before. :-) And although it sounds cheesy, I'm really glad I've finally come to my senses and recognized how wonderful it is to be able to share all the different parts of my life with you, even the ones I'm not particularly proud of.... These phone calls do me a world of good. I wish I had been doing this all along, but now is as good a time as any to start. You have helped me more in the past couple of months than I would be able to help myself even if I had lifetimes to do it."[104]

I answered him that being gay would be difficult, but I would love him no matter what:

I'm not surprised that you are gay, but I admit that I've been hoping that you weren't. I remember worrying about the possibility when you were younger and then realizing that of course I would accept it. I would not jeopardize loving you for any reason. There is nothing that would prevent me from supporting you 100%. But it is a little hard because it will make things tougher for you. There may not be a stigma at Stanford, but the world is mostly heterosexual, and you'll have to size up every new situation before you reveal that side of yourself. It will require caution and more protection of your privacy until you feel secure. And I know, especially now, you'd much rather be up front and at ease. Lib has said that even Burlington is hostile. Her friend Peter used to get nasty comments when they went downtown. I'm scared that you would have to endure anything like that.... I'm sure I'm not telling you anything new. You've probably thought about it constantly.... I am grateful that you are at ease with it. That's all that matters to me. The rest of us will adjust.

Thank you for being so "self-absorbed." Your self-absorptions mean everything to me. I am fascinated to hear your inner thoughts. I am getting to know you again, maybe even really for the first time, and I am so thankful that you talk with me. It's a privilege most parents don't have. Your conversations have given me some of the warmest feelings I have had. You are giving more than you get. I hope you find that in another person some day. I love you.[105]

Privately, I didn't understand why coming out was so difficult for Pat. I didn't understand the depth of his fear. I had always tried to be accepting of everything he did. Why would he think that would stop or that I would reject him? There seemed to be a flood of emotions that revealed more than being gay. The answer lay in the notes when Pat told his psychiatrist about coming out to me. He felt "dissociated ... 'like someone else was talking.'" He was afraid Bob and I would threaten to stop paying tuition as his boyfriend's parents had done. He actually thought we would turn our backs on him and stop paying for a school he had worked toward all his life. He worried about something we never, in the least way, indicated. But that did not stop him from worrying all the same. I told him we would never do such a thing. We would never abandon him like that. Ever. But that's how fearful he had become.

Pat's psychiatrist tried to get him to accept his mistakes, "learn from negative outcomes," and schedule "fun time." He should even schedule "worry time." When suicide crept into him, she offered a "contract for safety" and made him promise he would ask for help. He told her he had a long history of being anxious. His first memory was feeling helpless in a third-grade art class upon being told he was gifted. He felt he shouldn't waste it. He strove for perfection in school, work, and relationships, which meant that he was obsessive about everything. He wondered if he could be attracted to someone who wasn't "perfect." He didn't know when to stop working. He couldn't relax. He was anhedonic, a term I had to look up. It meant he could not experience pleasure. He felt worthless, hopeless, and disappointed even when he excelled. College gave him too many options. He didn't know which ones to pick.

He dressed casually and looked in control, but his mood was up and down. Some days he was suicidal. Some days he cried. Some days he was stable, his affect "bright." He tried socializing more in the dorm, but worries haunted him. He was afraid others might think he was "an arrogant loser." He was afraid of falling in love, afraid he couldn't control the outcome. He began sentences with: "This may sound silly...." His psychiatrist upped his Zoloft and Wellbutrin and gave him a supply for Germany that summer. And if things worked out, he would take a year off and explore his emotional side—away from grad school, away from stress. He promised to find a contact in Germany for emergencies and to continue phone appointments with her. As if to prove his new independence—his "individuation"—he was fifty minutes late to their final session.

Her last notes were a series of telephone calls from Berlin during which Pat denied being depressed or thinking of suicide. He was socializing and reading. He was having a little trouble managing free time, but his programming job at Siemens was "relaxing," and for the first time, he felt confident. He enjoyed being "in the real world."

Pat's emails to me were calm and articulate. He made friends at Siemens—"the easiest job I've ever had." He was "doing fine and having fun" and planned to stay another year. There were emails about canceling phone contracts, sending charge cards, an extension to grad school admission, and a State Department warning against traveling in Europe after the London train bombings in July. Pat was not concerned. Everything looked normal on the subways he was riding—no terrorists lurking on street corners as I imagined. He didn't even see panhandlers. "I think they scoop them up and give them housing," he said. "Germany is pretty advanced that way."

He talked about "stretching" his medication. "It's pretty crucial to have it." But he refused to get a doctor to renew the prescription in Germany. I kept cheerleading from the sidelines. "Great news about your apartment. Do you have roomies? Am I being too nosy? Same old me. Shameless personal questions. But I'm just so happy that you sound good and I want your whole life to be perfect—just like you. XX"

Then more emails about doctors' appointments when he came home for Christmas—the dermatologist for his acne, the ophthalmologist for his contacts, and Dr. Danenhower for Zoloft and Wellbutrin in consultation with his psychiatrist. He hated "having to learn about all of this crap and have it floating around my head all the time :-)."[106] After Christmas, he wrote about a "mini breakdown" from D_____'s rejection on New Year's Eve. I asked him to get a psychiatrist in Berlin. I tried calling but couldn't get through. On January 26, 2006, he thought Humboldt's need for paperwork meant more rejection. I sent three emails cheering him on. He never answered.

It took almost a year for Pat's supervisor at Siemens to write about Pat's death. Guenther Siegl said he needed "time and peace to collect all thoughts . . . because it isn't emotionally easy." In the middle of January, Pat was absent for a week without notice. He returned, explaining "that he had much stress within the last few days." Dr. Siegl said it wasn't a problem, but please let him know when he would be gone so that he could be sure Pat was alright.

At the end of January, Pat was absent without notice again. Siemens employees called Dr. Siegl, frantically, saying they had heard Pat had killed himself. "That was so unbelievable and shocking news that at first I didn't want to think this is real. Unfortunately, in the afternoon this bad message became reality." He found Pat's last email apologizing for missing work because of family problems and promising that he would return the next day. "The text was very strange and probably already written under the decision of the forthcoming suicide," said Dr. Siegl, and by the time he read it, he said, "Patrick was already dead."[107]

The plaque on Patrick's bench, Stanford Center, Berlin, 2016

Pat with Shrek, Worldcon (comic book convention), San Francisco, 2005.

Reckoning

The tragedy of Patrick's death lies in the insidiousness of the disease that disconnected his knowledge from his everyday life and lost it in its inscrutability, and in the fact that we other people don't yet know how to clearly perceive this human condition for its treacherousness nor yet how to securely, respectfully, and with humility embrace each other's private worlds within our shared lives.

—Ann Warde
Patrick David Wood: Piano Solo and Trio, 2011

The psychiatric notes taught me about my son, but they also taught me about me, and I didn't like what I learned. Pat was right. I had not been close enough. He and I had talked a lot about what was in the notes—the thoughts of suicide, the "worship from afar," the inability to stop working. But somehow, in a normal tone of voice and with even a little laughter, he seemed to express his thoughts at an arm's length. They seemed to be outside of his head where we could look at them and turn them over so they weren't the demons inside. Conversations about the first time he had sex (an obligatory affair "just to get it over with"), the boyfriend he had at Stanford, the roommate who sold marijuana out of his dorm room, the time he abandoned a sketchy sexual encounter by slipping out the back door of a Berlin club— all these were verifications of his mental health and our closeness. Who else but a trusting son could share these stories? Who else but a caring mother could be chosen to receive them? But the calm, funny person who told them was really Pat's forced attempt at relaxing. The pressure I never thought I put on him, he felt intensely. The very gifts I admired were killing him—the perfect SATs, the music awards, the 3.8 GPA. Of course, he can do what he wants, I told myself. He's earned it. The options Bob and I gave him—the college of his choice, the help to live anywhere—were the problem. *I* was the problem. On long phone calls from Berlin, I gave him too many choices, too many paths for his brain to wander. Bob and I relied on doctors. They relied on Pat, and Pat was not reliable. We had all been colossally wrong and colossally right.

I drifted with the unknowable like a cloud. Should I have encouraged Pat to go to Germany? Should I have made him come home? Should I have suggested he stay at Stanford? If he had cancer, the answer would have been obvious. Doctors would have said no, don't go, and so would I. Parenting would have kicked in. He would have come home or been admitted to a hospital, and I would have treated him like the patient he was. Instead, I didn't see a disease. I didn't think that thoughts could kill a loving, gentle person. Surely, thinking was not affected by the neural connections that Kramer talked about—the over-active stress hormones, the cells that dried up, the shrunken hippocampus. I didn't see anxiety manifesting as a vulnerable physical entity. Anxiety was ephemeral, intangible, but controllable. You figured out what wasn't working, and then you changed your thinking. And that misguided reasoning made me let Pat decide where he wanted to be. I let a severely damaged brain make the worst decision of its life.

In 2017, eleven years after Pat's death, I sank with my wrongness, my total misreading. Was he protecting me, deceiving me? Conversations came back to me. "I'm not giving myself another chance," he had said about going back to Berlin after he graduated. "It would be *soooooo* easy," he whispered the following Christmas when we talked about Werther's suicide. His voice was detached, his stare straight ahead as if he were in a mental tunnel. His lab tests at Stanford Hospital were negative for drugs. But now I realized that another kind of addiction had crept into his voice. It was the lure of permanent relief.

In reality, it wasn't easy. Suicide deaths increased 25 percent nationwide from 1999 to 2016.[108] In 2019, more than 47,000 people killed themselves in the United States. They more than doubled the number of homicides. Suicides were the second leading cause of death for ten- to thirty-four-year-olds, and within that age group, LGB high school students seriously considered suicide at more than three times the rate of straight students.[109, 110] Suicide was the scourge of young gay people, but it was never easy. In fact, it was extremely difficult. Only one out of every twenty-five suicide attempts in 2019 was completed, according to the American Association of Suicidology. In other words, 47,511 died by suicide, but twenty-five times that number, or 1.4 million, tried to kill themselves and survived. And that figure was low. It did not include survivors under eighteen years of age.[111] That meant, whether on purpose or by accident, the overwhelming majority of suicide attempts were not completed. My mother, for example, failed many times. Throughout my childhood, she was drunk for weeks at a time and probably close to death. The last year of her life, she was in an emergency room or a detox center four times for drug and alcohol overdoses. The fifth attempt that year was fatal but far from easy. She drank alcohol and consumed prescribed tranquilizers called meprobamate and diazepam. According to the autopsy report, traces of it were found on her lips, tongue, esophagus, and in her stomach. Her liver, spleen, lungs, and kidneys were congested. Her arms, legs, and stomach were covered with purple and greenish-yellow bruises, maybe from falling to get to the bathroom, but enough to warrant a homicide investigation. Police and paramedics discovered her body covered in blood. A medical examiner was called to the scene. Her fourth husband, John, was suspected but not arrested. She suffered a deep cut on her forehead. Her bed was soaked in blood.

The bed was gone by the time I arrived in Fort Lauderdale two days after she died. My mother's older sister Harriet had come down from Boca Raton with her husband Jack and gotten rid of it. But the signs remained. I cleaned vomit in my mother's bathroom.

I cleaned bloodstains where she had placed her hand, her foot. I cleaned a trail of blood from her bedroom to her bathroom to the kitchen. I threw out bloody clothing soaking in a pail in the kitchen. John said he was helpless to keep her from drinking or taking pills. As a former alcoholic himself and a counselor in a detox center, he had treated her for alcoholism ten years before. She had been sober after that with years of a rising art career and a stable home life. And now John, in his mid-sixties, had given up. He stopped looking for the vodka and pills she had hidden. He stopped trying to keep her in bed. She would shuffle around the house and fall without being able to brace herself. Her face was cut and bruised from falling on it. A friend at the funeral gathering said she and my mother were convinced they could have a few drinks and stop when they wanted. The friend tried it and woke up six days later. She survived because she didn't take pills like my mother.

Another friend said my mother had almost died the previous winter. He had put her in an ambulance and taken her to the Hollywood hospital. The doctor said there was a serious drug problem. The friend offered to take her to a hospital again a day or two before she died, but John was afraid she would be furious. The last trip had cost thousands in hospital bills, and John didn't want to risk any more animosity. He didn't want to risk her anger for the expense of keeping her alive. I could have blamed John for letting her die because he did let her die. He sat in the Florida room and let her drink and take pills and fall against the aquariums she had set up in her room until she fell one last time. But he was also losing his own life. He gasped with pain and shortness of breath until his heart gave out four months after my mother died. The two of them essentially died together.

Beyond John's heart disease, I understood why he couldn't save my mother. I knew what he had gone through. I grew up with her drinking. I also felt helpless. I watched her descend much of my life, and then I watched her revive herself after Grandmère or Harriet made her go to detox centers. I might have been the one to let her die any number of times. It would have been a giving up similar to John. And now there was no one to blame, no one to hold accountable because that person was already dead. My mother's suicide was a lifetime of pain. It was an up-and-down slog of trying to die until she didn't have to try anymore. It was anything but easy.

Carbon monoxide poisoning was especially complicated. It required a contained space and an isolated location with no interruptions. Automobiles were once widely used, but since 1975, catalytic converters have been required in American cars. They reduce emissions by turning the carbon monoxide in exhaust fumes into less toxic compounds. Pat probably knew this, and he also probably knew that charcoal-burning had become widespread in Asia in early 2000.

It began with Jessica Choi Yuk-chun, a thirty-five-year-old insurance executive who was the first person in the world recorded as dying by charcoal-burning.[112] In 1998, she sealed the windows and doors to her bedroom. She lit charcoal in a barbecue grill and lay on her bed to die. By 2005, 300 people a year in nearby Hong Kong were dying by the same method. It was the second most common method after jumping from tall buildings. It prompted Chinese psychiatrists to study charcoal-burning suicide and interview those who had survived. In a 2005 *South China Morning Post* article, study co-author Dominic Lee Tak-shing said that most of the survivors tried charcoal-burning because it was thought to be less violent and less mutilating. "Imagine going to the top of a high building and looking down before jumping. It's painful and very disfiguring and people don't like to have their bodies in pieces and in a mess when they go. Charcoal-burning is perceived as an easy solution because they believe they can die without pain."[113]

But perception was not reality. After their attempts, survivors told a different story. Death by carbon monoxide was not always painless. "It is a suffocating experience which is extremely unpleasant," said Dr. Lee. "The process involves displacing oxygen almost like being strangled and people who survive say it is not something they had anticipated or thought carefully about."[114]

Carbon monoxide (CO) poisoning is a deliberate, intentional process. It is not impulsive like using a gun or jumping off a bridge, which takes less planning. It is a strong indication that Patrick was determined. He *committed* suicide, which some say sounds too much like committing murder and that those who kill themselves are victims, not murderers. I say it actually was murder. Pat may have committed it in order to escape pain, but it was more murder than cure. No one else ordered the charcoal. No one else stuffed the cracks in the walls with Kleenex. No one else used lighter fluid to ignite three pans of charcoal and let them burn long enough until they filled the bathroom with a high CO concentration. And no one else drank the vodka and pills to fall asleep. To me, the term *commit* was a revelation. *Commit* was the verb "to carry into action deliberately."[115] Patrick was the subject of the verb. *Commit* showed his intent. It showed that he did it. Not me.

Carbon monoxide attaches to the hemoglobin in red blood cells and robs its ability to carry oxygen in the bloodstream. Cells become oxygen-starved and die in a process called hypoxia. As cells die off, the victim loses consciousness and can die within minutes. But if the CO concentration is not high enough, the victim may experience vomiting, chest pain, and suffocation before death.[116] The victim has to lose consciousness early in the process, or carbon monoxide poisoning will not be painless. In Pat's case, that meant he had to get the charcoal burning long enough to saturate the air space and time the ingestion of sleeping pills and vodka so that he wouldn't feel sick to his stomach or be starved for air. If he didn't plan precisely, the process could have left him clinging to life and permanently disabled. Survivors can be left with dementia, psychosis, paralysis, seizures, and irreversible comas.

One solution offered on the alt.suicide.holiday website, which promotes "suicide choice," was to get the charcoal burning long enough outside or on a balcony before bringing it into a contained space. The materials were simple and the result painless, the post offered. "Light the coals outside," it said, "and let them burn down till they're gray. Place the grill in a room without windows, drink a bottle of Nyquil or sleeping pills, and go to sleep, never to wake up.... The gas from the coals will displace the air in the room with carbon monoxide.... Try it out."[117]

When Pat googled suicide methods at a Stanford library in 2005, he would have found the alt.suicide.holiday list, including poisons, depressants, carbon monoxide inhalation, constriction, drowning, decapitation, electrocution, exsanguination, guns, falling from heights or in front of trains. He would have found combinations of methods meaning decapitation from jumping with piano wire around your neck or shooting yourself and drowning. He would have found first-hand accounts of gassing and hanging—the gasping and rapid pulse of a bag over your head, for example, or the rope tightening around your neck until you black out. The descriptions made me gulp for air while I was reading them.

Get over your fear of pain, the site says. What are you afraid of? You should experiment with "pain play" so you realize pain is temporary, and you can think about suicide more clearly. Death is a "holiday." Death can be "pleasurable. What if death could be the ultimate experience a human being could engage?" the site continues. "Pay a few thousand dollars and suddenly a whole circus of possibility opens up. Death during sex, at the height of euphoria; death while engaging all the nastiest (or alluring), most forbidden (or desired) pleasures of the world.... Oh yes, and not to forget the classic: Goethe's *Sufferings of Young Werther*."[118]

Reading a book about death can get you used to "self-termination," the site explains. It might have inspired Pat to read *The Sorrows* on the night he died. It might have coaxed him into an apartment with a balcony. Maybe that's where he first lit the charcoal as he looked down on the street below. Maybe he let it burn a while so that when he brought it inside, the smoke from the white-hot coals would fill the bathroom quickly, and he would be sure the CO concentration was high enough before he locked himself inside. Maybe that's why he rented the apartment in the first place. It was in a nice section of Berlin, he told me, closer to his job at Siemens and two blocks from Ryan and Steve. But maybe the real reason was that it had a balcony to begin the process of killing himself.

The alt.suicide.holiday website flirts with the vulnerable. It whispers in their ears and promises the trip of a lifetime. It gives them false hope of an easy death. It seduces with the unknown. But carbon monoxide is not the simple death the site describes. The planning is complicated. Much can go wrong—the agonized breathing reported by survivors, and maybe worst of all, the danger to unintended victims. High concentrations of CO can cause explosions. A light switch can interact with the CO gas and spark a fire. Carbon monoxide can leak through walls and kill accidentally, especially in multi-story apartment buildings like the one in which Patrick died. Over 400 victims die unintentionally from carbon monoxide each year. Many more check in to emergency rooms with vomiting, weakness, and chest pain, the flu-like symptoms for which CO is known and which make it hard to diagnose.[119]

In *Final Exit*, Derek Humphry advocates euthanasia for unbearable physical ailments but does not recommend CO poisoning for "self-deliverance." He includes CO suicides in the chapter titled "Bizarre Ways to Die." He pleads that his book should be used for the reason it was intended—to help those with terminal diseases who no longer want to live. Readers thinking of suicide because of mental ailments should get help. But in the end, he says that if the book is used for the suicide of a physically healthy person, the decision to live or die is "the ultimate personal and civil liberty.... Self-destruction of a physically fit person is always a tragic waste of life and hurtful to survivors, but life is a personal responsibility. We must each decide for ourselves."[120]

Sherwin Nuland takes a stronger position in *How We Die: Reflections on Life's Final Chapter.* "Taking one's own life is almost always the wrong thing to do," he says, unless it is to relieve the infirmities of disease or old age. His measure of rational suicide is that the reasons "must be as defensible to those whose respect we seek as it is to ourselves. Only when that criterion has been satisfied should anyone consider the finality of death."[121] In other words, I would have had to agree with Pat's decision, and by that standard, Pat's reasons failed. They weren't defensible. But Pat had reasons which were defensible to him, and as much as I disagreed, I had to trust that he was making a rational decision for himself. I needed to understand those reasons in the hope that they would be somewhat defensible to me. I wanted the trail that Pat followed to make sense, even if that trail should never be followed again.

Beyond the physical implications of CO poisoning—the preparation, the risk of failure, the danger to others, the fear of struggle—Pat had to be desperate enough to take those risks. He had to become used to the idea of suffocation. He had to reverse twenty-three years of good health—the wholesome meals, the vaccinations, the fluoride treatments, the eye exams, the sports, the Invisalign braces which he bought with his own money. He had to want death more than the pain he felt. I admit that he had that right. His life belonged to him. He could not be expected to live because I wanted him to. The right to die is, as Humphry says, the ultimate civil right. But what is the difference between physical and psychological disease? Are they not both painful? Are they not both terminal? And because of the altered brain anatomy discussed by Peter Kramer, are they not both physical? If the answer is yes, how should I have argued against Pat's right to die? Bob and I had fought against that right since Pat was a baby. We had moved into our house when Patrick and Libby were seven months old. One of the first things Bob did after the cribs and changing tables and clothes were unpacked was put carbon monoxide monitors outside the bedrooms. He knew the oil-burning furnace was old and that CO was undetectable and deadly. He checked the batteries in the monitors regularly to make sure they were working. As I was typing this passage, I looked up from my computer and across the hall toward Pat's bedroom. There was a smoke detector blinking near his door and a carbon monoxide monitor a few feet away. Who would have thought that Pat would grow up and kill himself by the same method that Bob had tried to prevent?

Patrick needed to live for himself. He had to want life more than the pain he felt. He had to want life as much as we did. We raised children so that they had the tools to survive, so that they had the education and the goodness to succeed. At the risk of stating the obvious, we did not raise children so they would grow up and kill themselves.

I know now that I should have let Pat talk about death when he said it would be easy. I should have taken him seriously and encouraged a discussion, even when he sounded normal. I should have told him I was there for him, that I would do anything to help him stay alive. I assumed he knew that, but I didn't understand that the pain of suicide runs over assumptions as if they were never there. I should have made a distinction between him and his brain, which sounds ludicrous, but I should have tried. I should have told him that suicide was disease talking or maybe family ancestors talking, but not him. I might have helped him blame something or somebody beside himself. I might have helped him understand that the source was beyond his control, but it could be treated. He would not have believed me. He had been under treatment for much of his life, but I should have taken him to get help anyway. I should have physically taken him instead of suggesting it on the phone and accepting his refusal. And when the immediate danger was past, maybe I should have asked him: How do you know that death is better? Maybe death is worse than you imagine. Maybe it's like Dante's *Inferno*, where people who die by suicide are punished for rejecting their God-given earthly bodies. They are cast into lower hell like wild seeds. They become trees filled with blood in the foul-smelling seventh circle of hell. They are dismembered by birds with human faces. They look at their former bodies hung on thorn bushes. They cannot keep what they have thrown away. They cry through branches that bleed.

Farther along the seventh circle, homosexuals are cast with sodomites. They roam a barren wasteland for their sin of barren sex. Dante meets a former mentor, a "radiance among men," who taught Dante how to make himself eternal through art. His features are now burnt by hell. Dante greets him warmly. He has a soft spot for the great men and scholars who were scorned on earth for their homosexuality, but he casts them in the canto on "The Violent against Nature."[122] In Dante's world, Pat's death was worse than life. It was a violence against himself and against nature, and by the time Pat found out about his torturous fate in Dante's hell, it would be too late.

Pat maybe didn't care what Dante or God or anyone else thought about suicide. He wasn't religious. He maybe didn't care what I thought, at least not at the end. At that point, I was as far away from his mind as I was from my mother when she was drinking. But even so, what if he didn't find the peace he was looking for?

And then there were other arguments, which had nothing to do with religion or literature, but which might have appealed to Pat's logical mind. What if I had repeated that rejection was not a predictor of the future, that rejection would be temporary? It would pass if he gave himself more time, and each time it passed, his strength would return. He would trust that he could handle it. He would know he could handle it if he waited until he was eighty-nine years old.

What if I had used the logic of one of my editors who suffered from depression. Perfectionism made it worse, and she played with the notion of dying. But the thought of dying was a romantic notion—a fantasy that stopped short of figuring out how to kill an otherwise healthy body. The future saved her—the not knowing what she would miss, until finally, she didn't care if life was glittering or joyful, as long as it was life.

Pat would have struggled in the future. No question. He had struggled as long as he could remember. He once told a psychiatrist in high school he might have been depressed his whole life. His brilliance in math and his career in computer science were not enough to make him want a future. He had too much evidence that his enormous gifts were not worth the struggle. His depression overrode his hope to teach on a college campus and smothered job offers at BMW and Siemens. It slammed the glittering future he would miss. But each depressive episode might have descended less, might have been monitored better, might have responded to medication, might have been shared with a partner. Each disappointment might have lightened with curiosity about the future—the not knowing what he would miss.

What if I had used the reasoning in Jennifer Michael Hecht's *Stay: A History of Suicide and the Arguments Against It?* Hecht says that when you kill yourself, you are really killing two people. You are killing the person you are at the moment of death, and you are killing the person you will become. You are killing the future you—the person you don't yet know, a different you, a person you will never discover, and maybe most convincing, a person who might be happier.

Beyond those two people—the present you and the future you—Hecht points out that you could be endangering others, that individual suicides lead to other suicides. They provide a blueprint for those who are vulnerable, and they increase the sadness and depression of those affected. For every suicide, between six and thirty-two people are directly affected.[123] These people are almost twice as likely to be diagnosed with depression and anxiety. They are more likely to report long-term suffering and increased suicidal thoughts.[124] Some kill themselves.

Former student Sara M_____ explained her thoughts about the effect on others. She had attempted suicide when she was recovering from one of many operations for cerebral palsy. The pain was excruciating. She couldn't walk. Her roommate left her in a San Francisco walk-up apartment, and she didn't want to be a burden to her parents. She convinced herself that death was the answer. But when she survived an attempt to hang herself, she realized that she couldn't hurt her parents that way. She needed to live for them and for others who navigate their own darkness. "It's similar to a suicide bombing," she said. "Many innocent people become victims. It's like collateral damage in a war zone, and the brighter the light, the darker the shadow." Sara's cousin, for example, had killed himself in Germany while getting a PhD in mathematics.

For highly-publicized suicides, fictional or nonfictional, the increase in suicide deaths is well-documented. In the Netflix series *13 Reasons Why*, for example, high school student Hannah Baker blames thirteen people for her suicide in tape recordings after her death. Within months after the show was released in 2017, suicide among ten- to seventeen-year-olds—those close in age to Hannah—increased almost 30 percent, according to the National Institute of Mental Health.[125] The increase did not mean that the show caused the suicides, but the science was in. Prominent, graphic suicides resulted in more suicides.

Even describing Patrick's suicide might be a risk. By writing about the method he used, I might be giving readers a model for their own way out of misery. But if anybody thinks this is a path to follow, think again. Consider working all your life to be brilliant and gracious while suffering the worst pain you can imagine. Consider fighting that pain with many trials of medication, with side effects that you didn't like and therapy that didn't work. But you kept trying. You kept hoping until, after twenty-three years of trying, you were still out of control. Misery dominated. Nothing was working. No one understood you. They told you everything was going to be all right, but it wasn't, and you were alone with your own truths, your own hopelessness. You fought those truths most of your life, and then the power to fight became less than the power of pain. If that is a model for anyone, then you do not understand the full impact of suicide.

I have tried to concentrate not on Pat's methods but on the torment of his depression and the devastation afterward. In one case, that devastation was actually a deterrent to suicide. Years after Pat's death, one of his friends thought about killing himself. He suffered from depression, but he stopped short of an attempt because of what happened to Pat. He could see the excruciating pain that Pat endured and the damage to those left behind, including the damage to himself. The idea that Patrick could imagine the effect of his suicide on others is probably wishful thinking. The pain of depression closed his mind. But, along with the decision to die, we need to know the arguments to live. We need to know that suicide puts others at risk. One of the first questions my doctor asked after Pat's death was whether I thought of killing myself. I didn't have it in me, I answered, but the point was made. Suicide is a risk for family members. If Pat realized he could endanger others, if he realized he could create his own Werther effect, he might have gotten past one more low point. He might have waited until the urge to kill himself lost its hold, until medication eased the misery, until enough time passed that he became the older person whom he had spared from death. The more times he chose life, the more perspective he would have gained.

Instead of having those conversations when Pat said death would be easy, I panicked into speechlessness. And after a brief silence, the two of us in the car on the way home after dinner at a pizza restaurant, Pat realized that I didn't understand what he was planning. He hid that part of himself from me, which probably drove the sadness deeper, the secrets bigger, the choice more obvious. He was ready to leave. He never said goodbye. He left no note for his family or Ryan and Steve—only for the police and firefighters who found his body and for the boy who rejected him. "Tell D_____ I'm sorry," he said in the note on his coffee table. "Tell him I will miss him." He said it as if he would be capable of feeling after he died, as if the pain of rejection was so great, he would carry it with him into the afterlife.

He wrote to those who didn't love him. He narrowed to the immediate source of pain. He disconnected himself from the life he had. He would never again see his twin sister, his family, and his friends. He would never again hear music, dream of mathematical solutions, love another man, read the classics, get his doctorate, or become the college professor he wanted to be. He was ready to give up a glimmering future. By the time he made up his mind to kill himself, it was the most selfless thing he could have done. By that time, there was very little self left to kill.

How could any of that be easy?

I drifted toward his darkness, his isolation, his self-deprecation. His gifts weren't talents anymore. They were life-long battles against the demons that told him he wasn't good enough. They were the opposite of triumph. They were Pat's compensation for the worthlessness that plagued him—his refuge from depression. If he couldn't accept himself, he would prove himself. He would be perfect. He would be untrodden snow.

His whole life became tainted. The times he slumped in his chair, the times he slept late in the day, the times he slammed his door. I had taken those times as rebellion, as being bored with his parents. Now I saw them as symptoms of a terminal disease. The awards and the A-papers were death sentences, and I was the executioner, watching him from afar, marveling at his talents, wondering if they were too much, but enjoying the halo of success. I took pride that he did everything right, that he stayed up all night to make his math homework look like a textbook, that he sat through the *Die Meistersinger* twice in Munich. The whole six hours. Two times. He was my shining Patrick, my glorious star. "How do you do it?" envious parents had asked me. "I don't know where it comes from," I answered, basking in their glow. "It doesn't come from me." But secretly, I took credit. I must have done *something* right. I gave him the environment. That must have set the stage.

Actually, maybe I benefitted from Pat's depression. Maybe I misinterpreted his kindness and sensitivity—the charm that Kramer talks about—as marks of goodness instead of coping skills to avoid conflict. Pat's perfectionism and his need to please made him do the right thing throughout his life, and that made parenting easy. He rarely complained about any request. Clear the table? No problem. Bake cookies at Christmas? I only had to ask once. Maybe I was guilty of believing Kramer's myth that depression was attractive, even desirable for creativity. I was seeing greatness. Pat was seeing failure. And the greatness that we had both misinterpreted became Pat's war against himself. Each time he climbed higher, higher than he thought anyone could, there were footprints. Someone had been there before him. Someone had climbed higher than he ever could. There was no untrodden snow. And it killed him.

I stepped behind the curtain of depression to feel what it was like. But I could not feel it, even when it was spelled out for me in the psychiatric notes. I could only turn it over in my mind. I did not obsess to Pat's highs or lows, and that became my one small defense. I had been honest with him about not understanding what he was going through. I couldn't understand it because I couldn't feel it, and I had told him that in so many words. When he asked if I wanted access to his therapist, I answered, "These are your private conversations. I want you to feel free to say anything." It was my way of saying this was over my head, that he was over my head.

One memory brought me back to a low point I should have kept in the front of my mind. Bob and I flew from Connecticut to see Pat graduate in June 2005. Colin and his girlfriend, Julie, flew from Seattle. Libby flew from Vermont. My father and Anne flew from Los Angeles. It was the year Steve Jobs, dressed in a black graduation gown over blue jeans and sandals, gave the keynote speech at Stanford. Graduates poured into the football stadium dressed like video game characters, hula dancers, and cardboard box dominoes, which fell against each other in a line. They ran, sauntered, and stumbled around the track on the edge of the field and then landed in their white chairs in front of a shaded stage. Cheerleaders flounced, and a raggedy band played. A Stanford tree mascot hopped in front of them. Homemade signs read "iGrad," "Thank you Mom Scholarships," and "Will Read 4 Food." The swim team played frisbee in red speedos and graduation caps, but when the ceremony began, they sat still and listened. President Hennessy spoke. Jobs took the stage and talked about dropping out of college and finding what he loved. Those events did not seem practical at the time, he said, but he trusted that those "dots" would connect in the future, and they did. He and Woz started Apple in his parents' garage when he was twenty years old. He was fired from Apple ten years later, but he recovered by falling in love, starting a company named Pixar, and returning to Apple, which he transformed into the world's most innovative company. Then he dropped the bomb that he had recently been cured of pancreatic cancer. "Remembering that you are going to die is the best way I know to avoid the trap of thinking you have something to lose," he said. "You are already naked. There is no reason not to follow your heart." He went on about death being the best invention of life because it clears out the old, and someday the students in front of him would be cleared out, too.[126]

The stadium was quiet, absorbing the weight of Jobs' candor, but I barely heard him. I was worrying about Pat and the strained expressions on his face while we were there. He slept much of the time during the several days of speeches from prize-winning professors and gatherings of happy parents. At one point, we roamed the Stanford bookstore for souvenirs. I looked for Pat to see what he was reading so we could yak about his new favorite author. He wasn't in the bookstore aisles. I looked at the snack bar on the second level, and there he was, by himself, staring into space—no food in sight, no friends. I kept watching. He kept staring vacantly into nothing. I panicked. What should I do? Ask him if he was okay? I knew he wasn't, but I didn't know why he wasn't. How would Bob find me if I went upstairs to where Pat was sitting? I was afraid of getting caught between separate parts of the family, of confronting something I didn't understand. I hesitated, and when I looked back up at him, he was looking down, reading something. I latched on to that as if he had suddenly righted his rudderless mind and kept it on course.

Normalcy settled through me like a drug. I put off the hard questions, played over the anomalies, and didn't sound the alarm that was clearly evident. I wrote to Pat later that I knew graduation was hard for him:

You were a little shaky. I just wanted to hug you all the time, but I know that's not what you need. You need a good situation, a few (as we used to say in the sixties) asshole buddies, and you need to be you without any input. I'm so hoping that is happening for you now. I've learned from "Noonday" [*The Noonday Demon* by Andrew Solomon, which Pat recommended] that you need three things in place: meds, talking therapy, and physical/social routine. They are no guarantee but I am understanding a little better that your chances are better if you maintain all of them. You've got two of them in place this summer, and if you need to call your psychiatrist, do it and the heck with the cost. I will be happy to help.

I hoped that would pierce his sadness, and then I told myself the bromides that I had felt when I graduated thirty-four years before him with a lot worse GPA—freedom, choice, exploration. But Pat had already explored. He had climbed farther than I ever had. He had ascended, and when he reached the summit, he saw that others had been there before him. Others had climbed higher than he could. His mind panicked. Footprints trampled him. He would not risk another lockdown in a hospital he didn't like. He would not climb anymore.

Death and grief, 2006.

Libby, the author, and Patrick, several months after he was
released from Stanford Hospital, Stanford graduation, 2005.

Dr. Hu

Because I am in love with the idea of a special, unique event, an instantaneous change in my entire personality that will solve all my problems, I can't convince myself that I could start to solve them gradually.

—Patrick Wood
"Being Shy," 1999

Dr. Rona Hu was the medical director of the fifteen-bed inpatient psychiatric unit at Stanford Hospital when Pat admitted himself in 2005. She was also the attending doctor, whom Pat liked and saw almost every day during his admission. She became an associate dean of academic affairs at Stanford University School of Medicine in 2020. She specializes in schizophrenia, bipolar, and depression and is a clinical professor of psychiatry and behavioral sciences. Visitors enter the unit, known as H2, through two locked doors and register at a nurses' desk, where items that could be used for cutting, stabbing, and strangulation are handed over. Patients are allowed to read, attend group therapy, play board games, have visitors, and make phone calls from two phones in the ward. Their rooms look like typical hospital rooms with curtains separating two beds.[127]

Fifteen years after Dr. Hu treated Pat, she talked with me about gay life, depression, and suicide, and she remembered Pat fondly. "He was so lovely. Everybody liked him, everybody in the hospital. I wish I could say that all of our nurses and all of our staff like all of our patients, but it's not true. Some of them are difficult, but he was so sweet, and so everybody—gay, straight, old, young, male, female—everybody liked him. We get a lot of Stanford students, but Patrick stood out. A lot of them are stressed about perfectionism and grades. And a lot of them are convinced that they need to make a difference in the world. So that's not that unusual, but I think the combination of things that Patrick had—his being gay, his sensitivity—he was really an exceptional person in a lot of ways. And I remember wishing that I could infuse him with acceptance and time. Depression makes it hard to listen. Depression makes it hard to believe when somebody tells you that this one person isn't going to be the only person that you ever love and that the pain of heartbreak doesn't go on forever."[128]

Pat was similar to a boy Dr. Hu had dated in high school. B_____ had wavy blond hair and blue eyes and was also gay. When B_____ came out, his mother feared that he wouldn't grow old with someone, that he and his partner would break up when he wasn't attractive anymore, and that he would never have children. "Being gay is something no one would choose because it's difficult," said Dr. Hu, "but you can also get through the difficult parts to the good parts." In B_____'s case, that meant children and a long-term partner.

B_____ had a sensitivity, which helped him support a mutual high-school friend named S_____. S_____ went to an Ivy League school and then Johns Hopkins Medical School but became schizophrenic and had to drop out. He went back to his high-school job taking tickets in a movie theater but had to leave that as well. "He was very strange by that time," said Dr. Hu. "He had a blank expression like he had completely checked out of his body."

At a restaurant with B_____ and Dr. Hu one day, S_____ started laughing at two women at the next table. He kept repeating, "Two women eating chicken. Two women eating chicken," and laughing loudly. The women were upset, and the three friends had to leave their food and walk out of the restaurant with people staring at them. It was the last time Dr. Hu saw S_____ before he killed himself months later. "I know that I didn't 'make him' kill himself. I know that," said Dr. Hu as she held a Kleenex to her eyes. "But I also know that I feel like I could have done more to help and that I gave up on him. B____ is someone who didn't give up on him, even until the end. Maybe there's a correlation between being gay and that sensitivity."

When another friend, J____, came out to his family, his football player brother beat him up and put him in the hospital. He later died of HIV. "So Patrick touched me in a number of ways," said Dr. Hu, "having lost someone to suicide before him, and then having lost someone gay to HIV.... I feel like if I can make some changes that are helpful, then that's one way of apologizing to S____, to J____. It's not about absolving myself of guilt or anything like that, it's just this sense of, I can do something now that maybe I couldn't do then. Maybe I wasn't mature enough, or I didn't know enough. I've had patients since then who have died, and I feel like if they're entirely senseless tragedies, if I can take something from that and help somebody else, I feel like that's what I need to do."

Dr. Hu stressed the vulnerability of gay people, beginning with a delay in sexual development. Relationships are often put off until they arrive as students at Stanford. For gay men, nine out of ten other men won't be attracted to them. "And in that nine out of ten that won't, some of them will beat you up or shame you." She said her gay friends in medical school talked about crushes as if they were still in junior high school. "'Do you think he likes me? He might like me.' That kind of thing." But gay men didn't have those conversations in middle school. "So a stage in development that we went through with the sanction of society, gay men couldn't do in middle school, or gay women for that matter. It wasn't safe. So, for Pat to fall in love during college, I'm assuming that he didn't get the same experience in high school, that if he had crushes, it wasn't safe to act on them. We got some of these crushes out of the way early, when everyone else was having them. And so the very first intense feelings at the first stirrings of hormones happened early and with a whole societal backdrop."

Stanford probably has to do more to reach out to gay students "upstream," Dr. Hu said. "By the time someone comes into the hospital, they're in so much distress. Gay kids are almost always products of straight marriages. A lot of times, it's not even fear of hatred or disapproval. It's the fear of disappointing parents that there won't be grandkids now or that they're not living the life that was envisioned for them. Even the best of coming out takes a bit of processing. Most straight parents don't hug them and say, 'I'm so glad you're gay.' After the coming out, it's not completely done. There's the gradual thing of 'I wonder if they're tiptoeing around me because of this,' or 'I wonder if they're still disappointed.'"

Pat's processing was more like a war with himself. That was the message from the NRA magazines on the right of the coffee table in his apartment and the gay magazines on the left. But maybe worse than the war with being gay was being a perfectionist. That war did not allow failure at anything, gay or straight. "It can seem like a good thing in the short term to be a perfectionist," said Dr. Hu. "But it's not really sustainable. It leads to all kinds of problems in the long term, one of which is just the unforgivingness of one's own self. But then the other is to be very secretive and to present only the best to other people." Perfectionism can be internal, like Patrick's, or external, for which Asian culture is known. But the danger, she pointed out, is that "Asians tend to have undiagnosed and untreated depression." Worst of all, in a 2017 "Health in High Ability Students Webinar," Dr. Hu cited a study showing that perfectionism predicted suicidal ideation above and beyond hopelessness and depression among Asian Americans.[129] "If Pat had always been a perfectionist child," she said, "that's at least partly inborn, but then, as a gay young man, he probably didn't feel safe putting himself out there until it was his best effort. Perfectionism has this sort of illusion of control as in, 'If I could just get this perfect, then it would be something that could not be undone.'"

I found out later that, according to the American Psychological Association, perfectionism means overly high standards and self-criticism. It means you are never good enough. Your expectations are unrealistic. Failure is inevitable, especially at Stanford, where you are competing with the best in the country. In 2019, Stanford was the hardest American university to get into. The acceptance rate was 4 percent. Out of over 47,000 who applied, about 2,000 were accepted—2,000, who might not have been perfect, but who worked very hard to look that way on paper. Their high school grades were stellar. Their average SATs were not far below Pat's perfect 1600.[130] They were the hardest working high school students anywhere, the ducks paddling furiously below the water while looking normal above the surface. Perfectionism was probably somewhere in their makeup. The danger was the impossible task of actually being perfect. That danger drove Pat's despair throughout his life—the misery after a flawed recital performance, the exhaustion of making his math homework look like a textbook, the indecision over boyfriends in Berlin. He said in the psychiatric notes that he didn't know if he could be with someone less than perfect, and even worse, if he couldn't be perfect, he didn't want to live. In other words, the worse his depression, the greater his need to be perfect—a solution that had often worked in the past.

Since Pat's death, Dr. Hu presses harder for a family meeting at the hospital, which probably 90 percent of Stanford students refuse. "Whether gay, straight, grades are good, grades are not good, whatever the issue is," said Dr. Hu, "Stanford students tend to not want to have a family meeting and break whatever news. They want to break the news to the parents on their own later, which I think, typically, they don't do. There have been times when, if it weren't for Pat, I would've backed off. And not just with students, but grown-ups, where the patient has literally been shaking, and we've worked out ahead of time that if they can't say the words, I'll say the words. Just let me know. But we're going to do it in the hospital because you have a whole team with you. If you haven't been able to come out up to now, then it's hard. If it had been easy, you would've done it. But you ended up in the hospital because you're suicidal."

She gave an example of a suicidal transgender student who was shaking with fear that her Asian Catholic parents would never accept a new identity. Dr. Hu offered to do the difficult talking. She explained to the parents that the daughter had made a suicide attempt and was depressed. "But part of why she's depressed," said Dr. Hu, "is that she feels like people don't understand her and maybe wouldn't like her if they knew the truth, which is that she's always felt like she was a boy. She would like to be a man instead of a woman." The mother responded by saying she knew a nice person like that. The father said, "I've always wanted a son." And then he offered to take the daughter to his barber. "The weight lifted off the shoulders," said Dr. Hu.

Pat had also declined a family meeting. He felt that being gay would destroy us and that we would never accept it. I tried to think how we had given him that impression. I remembered some anti-gay jokes floating around the household when he was growing up. I told Bob to watch his back, for example, when a gay couple moved next door—a couple who turned out to be wonderful neighbors. Libby remembered a few quick changes of the TV channel if a program with gay characters like *Will & Grace* came on. I never put those slights together with the delayed development, the sexual repression, or the need for perfection. But when I added them up with the genetic influence of both Bob and me having parents who killed themselves, I felt like Hannah Baker's mother, who doesn't foresee her daughter's suicide in *13 Reasons Why*. "The genetic effect is very strong for depression," said Dr. Hu. "Probably more for schizophrenia and bipolar. I've talked to many parents who feel guilty for the family history. But you don't get to fan through your genes and just give out the best ones to your kids like playing cards."

Dr. Hu advised the producers of *13 Reasons Why* that it should be sympathetic to Hannah but not cause copycat suicides. Her solution was to focus on mental health. Hannah needed to show visible signs of depression, like bad hygiene, vague conversation, and staring into space. The high school counselor needed to be sympathetic to encourage young people to get help. The parents needed to be more visible and have a good relationship with Hannah. "Many shows from the point of view of the teenagers depict the parents in ways that are very blaming, or the parents are stupid and clueless. You can have perfectly intelligent, nice parents, who love their daughter but still don't realize when she's becoming suicidal. I wanted that to be sympathetically portrayed, and I really thought they did."

One dispute was that Nic Sheff, one of the producers, felt strongly that the actual death should be portrayed. "My advice was not to portray it," said Dr. Hu, "but if they did portray it, to make it not peaceful, not happy, not sexy, or glamorous. 'And don't come up with any new means that no one's thought of.' The first iteration of the script was her naked, and I said, 'No, no, no, no, no, not naked. Not naked, not a swimsuit, not lingerie. First of all, she's in the house. No teenage girl is going to want to be found … you know? Second, for the purposes of the show, it's too sexy. Also, in terms of realism, she's depressed now.' I said, 'Find the oldest, baggiest sweatshirt you can find.' And they did."

In spite of the nearly 30 percent increase in copycat suicide after *13 Reasons Why* aired in 2017, Dr. Hu pointed out that the increase started the month before the show was released. It also affected young boys instead of girls Hannah's age. Nevertheless, the increase was alarming enough that the death scene was eliminated. After the first season, Hannah's mother notices water flooding out of the bathroom. She opens the door to find Hannah already dead in the bathtub, with only the back of her head showing.

13 Reasons Why won praise for probing the issues of sexual assault, bullying, and suicide, but it was also criticized for its shallow portrayal of mental health and for blaming others for Hannah's death. And that brought me to my main question for Dr. Hu: When would a biological test for depression be available? A blood test, for example, would establish depression as a legitimate disease. It would help us to stop relying on dramatic Hollywood portrayals for answers. It would help parents understand that their children are genuinely sick. It would erase the stigma of depression as an overly sensitive personality. It would distinguish between normal sadness and the pathology which leads to suicide. Dr. Hu agreed that we need a biological test but said the time to act on other factors is now. "Until there is some sort of blood test or marker, we can still work on stigma in other ways—both awareness that this exists, but also, take the blame away from the person having depression as some sort of moral weakness or lack of willpower or character flaw. I'm hoping there will be a biological marker at some point. Probably once it happens, it will be helpful in decreasing stigma. I don't want to wait for that. I feel like there's a lot to be done on both awareness and stigma."

In the meantime, most patients do well with medication and therapy, including the popular cognitive behavioral therapy, which uses coping strategies to counter irrational thought. Insight-oriented therapy, basically self-awareness through personal history, has become "less popular because it's more difficult to quantify," said Dr. Hu. "And yet I feel like we shouldn't throw out anything that's actually very helpful. Our experiences do affect us, do change us. When we learn emotionally from things that have happened, that changes our coping as well."

Medication and treatments include:

Electroconvulsive therapy (ECT) - still the most effective for suicidal depression. It requires hospitalization and anesthesia to induce a seizure. It might cause memory loss but "can be lifesaving."

Transcranial Magnetic Stimulation (TMS or "ECT light") - which is less invasive, requiring no hospital stay and no anesthesia. Patients are fully awake and can read or watch TV during treatment.[131] A coil placed on the patient's head generates a magnetic pulse to stimulate targeted areas of the brain. It feels like somebody tapping on a bike helmet.

TMS might have been a good option for Patrick, but it wasn't available when he was hospitalized in 2005. At that point, Dr. Hu might have tried ECT. "It's possible that if I had known how suicidal he was, I would've been more aggressive. Most of the people who get ECT are not young people. Some are. If he had been up front about how suicidal he really was, maybe we would have pushed for something like ECT. I think if we'd had that coming out in the hospital and then got you signed up for PFLAG right away.... I do wish we could've done that. It's sort of an impossible question."

Of the antidepressants:

Lithium - "has definitely been under-used. I don't think they've found anything that beats it for suicidality. Low doses of lithium are probably helpful for a lot of people. It's filtered through the kidneys, so there's a range above which it can become quite toxic. People will start getting very serious side effects, nausea and vomiting, and then they can get kidney toxicity. A serious overdose could kill people. It fell in less favor for a while because of this fear, but with careful monitoring, it's probably more effective for suicidality than antidepressants like SSRIs."

Selective Serotonin Reuptake Inhibitors (SSRIs) - "are not over-doseable. They became popular, not because of their efficacy, but because of their safety. The older ones that they replaced, the tricyclic antidepressants, were very suicidal, very over-doseable."

Monoamine Oxidase Inhibitors - are good for patients who don't respond to SSRIs. "If they're willing to give up Spanish ham and aged cheeses, then they do really well."

Ketamine - a popular, low-dose anesthesia that improves mood faster than antidepressants and is known to help treatment-resistant depression. It's a temporary lifting of depression, she said. "You're better, and then you're not. But if researchers can improve consistency, it will be a good treatment."

Early in Dr. Hu's training, the psychopharmacologists and the psychotherapists argued about using medication. She said, "The idea was that, if something was biologically caused, then you needed to use medications. If something was psychologically caused, then you could only use psychotherapy." When one of her first patients came close to killing himself after a year of therapy, a supervisor implied that using medication "was basically like a failure." The patient had written suicide notes and had the hoses to kill himself by carbon monoxide poisoning from his car. Dr. Hu said, "It was only after being in the hospital and starting him on Prozac that we were able to get any psychotherapy work done because he was so depressed he couldn't hear it. Once we lifted his mood biochemically, we kind of put a bottom on it. Therapy by itself wasn't enough. And I don't think it was just that I was not good enough. It was that he needed the medication to be able to withstand the therapy. When patients are feeling terrible, they don't remember what it was like to feel good. It's like state-dependent memory where they doubt what they were feeling. And it goes both ways. When they're feeling better, they don't know why they over-reacted to the low."

The ability for patients to hide suicidal feelings has put Dr. Hu at odds with medical students and residents who think nobody should be placed on a 5150 mandatory hold. She was on call recently when a resident didn't want to keep a 5150 placed by police. The patient seemed normal and said he was fine. The family said he was fine, too, and the resident wanted to give the patient the benefit of the doubt and let him leave the hospital. But there was no other explanation for what the patient had done with his car except an attempt at suicide. Dr. Hu had to argue with the resident to keep it in place. "You're not saying he's a bad person if he has symptoms," Dr. Hu said. "You're saying that he has an illness. The family says he's fine because they want to believe that he is. Nobody wants to be in the hospital for the weekend or for whatever, but we might have to, to save his life. It would be awful if everybody had to make the same mistake every time in order to learn. We need to convey to people how serious this is before someone dies."

Dr. Hu was right. We could not rely on the patient to confirm a diagnosis of suicidal intent. I knew from experience. I had made the same mistake as the resident. Pat said he was fine. I thought he would be fine, and I gave him the benefit of the doubt. I let him leave, and it was awful.

"The 5150"
By Libby Wood

After grad school in psychology, I moved to Hawaii in 2017 and lived alone for a year. I surfed a lot, mostly an improvised effort to heal, similar to a cross-country bike trip I rode with my partner Linden Crawford in 2008. I immersed myself in the ocean and found it to be a transformative conduit for grieving. It took me out of my head and allowed me to be in my body. I cried a lot that year. I moved back to California and became a clinician at a psychiatric crisis unit and inpatient hospital in Santa Cruz. During my interview, I was invited to tour the facility and had the privilege of walking around what felt like a sacred and lonely institution. The staff was serious and a little on edge, as if they were ready to respond to anything, especially a crisis. They carried themselves with gravity and intention. It was like being in a library that demanded professionalism and respect because it had people like Patrick walking around.

The clinical director said, "You're going to be the first person to greet people on the worst day of their life." I wasn't sure how I felt about that statement, but I knew I was in the right place. I wanted to be the person for someone like Pat when he was hospitalized at Stanford. I wanted to be the person who could provide clinical excellence, and this goal kept me striving for greatness and connection.

I became certified to commit children and adults who were a danger to themselves or others in three counties in California. I determined whether persons needed to be placed on a mandatory psychiatric hold for seventy-two hours according to section 5150 of California state law. The job was demanding, perplexing, heartbreaking, and sometimes rewarding. It's difficult to manage long-standing issues in seventy-two hours, but I began to love the work. It was rich with meaning about Patrick's five days at Stanford Hospital. I found myself under wonderful training from clinical and medical directors, gaining expertise in developing my clinical intuition. In many ways, the training cultivated my competitive and professional nature. It was similar to my approach at the University of Vermont, where I majored in art and played soccer and lacrosse. It was similar to surfing. I wanted to be good at everything.

Training for the 5150 allowed me to be both present and absent, to be close and yet distant from Patrick. It made me lean in to my fears of suicidality, psychosis, trauma, and other psychiatric presentations I'd never imagined before. When friends and family asked what I did for a living, I told them it was hard to explain. I asked if they'd seen the film *One Flew Over the Cuckoo's Nest*, where Randle McMurphy pretends to be psychotic to avoid prison. It was easier than watching the disturbed look on their faces when I tried to paint a picture of a psychiatric ward. For all I knew, some of them might have been hospitalized themselves.

I went on to work at emergency departments in other hospitals, writing 5150 holds when necessary. I learned to make decisions under pressure and maintain a calm, deliberate, and kind approach with patients and colleagues of all ranks. I learned to build rapport swiftly to relate to patients, assess risk, and gain trust so we could plan for eventual discharge and family resources. I wanted to amplify Pat's legacy—an insatiable desire. But I held on to a fantasy that if I could be excellent and strong enough in this field, he might appear.

I worked in the acute psychiatric landscape for four years, hoping to see my twin walk in the door. At the same time, I hoped someone like him would never walk through those sturdy, locked doors, imagining that make-believe person out in the community in love, spending time with friends and family, enjoying a book on the beach, laughing to himself aloud while reading some heady novel, just as Pat so often had. Maybe that's why I kept going to work—to help people like Pat and their families get back to that place. I wanted to have a role in diffusing the pain and lift the voices within the family system that felt unheard or shy or afraid to share how much they were suffering.

I worked with patients during a global health emergency when psychiatric hospitals took COVID-19-positive patients during the pandemic. It was a new disease that was potentially lethal, but when a COVID-positive patient was on the unit, my task was to assess their psychological well-being regardless of the health risk. My job remained the same—to follow protocol, assess the patient, and protect them as well as myself. I tried not to become a carrier and endanger patients. I wore a face mask, face shield, gloves, gown, scrubs, and in between every patient, I changed all of that protective gear. Picture an astronaut, and that comes close.

Two years into the pandemic, I got a miserable case of COVID anyway and had to leave work for ten days. I was incapable of doing anything, and maybe because of the brain fog, I didn't feel the insecurities, the failures, the guilt, and the regret. I was blank. And when I finally got the energy to sit outside my house, I remember a butterfly floating past me and landing on a butterfly bush. It felt like the first real break in years.

The most important part of the protocol in assessing whether a 5150 was necessary was to creatively develop a bond with patients, gain trust—called a therapeutic alliance—and evaluate risk, which included assessing the patient, contacting family members, and collaborating with staff on the unit for multidisciplinary observation. I would ask floor staff and everyone, what have you noticed about so-and-so? Anything you feel that I should know?

Communication with staff was crucial. And then came what I call my clinical gut. That was my tuning fork. It was activated as soon as I clocked in for work in the staff lounge and used my fob key to get on the unit. I was surveying the scene, like any accident, like any crisis, and then I went into the chart room to read notes from the previous shift.

My assessment began once the patient was admitted to the crisis unit. At first, patients met with nurses, who assessed the medical part of their history, and the whole time, I was observing their affect and behavior, how they engaged with staff. I was assessing before any direct conversation with the patient. I was noticing signs that tipped the scale regarding disposition. Was the patient distraught, in shock, or catatonic (meaning psychotic)? Were they amenable to having a conversation? Were they able to engage in assessment? Did they need more time before they could articulate what led them to a psychiatric hospital and speak to someone they didn't know? When the time was right, I introduced myself. "Hi, my name is Libby, and I'll be meeting with you."

I tried to assess for safety and build rapport at the same time. I read as much of the file as possible so I knew the background and could connect to the patient. I invited the patient to describe what led them there. I asked what they felt they needed. I assessed if their presentation warranted a locked psychiatric setting. I created a shared language with family and friends—everyone involved. Was the patient okay to go home? Was the home safe? Were supports in place? Was everyone on the same page? I would say things like, "I think it's important for us to have a shared understanding of the suffering," so that everyone knew the plan and agreed to it. For example, in caring for the patient at home, the family might agree to hold vigil for the patient—essentially monitoring the patient on discharge. Even if the patient was well enough to go home, there was a serious safety plan in place, including a sweep for ropes, bleach, knives, sharps, and pills. Sometimes I requested that the family agree to take the door off the patient's bedroom and monitor them for forty-eight hours after discharge. When the patient was in the bathroom, maybe the door could not be closed all the way. These were high-risk people.

Most importantly, I emphasized connection and love. Relational connection can feel distant for depressed or psychotic patients, especially for people like Pat They might feel the cognitive distortion that they're unlovable and people would be better off without them. I stressed a plan for human connection. The family might agree to spend quality time together, eat meals together, make some of the patient's favorite food, or go for walks.

I went from psychiatric crisis hospitals to my own practice in therapy because I wanted to work preventatively with people and their families. I wanted to use the knowledge I gained in emergency settings to be more effective in assessing and treating risk on an outpatient basis. I wanted to understand people on a deeper level, and that led to studying analysis with the Palo Alto Psychoanalytic Psychotherapy Training Program (PAPPTP) at Stanford. For three years, I walked the same halls of the psychiatry building that Patrick might have walked when he met with his psychiatrist. I learned concepts of self-awareness and transformation he may have pondered before he ended his life. Stanford analysts taught me to be curious about the myriad depths of meaning and how connection and metaphor may transform a dormant drive into action. Their guidance led to my pursuit of a PhD researching the effect of psychoanalysis on depression and suicide. Analysis explored the roots of suffering. It examined experiences of the past that affected the present. It allowed patients to make sense of their world. I've learned the curative impacts, warmth, and qualitative depth of analytic treatment as both a student and a psychotherapist.

When I have a difficult case in my private practice, I consult with the Palo Alto analysts. They help with complex situations. They taught me that when I sense suicide might be a concern without the patient explicitly saying that, I listen to what the patient is not saying. I listen to what is said as well as not said to explore a more holistic meaning of their pain and know how to move from there. I look for symbols and metaphors in their answers. Sometimes patients leaning toward ending their lives create language for themselves. An example is that someone might say, "I'm feeling ready to go home." But what they mean is ending their life. That would feel like home to them. Analysis has taught me to ask what they mean.

After Patrick killed himself, my mother told me that while she and my father packed his belongings at Stanford, he said to her, "I'm giving myself a year." In the many conversations she and I had since Patrick's death, she remembered wondering, "A year for what?" She didn't realize he meant he would end his life a year after committing himself at Stanford Hospital. She didn't know he made a deadline for his death if he didn't find a boyfriend in Berlin.

When someone does share that they have suicidal feelings, I invite them to talk about it. I guide conversation and get a better understanding of the level of risk. How can we understand their pain better together? What is motivating them to keep going every day? What is motivating them to keep living? I imagine them as Patrick sitting across from me on the couch.

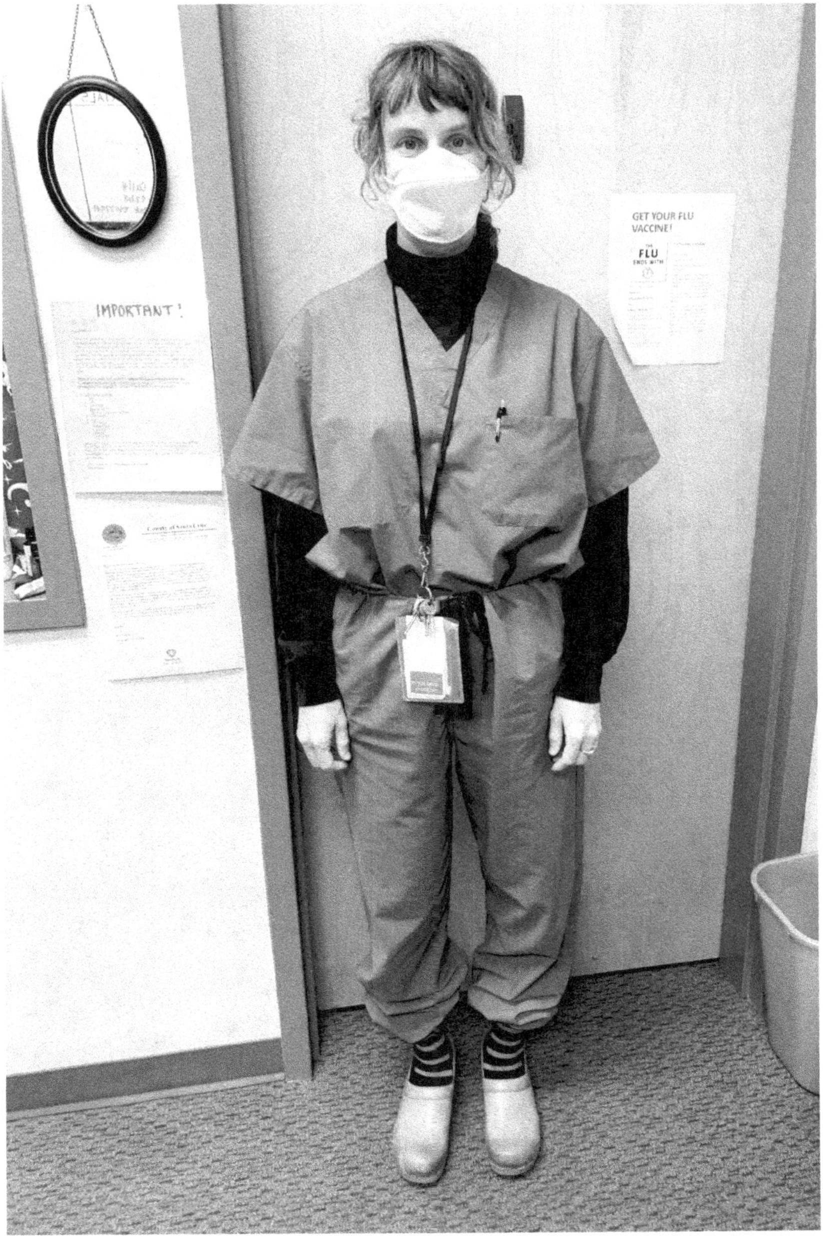

Libby, preparing for emergency psychiatric intake
during the COVID-19 pandemic, 2020.

The author with Klaus Wowereit, the mayor of Berlin, Gay Pride Parade, 2009.

Christopher Street Day

In Berlin, Patrick came to understand and embrace who he was, but he cared more about what he could and would become. This element of the essential Patrick is evident in a monologue from one of his favorite films, All About My Mother, *when the feisty drag queen Agrado proclaims, "A person is more authentic the more he looks like what he has dreamed for himself to be."*

—Ryan Wirtz
"The Essential Patrick," 2006

During the summer of 2009, after meeting with Pat's psychiatrists, I strolled with Libby, Linden, Steve, Joe, and Tibor through gay pride crowds in Berlin. Bob stayed home to take care of the animals once again. Colin was still in school in Tacoma. It was my third trip to Berlin since Pat's death. The pride parade was more like a pride saunter on a warm, sunny day, which stretched across wide boulevards and meandered past tall buildings. We stopped at one of the buildings and took an elevator to a bar on the top floor. "It's just a brief stop," Tibor said. I nodded and stood against a wall watching young people on barstools, chatting and laughing. I started to cry because Pat was not among them. Some of them looked at me and then turned back to their conversations.

I began to think a city-wide party was a bad idea. It felt like a city-wide funeral to me, but Tibor saw that I was standing apart and brought me a drink. I carried it outside to a balcony with Libby and Linden. The street below was lined with people and open-air tractor-trailer trucks. Beyond were the sloping roofs of the Berlin

Philharmonic, where Pat had listened to many concerts. He would have been here if he could, I said to myself. Instead, it had to be me.

Joe and Tibor led us back down to a wide street of slow-moving people, past the Sony Center and then Potsdamer Platz. Cars were prohibited on this holiest of gay holidays named Christopher Street Day after the 1969 New York LGBT uprising. It began the gay liberation movement in the United States. Steve stayed by my side lest pride partiers turn their blurry sights on the old mom wearing a Pat t-shirt and carrying a Pat poster. It showed a picture of Pat sitting in front of his Siemens office computer with the dates of his life. "In Memory of Patrick," it said. "1982 (USA) 2006 (Berlin)." We all had copies and carried them in front of us as we strolled in the afternoon sun.

We continued past a fire truck with men in black uniforms, standing on top and waving to the crowds. The classical columns of the Brandenburg Gate loomed ahead, its quadriga driven by the goddess of victory. The glass dome of the Reichstag building rose above a tractor-trailer truck with men in sailor hats and tight white shirts. The Soviet War Memorial in the Tiergarten was draped with revelers. They threw their backpacks on the Russian tank in front of it and sat on the gun turret. The Siegessäule Victory Column in the middle of the Tiergarten came into view behind crowds of people and trucks. Its 220-foot column, topped by the "chick on the stick," suggested the meaning of the day. DJs stood on top of a truck with a soundboard for music. Loudspeakers were nearly as tall as the truck. A banner above them said "Berlin Pride Festival." Someone below wore a full-length white dress with a veil on her head as if it were her wedding day, and in a way, it was. We were all celebrating the union of gay men and women. The road to the Siegessäule was lined with beat-thumping, open-air trucks decorated with rainbows, balloons, dancing sailors, and muscular men. It was named for the Russian assault on East Berlin protesters on June 17, 1953. Now, partiers waited patiently for beer and sausage. Leather-clad revelers with giant red mohawks looked at me casually. My somber face did not invite party mode. But some looked at Pat's poster and hung their heads. They realized that a man their age had walked among them and now walked no more. They put down their wine bottles, walked across the street, and gave me a hug.

Libby and Linden made sure I was okay and then disappeared to a smaller pride festival in Kreuzberg. I felt completely at home with Steve, who never left my side, and Joe and Tibor, who seemed to know everyone milling around us I had never felt better since Pat died. I was home, with Pat's people, who accepted me for appreciating the hardships they were casting off that day.

Joe, Tibor, Steve, and I stopped for pictures with Christian Krüger and a doctor who was there to celebrate but also to treat those who celebrated too much. The Siegessäule rose behind our group photos. We made our way past the lines in front of the booths on Strasse des 17. Juni and approached another line in front of a small red tent. It guarded the only opening in a high fence surrounding the Siegessäule. Pride officials sat at a table under the tent. Joe and Tibor went to the front of the line. The officials crossed their names off a VIP guest list, which allowed people inside the barrier. Tibor scanned the list upside down and returned to Steve and me standing farther back in line. "Many names were not crossed off the list," he said to Steve in German. He gave Steve one of the leftover names with a "plus one" next to it. "You are …" and then he told Steve the name in a low voice. "He'll probably never show up," Tibor said, and then he repeated the name. Steve nodded his head. I was the plus one.

We approached the guardians of the VIP list. We lowered our "In memory of Patrick" signs to draw less attention. Steve's quiet manner passed for a poker face. He told the official the upside-down name. "She's the plus one," he said in German. I said nothing. The official found the name and crossed it off the list. He attached white bands on our wrists and asked if they fit okay. We nodded yes, smiled thank you, and walked through the opening of the barrier. My knees stopped shaking. Steve's poker face relaxed. Joe, Steve, and the doctor raised their wrist-banded arms in triumph. We wandered in the VIP area, apart from crowds that waded through bigger crowds to pay for food outside the barrier. Picnic tables offered plenty of seating. The booths had no lines. A bare-chested man kissed another man near the barrier. A woman in front of him wore a mini-skirted dirndl with tall black boots. She looked like a Bavarian cheerleader. I wandered to a trailer of toiletten with no line, a benefit of VIP status.

"We get five free drinks," Steve said when I returned. He pointed to the five circles on our wristbands. Joe's wristband allowed unlimited drinks. He took an order and returned with an armload, which he warned were poured freely. The brown sugar, mint, and crushed ice blended smoothly with a full cup of alcohol. The sun was still strong at 9:00 p.m. We settled around a table. Tibor introduced me to friends at the table—young people in their twenties and thirties. He brought heaping plates of sausage and potato salad to the table. His purple artist's wristband allowed free food. He was a master of access to anything Berlin, including a backstage party for Blue Man Group at which Pat had partied all night.

A dark-eyed communications student at our table saw Pat's poster and winced in sympathy. Tibor introduced a man who knew Pat. He twitched one side of his face and ran his tongue around his teeth. He looked down at the table. "What I want to say to you is not possible to put into words," he said, "not here, not now. It's not possible to express the depth of feeling, so I'm at a loss. Pat was here. He was okay. And then he wasn't. I don't know how to react." More twitching and tongue circling. "It's just that he went through something that I didn't understand. When I saw him, he was happy. He was okay. I don't know the path he took. If I had known, I would have done something. I would have tried harder. But I didn't know anything about his depression. I wish I could have done more, but I can tell you that Pat was very social. He was in the scene. Everybody liked him. What he did wasn't because of us. I can promise you that."

A dark-haired Australian boyfriend with eyeliner leaned down for the man to light his cigarette. The man waved him away, and the boyfriend backed up defensively with his hands in the air. The man kept his eyes on me. The twitching stopped. He finished his thought. "I want to tell you something. I asked Pat to come home with me once, but he said no. So there, now you know. He may have died here, but it wasn't because of us. He had people who would help him. He just didn't ask us." The lanky boyfriend circled by, and the man lit his cigarette.

The day darkened, and a band played rock music on a stage at the base of the Siegessäule. A sea of people stretched in front of it to the Brandenburg Gate over a mile away. The mayor of Berlin appeared on the steps of the Siegessäule, a sweater draped over his shoulders. Klaus Wowereit was an openly gay and successful politician whom Tibor had met in a club. They spoke at the base of the steps and motioned for me to come over. Tibor explained to the mayor that he had once introduced him to Patrick, and now he was introducing him to Patrick's mother. I showed the mayor my Patrick sign and thanked him for his welcoming city. Berlin had strengthened Pat, I told him. It allowed him to be who he was. Tibor translated. The mayor looked into my eyes, held my arms, and kissed me on both cheeks. He said he was sorry, and I nodded my head in thanks. We posed for several pictures, and then he smiled in understanding and turned to other VIPs.

Dancing, free drinks, and bass-filled beats shot out as if from the guns of war on the Siegessäule. They seethed and pulsed and lit up the night sky with blue smoke from the stage. They exploded in a contrast of war memorials and portable toiletten, lusty queens, and Tiergarten sculptures—an orgy of identity that welcomed the dead and the living. Berlin's gay pride was expensive and garish. Seven kilometers of busy main streets were closed to traffic that day. Environmentalists complained of disturbing Tiergarten wildlife. Wine and beer bottles lay everywhere. An argument broke out near the VIP area. Police came running and separated the aggressor, who suddenly emerged smiling. Drag queens strutted. Leather, chains, and tattoos covered buttocks and breasts. "You don't like gay marriage? So don't fucking get one," said a t-shirt. Ambulances sirened their way through crowded streets to carry off partiers. A few vomited in the Tiergarten. The doctor friend was called to the scene.

I walked home with Steve down Tiergartenstrasse and then Stauffenbergstrasse, where Claus von Stauffenberg and three accomplices were shot for attempting to assassinate Hitler. We wandered into a dark cobblestone courtyard where a bronze statue, "Young Man with Tied Hands," memorialized von Stauffenberg and the Nazi resistance. The man was naked with his hands bound in front of him. A plaque in front of him said:

You did not bear the shame.
You resisted.
You bestowed the eternally vigilant symbol of change
by sacrificing your impassioned lives for
freedom, justice and honour.[132]

I placed Pat's picture at the base of the statue where humanity now prevailed.

Above: Tibor and Pat.
Below: Joe, Pat, and Tibor, Gay Pride Parade, Berlin, 2005.

Café am Beethovenplatz, one of Pat's favorites, Munich, 2009.

Munich

Patrick saw himself as an expatriate who wanted to break stereotypes and counter the negative attitude towards Americans that he saw pervading German society. But he did it all so subtly and gently. That was the essential Patrick.

—Ryan Wirtz
"The Essential Patrick," 2006

The 2009 German pilgrimage continued by train from Berlin through Wittenberg, Leipzig, Nuremberg, and Augsburg to Munich, where Pat had interned at BMW during the summer of 2004. He ate dinner in a beer garden that used beer steins for light fixtures with his friend Tobias. They watched nude frisbee in the English Garden, but Pat refused to participate. He wasn't going to take his clothes off in a public park no matter how much he believed in free expression. He watched *Die Meistersinger* twice in a square once dominated by Nazi parades. The first time, he brought a friend. The second time, he went alone. Not even his German friends liked Wagner that much.

Pat's BMW supervisor, Heidrun Belzner, showed Libby, Linden, Tobias, and me Pat's office building in the northern part of Munich near the Olympic stadium. BMW spread to many buildings across broad streets ribboned with traffic. We walked down a sidewalk and stared through a metal fence at a light-colored building. Heidrun pointed out the window of Pat's office and the canteen where he ate lunch. We could not go inside because of security, but we were content to see another Pat shrine from a distance.

We retired to an ancient, noisy restaurant in Munich where Beethoven used to dine—one of Pat's favorites. The dark back bar and bentwood chairs warmed the atmosphere of Café am Beethovenplatz as Heidrun talked about working with Pat. He had lived in the studentenstadt near BMW, which was boring and full of transients, but he chatted with other interns at work and went out with friends. He never missed a day of work and seemed to have a full life. She was shocked when she heard about his death.

He designed a traffic analysis program for the Department of Traffic Science and Technology at BMW that was still in use three and a half years later. He worked with traffic simulation software in Linux. He used the MATLAB programming language to analyze traffic data and simulation results. What once took half a day of entering numbers, Pat streamlined into fifteen minutes. He designed an algorithm to assess the quality of traffic data that BMW was processing to study patterns, accident rates, and fuel efficiency. His program made sure the data gave accurate results. It assured quality control.

He was a master at simplifying, and once he was on the case, you had better keep up because he would email you at home to make suggestions and get feedback, said Heidrun. Maybe this will work. Okay, not feasible. Let's try another way. He was more than an intern. He was a partner. He was a brainstorm of swirling ideas. His work evaluation was superior except for organization, maybe because of the juice bottles piled on his desk. The director of interns offered him a job. "How good was he?" I asked Heidrun amid the clanking dishes and loud conversations from the tables nearby.

"He was one of the best we ever had," she said.

Patrick, while interning as a programmer at BMW, Munich, 2004.

Pat, one year old, 1983.

Where Did He Come From?

I have discovered some crucial truths, the theoria to my agon.... I have established that knowing how to deal with other people is a learned skill that takes a lifetime of experience. Maybe I will never be as outgoing as other people, in part because it is in my genes, and in part because I got started too late on the process. My past has had a tremendous influence on my capabilities, and I have learned to respect that.

—Patrick Wood
"Being Shy," 1999

Friends, teachers, employers, and doctors from Berlin to Palo Alto were helping. They shifted my thinking from present to past tense. Pat no longer is. He was. The new present tense was books on suicide. David Vann's *Legend of a Suicide* punched me in the gut with its bloody, putrid plot twist. In the long fourth chapter called "Sukkwan Island," thirteen-year-old Roy reunites with his father on a remote Alaskan island. They live in a wet cabin, lose their food to a bear, and catch salmon to survive. The father sobs at night, blubbers about prostitutes, shoots holes in the roof, and makes Roy feel guilty about wanting to leave. Roy is desperate. He is stuck with a bungling father who tries to kill himself, who threatens both their lives. Roy takes action in a passage of the book that made me look up in horror. It was too much to take in. I looked down and read the passage many times. It got worse. When friends asked how I was doing, I answered with a copy of *Legend of a Suicide*. You want to know what it's like? This is what it's like. You will never forget that scene.

Leroy Aaron's *Prayers for Bobby* punched me again with Mary Griffith's Bible-drumming against her son's gay life. In 1983, when twenty-year-old Bobby Griffith jumped off an overpass to be killed by a tractor-trailer truck, her guilt made mine look small. Bobby is much like Patrick. He is gentle as a child, almost too obedient and sweet-natured. He has a space between his front teeth, and his sunshine-blond hair radiates goodness. He loves stuffed animals more than physical play. He sits dutifully in Mary's Walnut Creek, California church, loving God as a child. But the minister rants against gays and lesbians, and Bobby feels condemned as he grows older. When he comes out at age sixteen, Mary tells him homosexuality is not natural. God can cure it. She has seen it on TV. She encourages counseling through the church. She pins copies of scripture around the house so Bobby will try harder to be saved. She puts quotes about sinners being children of the devil above the bathroom mirror. She is desperate to save him from damnation, and worse than that, she is ashamed of her son.

Bobby takes to menial jobs and prostitution to make money. He moves in with his cousin to avoid Mary's preaching. On an August night, he walks to the Everett Street overpass across Interstate 405 in Portland, Oregon. He walks to the railing and looks to the south over the traffic below. He turns around and does a backflip into mid-air. He times his jump to fall twenty-five feet into the path of an eighteen-wheeler. The driver cannot swerve out of the way. The impact kills Bobby instantly. It scatters his clothes on the highway.

Mary realizes that Bobby did not decide to be gay any more than she decided to have hazel eyes. She asks God why he would send Bobby to hell for something he couldn't control. She answers by rejecting her faith and becoming a spokesperson for gay rights. On the Sally Jessy Raphael show in the early 1990s, she tells parents to be open-minded and let their gay and lesbian children know they are loved. That was brave enough on national television, I thought, but the next comment had me reaching for Kleenex. She asked President Bush, Congress, and religious leaders not to be, as she was, "an unwitting accomplice to an innocent person's death."[133]

With those plain words, Mary Griffith took the dagger out of her heart and put it in mine.

Stories like Mary's were helping. Pat's friends were reassuring. Psychiatrists eased the guilt. Science explained depression. Websites explained the lure of suicide as an addiction like any drug. But they were not enough. I was still obsessing about *why*. In therapy, it went something like this: Why does a person so brilliant, so promising, feel so horrible that they lock themselves in their bathroom, plug up every opening, even the cracks in the walls and the drains, take sleeping pills, drink vodka, and light three pans of charcoal?

He couldn't handle rejection. (This is my therapist talking). Gay people are the third most likely group to kill themselves. Psychiatrists and police are at the top. He was afraid of the future.

Me: Why?

Therapist: He wanted commitment. He didn't fit into the transient lifestyle of young gay men.

Me: Why?

Therapist: He needed more.

Me: Why?

Therapist: He wasn't prepared to live on his own.

Wasn't prepared? (This is me talking.) He graduated with honors from Stanford with a degree in math. He worked at Siemens in Berlin. He had friends. He had boyfriends. Everybody loved him. He went out. He traveled to Paris and Italy and Stockholm. He went to museums and concerts. He spoke German like a native. He played piano like a star. Why didn't he want to live?

The whys drove me to my mother's suicide. Was her life that sad? Did she pass that death wish on to Patrick? Did her genes dominate? I went back to her birth in 1927 when my grandpère was disappointed that he wouldn't have a son to go to West Point. My mother had a baby nurse at first and then a German governess when Grandpère was the military attaché in Belgium. My mother moved constantly because of Grandpère's army career. She spoke

German and French the first few years of her life and didn't really know her mother. My grandmère was busy with the house and friends and tennis and needlepoint groups and piano. Grandpère was working, so she didn't know him either. She knew him as the one who drove the car. The family would get into the car on Sundays. He would take them for a drive, and afterward, my mother and her sister Harriet would get out of the car and say, "Thank you, Papa. Thank you, Mama." And that was all they knew.

Beds were made and rooms cleaned. Bathroom habits were monitored: One French licorice reward for a modest bowel movement. Two for more. Tutoring or school followed. Madame Somebody for French or German. Somebody else for outings. Piano in the afternoons. Curtseys for introductions. Heads bowed, eyes down, skirts held to the sides, the right foot back, the knees bent. "This is Mrs. So and So." "How do you do, Mrs. So and So?" Sit quietly while the tea is served. At other people's houses, "fold your hands behind your back. You may not *touch* anything."

"Parade Rest," where my grandparents retired in Wilton, Connecticut, was a respite from thirty years in the army but not from regulation. Breakfast was at 8:00, cocktails at 5:30, dinner at 6:00, and be on time, or KIT TEN! (my mother's nickname) would ring throughout the house. When I was a child, we gathered in the pale blue dining room with a fireplace at one end and a mantel topped with porcelain horse soldiers. We sat on Louis XV upholstered chairs, mine with a New York City telephone book on the seat to raise me higher. Alice the maid served meals in covered silver dishes from the left. We spooned first and second helpings onto warm Wedgwood plates. My mother sat across from me, looking down while we listened to: "You may not have dessert if you don't eat all your dinner. Sit still, and do not speak unless you are asked. And for heaven's sake, clean your fingernails before you come to the table." It was an old-world, Victorian past that didn't explain my mother's suicide, but it put me in a previous world, without Patrick, with life varnished in a yellow glow that was remote, detached, and non-threatening. It made the search for answers more important than the answers themselves.

My mother's reaction to regimentation throughout many childhood homes, three high schools, one junior college, and several marriages, was to abhor the staid and formal, and she used that as a bludgeon when I made her angry. She would rise up to her five-feet nine-inches height and deepen her voice. "I'll send you off to Miss Porter's," she would threaten, her blue blood boiling. I should consider myself lucky to be in public school rather than finishing-school hell. How would I like it if Grandmère yanked me out of Highland Falls High School because of too many boys and then put me in Farmington with too many girls? Then there was St. Mary's in Peekskill, New York, with too many nuns. Ogontz Junior College in Pennsylvania was fine, but I would have a chance to go to a four-year college thanks to her divorce agreement with my father when I was five years old.

Why didn't she stay in school? Silence was her answer.

Grandmère's diary told the real story. My mother had blonde hair that curled gently to her shoulders. She wore bright red lipstick and long, curvaceous skirts like the 1940s starlets of her teenage years. She met my father at a summer dance at the Wilton Riding Club. He was tall and dark-haired with sparkling eyes and a broad smile, and somehow they managed conjugal visits. A few months later, she announced to her parents they had eloped.

We lived in Philadelphia while my father attended the University of Pennsylvania Medical School and then in Rochester, New York, where he worked the long hours of a young doctor at Strong Memorial Hospital. He was on duty for days at a stretch, taking catnaps at the hospital. He didn't have time for his young child and practically teenage wife. My mother wrote to her grandmother Flo-Flo, "Dave is terribly busy—he is interning at Strong Memorial Hospital, and I rarely see him."[124] We lived where houses were stacked cheek by jowl, and you had better not pick flowers from the neighbor's garden, or some Mrs. Italian Name would pitch a fit, and you would be reminded of it every time you went outside. If you wandered in the wrong direction, you would be warned of the mental hospital at the end of the street, where patients stared out of windows and howled at full moons.

In 1953, when my father was drafted near the end of the Korean War, he wrote to my mother from an air force base in Texas that the marriage was over. I came home from kindergarten one day, and my mother told me to get in the car. We were driving to Fort Lauderdale to be near my Aunt Harriet. My dad would come later, she said. But that was not true. She said it so I would stop crying and get into the car. I worried about my father until partway down the East Coast, the sun brightened, my mother rolled down the window of her green and white Chevrolet, and the worry faded. She covered her blowing hair with a blue chiffon scarf and drove with one hand on the steering wheel and her head held high.

We landed at the Driftwood Motel on Route A1A across from the Fort Lauderdale beach and then moved into a bungalow near Holiday Park. We had a little money from an Antoinette ancestor, and my father paid child support. We went to the beach most weekends at the Galt Ocean Mile, a barren stretch of sand and surf in the early 1950s. Man o' wars bobbed on gentle waves and washed up on the beach. Their dark blue tentacles spread across brown and green seaweed. We put on sandy shoes and jumped on their translucent balloons, which popped and hissed and lay in heaps. My mother gave me a camera, and we drove around in the golden light of the afternoons and took pictures of boats and palm trees on canals.

My mother painted from our photos, but she slept late in the mornings. I ate cereal or found bread and butter in the refrigerator and added sugar for a breakfast sandwich. I walked to first grade at Bennett Elementary School when I felt like it. Teachers raised their eyebrows when I showed up late, but that did not penetrate my six-year-old mind. I walked into a classroom of students at their desks, sat down, and found my place in the *Dick and Jane* book as if I hadn't missed anything.

I walked to school later each morning until one day, I met my classmates on their way home. "School's over," one of them said, and looked at me like I was stupid. I saw more kids pouring out of school and turned around and walked home. I hoped my mother wouldn't find out that I dawdled so long I missed an entire day of school, but we both got caught. The school called her for a meeting. We drove to school, she more dressed up than usual. I sat in the car while she walked into the main entrance without me. She returned with the pronouncement that I had to get to school earlier, and she made sure I did. She got up in the mornings to get me out the door on time. In the afternoons, I walked the few blocks from school to Wynn's Bar on North Federal Highway to meet my mother for a ride home. I stood behind her while she talked and laughed with her friends at the bar. She bought me a Coke, and I sat at a table nearby, or I wandered in the liquor store in front of the bar until she was ready to leave.

My mother set up her easel near the kitchen table of the first house and then in the Florida room of the second house on a canal in Wilton Manors. She painted boat wrecks, lighthouses, palm trees, and beaches. She turned to portraits and painted whomever she could get to sit for her, including me. She roughed out a sketch and brushed on the oils. I tried not to wiggle. The first day showed promise. She layered more paint. The likeness disappeared and so did the canvas. She said she was too close to the subject.

She took over another kitchen table with her paints and easel in the third house across from Stranahan High School. I walked across the street for tenth through twelfth grades except for a short diversion in Islamorada. School busses flooded the road in front of the house twice a day, and after school, students would pull their cars into the driveway and empty their ashtrays. The house was on a canal that gave my mother's second husband, Dick, easier access to the Intracoastal. He would pilot his twenty-two-foot inboard skiff to the New River, which ran through downtown Fort Lauderdale, and then the Intracoastal. He named it RiKiLi for Richard, Kitty, and Lisette. He cruised under the 17th Street Causeway Bridge, headed through Port Everglades, and steamed a short hop to the deep blue Gulf Stream that slid through the green Atlantic. He baited hooks longer than my hand, and when fish took the bait, he and my mother would grab the poles, wind the reels, gaff the fish, and flip them onto floorboards. Flapping, gulping, dolphinfish lost color as they lay in the sun.

We were a family until Dick stopped coming home to go fishing. My mother and I drove to his favorite bar one night. She waited in the car while I went in to ask him why he didn't come home. She knew I would embarrass him more than she would, and she was right. I stood next to him at the bar until he turned around on his barstool with a start. He didn't like being asked to come home by his eleven-year-old stepdaughter in front of his friends.

My mother and I stuck together through the disintegration of the marriage. When Dick stopped speaking to me, she confronted him. She would not tolerate his cold shoulder to me, but her confrontation escalated the break up. Their fighting began to shake the house as if they were slamming into walls. I ran into their room one night and screamed at them to stop it. They stumbled to opposite corners, Dick with no clothes on diving into a closet and my mother looking away from me. I ran out the front door and across the street to my high school playing fields. I hid behind a tree until the police came and Dick drove away.

After my mother's miscarriage, Dick packed up his boat and sailed away. He said the miscarriage meant God was punishing him for marrying a divorced woman. Bar friends and boyfriends appeared at the kitchen table. Jazz crooned on the hi-fi cabinet next to the table. My mother laughed too loudly, smoked Lucky Strikes, drank too much, and had an affair with the pool man. Opera boomed throughout the house when she painted. Her lips thickened. Her words slurred. Her eyes lost focus, and her mascara ran. She made dinner but sat heavily at the table. The knife and fork wobbled in her hands. She looked down at the table vaguely, and then she stood up and disappeared into her bedroom. My great-grandmother Flo-Flo weighed in that Kitten and Harriet changed husbands like shoes.

Alcohol shriveled my mother's frame. She didn't eat. She drank in bed and staggered to the bathroom on skinny legs. She leaned against the wall and shuffled barefoot along the terrazzo floor. Shuffle, shuffle. Stop. Silence. Shudder. Shuffle, shuffle. If I said she should quit drinking or get a doctor, she told me to mind my own business and leave her alone. If I said it again, she told me louder, and then she would tighten the belt around her bathrobe and hold on to the wall to shuffle to the bathroom.

A husband-to-be swooped her up and moved us to the Keys when I was a sophomore in high school. Captain Gerry took her for every bad check he could write. If she cooked hamburgers for dinner, he drove to the store, picked out lobsters, wrote a rubber check, and cooked them instead. She owed money for his bills at every restaurant, bar, gas station, grocery store, and dock in Islamorada. Four months later, more disappearing, more shuffling. She showed up at my school on Tavernier Key one afternoon as I was about to get on the bus. She pulled up to the curb and said, "Get in the car. We're going home." The back seat of her red Chevy Impala was loaded with our clothes. "Get in the car," she said again. We drove the few minutes to Key Largo where she stopped at a motel. She was too drunk to drive the few hours back to Fort Lauderdale.

We moved into a two-bedroom apartment dubbed Oatmeal Acres because of the old people there. My mother slept all day, and when she came out of her bedroom in the late afternoon, she smelled stale. She would tell me to heat up TV dinners, and if I told her we had run out, she'd accuse me of lying. I held the refrigerator door open so she could see it was empty. She looked down at the floor, tightened her bathrobe, and went back to bed.

I should have asked for help. I could have called Harriet, but my mother didn't want help, and I was scared of going against her. Instead, I took an easier route: I blocked her out of my mind. When I was in school, she didn't exist. When I was home, I heated

TV dinners or did the few chores she asked. When she slept, I stopped worrying. That made the problem go away.

Harriet called occasionally, but there were few visits. Harriet didn't like my mother's drinking, and my mother didn't like Harriet's second husband. Jack Holly was a car salesman and a race car mechanic. He had curly slicked-back hair, thick eyebrows, and a Southern drawl. He raced cars, ran junkyards, bet on horses, showed off his money, and said words like *darlin'*. But he was also the force who made my mother get into his car and drive to detox centers.

One of the rare visits with Harriet's family was a Christmas dinner at Grandmère's apartment in Fort Lauderdale. I drove over early to bring food. My mother said she would come later, but she never showed up. I started to worry and wanted to drive home to be with her, but Grandmère called my mother's psychiatrist friend and put me on the phone. He told me it wasn't my fault. My mother was manic depressive, which he explained as being either very happy or very sad. She was up and down, he said. She was unpredictable, and it had nothing to do with me. Don't feel guilty, he said. She loves you and wants you to enjoy Christmas with your family. It's not your fault, he repeated, and I could tell he had run out of explanations about my mother's drinking on the biggest family day of the year.

Grandmère paid for the private detox centers, which worked temporarily, and when my mother was home and healthy, Grandmère would plead with her to come for lunch at the Lago Mar, where she stayed in the winter. Lunch had to be *early* because at 2:30, *promptly* (insistence rising), she had an appointment, and she *couldn't* be late. Appointment was code for Grandmère's colonic. A Mrs. Swiss Somebody would come to her apartment and bring an enema to clean out the remains of the lunches.

By then, my mother had a studio full of art awards. She didn't want to stop painting so she would eat too much lunch at the Lago Mar. She bought an answering machine, which infuriated Grandmère. The messages became insistent. "I've come all the way down here to be with you, and you don't pick up the phone? *Really*, Kitten!" she ended with a flourish.

At that point, my mother would screech that Grandmère was driving her crazy, and when I offered a weak solution like, "Why don't you tell her you need to paint?" she screeched louder. She screeched how Grandmère would be impossible, how she would make a fuss and that would drive her more crazy. Then she raged about her childhood and the baby nurses, the German governesses, the French-speaking school where she spoke English, and the English-speaking school where she spoke French. She moved constantly when she was a child to diplomatic assignments in Europe when Grandpère was military attaché to Belgium. And then more moving when he returned to the States after the failed Disarmament Conference in 1935. In 1940, a year before Pearl Harbor, Grandpère became the executive officer of West Point. He was one of many retirees replacing war-bound West Pointers. He succeeded Col. Thomas J. J. Christian, who went on to command the 361st Fighter Group and died in a bombing mission in France in 1944.

Grandpère was second in command, basically the vice president of West Point, in charge of land purchases and new construction to prepare for World War II. He commanded the infantry, cavalry, air corps, field and coast artillery, engineering, signal, quartermaster, ordnance troops, and military police of West Point. He oversaw the largest land purchase in West Point history—163 parcels expanding the post by 10,520 acres in 1943.[135]

The move meant another temporary military house and raising two daughters on a campus teeming with female-starved soldiers. My mother would have to change schools. Again. Grandmère was miserable about moving. She wrote in her diary that the stream behind her newly renovated Connecticut home was *filled* with her tears. But my mother loved the freedom. She was the executive officer's daughter, and she had carte blanche to go where she wanted. She could look down on the Hudson River from her three-story brick officers' home. She could run up Thayer Road, past the colossal stone buildings of the academic area, and then out on the broad, level parade ground of the Plain. A few minutes farther put her at Trophy Point where she could look north to the Hudson River as it cut through the highlands. She could race down Flirtation Walk and lie on top of Kissing Rock and make smacking noises as cadets kissed their dates. She blended easily with the Black and white students and the football spirit of Highland Falls High School. But Grandmère had grander plans than mingling with locals and spying on cadets. She put my mother in boarding school at Miss Porter's with no boys and less worry.

The girls were snobby. My mother hated them and ran away twice. She ended up at lonely bus stops and drugstores in the middle of the night with Grandmère and Grandpère in pursuit. She was happier at St. Mary's in nearby Peekskill, New York, but Grandmère continued her assaults on commonality. "She wouldn't let me go anywhere!" my mother shrieked. "She wouldn't let me wear lipstick in high school. High school! She sent me away to Miss Porter's. I hated it! Do you know what she used to do to me? She used to beat me with a coat hanger! I can't take it anymore!"

My mother tuned out Grandmère's pleading for lunch dates with vodka. If her husband, John, hid the bottles, she drove drunk to the liquor store. If she sideswiped somebody, she took taxis. She blamed her drinking on her mother, and I believed her. There was no other reason I could see. She was a prominent artist in South Florida, at the top of her career with newspaper articles full of exhibits and awards. At a Parker Playhouse exhibit, the playbill described her paintings as combining the land and the sea from the somber New England coastlines to the "sandy, palm-fringed shores of Florida, full of warmth and sunshine. There is great strength and feeling in her work which frequently invokes in the viewer a nostalgic remembrance of similar scenes in phases of one's own past."[136] Art critic Schubert Jonas said my mother was "one of Fort Lauderdale's best and most consistent water color painters." In an interview, she told Schubert she tried to capture the "present, the past, the time of day and the season, the sounds, smells and everything that goes to make up the memories we have of places we have seen and visited. The great challenge is to transfer it to the paper so that in the end the painting conveys these qualities to the viewer."[137]

My mother had been painting and drawing since her high school days at West Point. She had achieved her life-long dream of becoming a recognized artist. She was a charter member of the Florida Watercolor Society. She and John went to art shows and formal exhibit openings. They had parties for visiting artists, my mother not tempted by the alcohol being served. In the evenings, she and John watched TV in her large house near the Intracoastal. They sipped coffee while several of her eleven Chihuahuas lay on their laps.

The one exception to the high point of career and marriage was Grandmère. She could be imperious and demanding, her full-throated voice wavering up and down like an opera singer. It rose along with her eyebrows and her entire being and interrupted my mother when she was in the middle of a sentence. She would look away and then down at her watch with fake surprise. "Oh dear! I wonder what time it is!" And then a low giggle while my mother was left with her mouth hanging open.

Grandmère's full throat rose against Harriet while she drove us from Greenwich to Nino's restaurant in Bedford Village, New York. Harriet swayed the car gently on country roads to protect Grandmère's right arm, healing from a fall on Martha's Vineyard. But one curve caused a Grandmère eruption. "You're driving too fast! You're hurting my arm!" A few minutes later, after Harriet slowed down, "Can't you go faster? We'll be late for our reservation!"

Grandmère's full throat rose against waitresses in many restaurants. "Bring the coffee now. Not too hot. Could you turn down the air conditioning? It's *freezing* in here. Kitten, are you warm enough? And do you have more bread? We've been waiting. Lisette, dear, remember to put your napkin on your lap. Do you need to wash your hands? *Do* tie your shoelaces before you go, and be careful of the waitresses. Don't get in their way."

The iced tea had to be *very* light, the soft-shelled crab *very* soft, and the pasta not *too* soft. *Al dente*, she would enunciate as if the waitress was hard of hearing. My mother and I could make fun of her. We mimicked her queenly, "Mon Dieu!" We snickered like school children, but my mother had to deal with her every day. She made me think that if I were a supportive mother, if I were a friend to my children like she was to me, they would be free from overbearing dictates. They would be free from my mother's misery.

In the fall of 1979, when Colin was six months old, I brought him to Fort Lauderdale to meet my mother. It was before the days of infant car seats, and Colin sat on my lap as the three of us drove home from the grocery store one day. My mother stared straight ahead and started talking about what she wanted when she died. Of course, I thought. This was the conversation that happens when families start planning long term, when they start planning for next generations. Colin stared out the car window as my mother said she had been to a lawyer and made some arrangements. She wanted to be cremated when she died, and she wanted her ashes to be spread over the ocean. I could have anything I wanted from the house—her paintings, her jewelry, her silver, her antiques, but she wanted the house itself to go to John.

I agreed. It was her house. She could do what she wanted with it. I had no attachment to it. I had never lived there. She had bought it long after I left for college in Connecticut, and Bob and I had our own house. John would need it more than I did in the unlikely event that she died before him. She was thirteen years younger. I told her she could give the house to whomever she wanted. She let that comment sink in. She kept her eyes on the road, and then she added, "I'm thinking of killing myself."

I didn't answer right away. I had Colin on my lap—a new life in the family. I couldn't fit death into my head. I was scared, but only briefly. It didn't make any sense. She had been sober nine years. She was making a living with her art. She was getting first-place awards. She couldn't be serious. I blurted an answer, "Mom, don't say that!" She stopped talking. We pulled into her driveway and brought groceries into the house. Colin and I returned to Connecticut a few days later. It was the last time I would see her before she died.

Later that fall, a friend stopped to say hello at the Delray Mall Art Exhibit. My mother was sitting amongst her easels and artwork displayed along the walkway, her face tanned from decades of sunbathing, her blonde hair in a pony tail, a soft drink in her hand. She said the sugar in soft drinks helped her stay away from alcohol. She wore a dark windbreaker and sandals. She brought a big straw bag and kept it open beside her so her oldest Chihuahua, Little Bit, could poke her head out. The friend congratulated her on being a grandmother. My mother smiled and said she was happy about Colin.

But my mother was facing another winter of Grandmère, who was widowed from Grandpère and looking for company. She would be flying from Connecticut and have a retired policeman, Officer Franco, drive her Oldsmobile down soon after. She would settle in at the Lago Mar and start pleading, "Kitten, darling, let's do this," and "let's do that," or "let's have lunch and walk on the beach or have dinner with John."

My mother was grim with dread. She could not concentrate on transferring the present and the past, the seasons and the sounds and smells of memories to her watercolors. She could not create the warmth and sunshine of palm trees and beaches for art shows. She could not revel in the joy of her paintings like "Rooftops," which lifts sagging roof lines to spiritual heights of towers and birds in the sky, where chimneys wobble and windows lean in rapture. She could not climb the pale steps of the "Blue Staircase," which spiral up from the gray and dark below to the yellows and blues of the sky above. Instead, she screeched to Grandmère's sister Queets about the prospect of too many lunches. Queets replied that my mother had to take hold of herself and not be so sensitive. The "terrible difference between generations is hard on everyone," and maybe a psychiatrist would help.[138] But the difference was all my mother could talk about. She erupted on phone calls to me in Connecticut. Why couldn't Grandmère get along as well as she and I did? I wrote to Grandmère in January 1980 that my mother needed time to paint. Her art career was a business, and she needed more time to make it successful. It would be better if Grandmère stayed away. But in her dramatic tone, Grandmère said it was difficult after all her years of "love & devotion." She had already signed a lease at the Lago Mar, and she was "comfortable" there. Little had sunk in to her matriarchal mindset. I was getting a taste of why my mother was screeching.

Five months and several trips to a hospital and detox center later, my mother stumbled back and forth to the bathroom. She fell against the large goldfish aquarium she had set up in her room. The sides and corners of the tank were covered in her blood, and there were bloodstains on her glasses. "There must be an END to it," Grandmère wrote in her diary, and on June 2, 1980, there was. My mother stumbled around the house that morning, but about 3:00 in the afternoon, John went into the bedroom to find her wedged between a fish tank and her bed. She was soaked in blood from falling against the aquarium. He watched her long and hard to see if she was breathing, and then he gulped nitroglycerin for his heart condition and called the police. They made him sit in the Florida room while they searched the bedroom. A medical examiner tried to revive her, but she had been dead several hours. Her face was bloody, and there were traces of blood in her room. Her death looked suspicious. The police called a homicide detective, who determined her death was accidental, and she was taken to the Broward County morgue about 8:00 or 9:00 p.m. She was fifty-two years old.

Grandmère told John and Harriet not to call me. She wanted to tell me herself, and in a shaky voice the next morning she said,

"Lisette, dear, I have something to tell you. Kitten is dead." I dropped the phone and fell to the floor. My father was visiting. We had planned to see the tall ships that day with Colin in Boston. Instead, he lifted me up, and I sobbed on his chest, then on the wall, then walking in circles. Bob came home from his job in a wire manufacturing company. He and my father would take care of one-year-old Colin while I flew to Fort Lauderdale to arrange the funeral. My mother had drunk herself to death, I said to myself. It must have been accidental. She had wanted to go away for a while, to disappear, and then come back as she always had. This time she didn't come back.

That night I dreamt that my mother called and told me to push a button on her coffin so she could get out before she was cremated. She was playing a trick on Grandmère, and I shouldn't tell her my mother had escaped. It was my mother's ultimate scheme. But the next day in Fort Lauderdale, it was clear the scheme had failed. I traced my mother's footsteps in drops of blood on the wall-to-wall carpet of her bedroom. I touched a bloody imprint of her hand where she gripped the bathroom door frame to steady herself.

"If you think it's bad now," Harriet said, "you should have seen it right after she died. Pills and booze hidden everywhere! Don't try to understand it, Honey. There's no explanation. Besides, she's happier now than she was on Earth, believe me. Don't worry. You'll feel better in time if you remember she's better off."

I knew Harriet was trying to help, but better dead than drunk was not my idea of better off. There had to be an answer. It may have died with my mother, but she had her reasons. I turned to John to understand them. We sat hunched over cigarettes and coffee the morning of the funeral. John's eyes watered and looked down most of the time. His alchy glow from former drinking days had degenerated into long fingernails, gaunt cheeks, greasy, thinning hair, and a pot belly on two spindly legs. I was not much better. The swollen, fleshy look of my eyes had spread to my whole complexion. But deterioration was one of the privileges of grief.

It was one of the many we earned that day along with sitting in the first row at the funeral parlor, my mother's brass urn in front of us, surrounded by flowers. She had told me she wanted to be cremated. I had no idea she meant within months after she said it.

The warring factions of my mother gathered awkwardly in isolated groups, waiting for the service to begin. Rich relatives and boozing buddies eyed each other from across the room. One of my mother's buddies looked like the drunk piano player she dragged home one night. He played honky tonk on the baby grand piano Grandmère had given my mother. He balanced his cigarette on the edge of the piano and left burn marks.

A friend and neighbor of twenty years walked up to the podium. "Kitty," he said, halting and starting again. "Kitty loved everybody. She could eat with kings and paupers alike. Rich or poor, it didn't matter. She was a friend to everyone."

I rode home from the funeral with the urn on my lap. It was heavier than I expected. At thirty-two years old, I had no idea about urns and ashes. I had never lost a loved one. I didn't want to know that bits of bone remained from the cremation and added to the weight of the ashes, especially not my mother's ashes. But that day I learned that a whole, loving person could be reduced to a small container that fit on my lap, a person to whom I had spoken the week before. John had called to say he couldn't stop my mother's drinking this time. She was out of control. He had no choice but to put her on the phone to me, hoping I would say something that would make her stop. I heard nothing but breathing. I waited. Nothing. I said, "Mom, what the hell are you doing?" No answer. She handed the phone back to John without a word and stumbled away. That was the last thing I would say to her before she died.

I put the urn on the mantel of the fireplace in my mother's dining room. I placed the funeral flowers beneath it, and after friends and family left the house, the flowers pierced the gloom of the evening silence. John and I drew on our cigarettes, stirred coffee in mugs, and stared at the urn. John sat behind an ashtray piled with cigarette butts popping nitroglycerin pills for his heart condition. Within months it would have him in an urn matching my mother's.

I reached for another of John's Gauloise cigarettes and said, "I think I'm going crazy."

"So, who isn't?" John said, and his hand shook as he gave me his matches. "As long as you don't like it, you'll be okay."

I told him I hated it. It scared the hell out of me. "Then you're going to be okay," he said. "It's when you like going nuts that you are nuts."

"So, you think you're nuts," I said, "and you don't like it. Then what do you do?"

"Well, you can either drink or figure something out. You'll figure something out. And don't let your family get to you. Grandmère and Harriet both wrecked their kids' lives. Don't forget that. Stay away from them if you have to. That was the problem with your mother. She had her own life. She didn't care who she was with as long as they were good people. They looked down on that, and she let them get under her skin. Stand up to them, that's all."

But I didn't have to stand up to them. In time I stood with them, as Harriet, Grandmère, and I tried to understand why one of us in the family drank too much and the rest of us didn't. Grandmère's method of understanding was to ask a medium to contact my mother. The medium told her, "Don't worry. Everything will be all right." She repeated his message to me in a commanding tone, as if we could seriously trust someone who talked to dead people. But that's how desperate she was to understand my mother's drinking.

The medium told her to instruct a gatekeeper to let my mother come through. Gatekeepers were always Indians, and if she didn't know his name, she could call upon White Cloud, who would let only the good come through. The medium passed along messages from Flo-Flo and Grandpère, and by the way, Mount St. Helens would explode three times and then go silent. My mother was happier than she had ever been. Her death was not Grandmère's fault but partly the result of the threatened divorce, which John must have hurled to snap my mother out of her stupor. And then a consolation: Grandmère had done more than her duty. She should not look back. She should lift her head and move forward.

She deeply tried. She lingered on lonely trips to Germany—Baden-Baden for the mineral baths that did not cure and Oberammergau for the Passion Play that did not inspire. She passed away two years later at age eighty-two. I could only summon her death in fleeting moments. Patrick and Libby were one month old. Colin was three and a half. I was overwhelmed with infant twins and a young son, and I was empty from my mother's death two years before. Decades later, I scoured Grandmère's diaries for clues to my mother's death. One held an index card with yellow edges. It listed nineteen "Nightmares of My Life": My mother ran away from school. Harriet married Chick Andrews. Harriet divorced Chick. Harriet got cancer. Kitten divorced David and then Dick and then Captain Gerry. Grandmère's father died. Grandpère died. Kitten drank. Kitten married John. Kitten died from an overdose of sleeping pills and vodka.

I sat upright. A bottle of sleeping pills had been on the window sill in Pat's bathroom in Berlin. A bottle of vodka had been on the floor. They deadened him until the smoke could kill. My mother and my son had used similar methods to kill themselves—the same alcohol, the same combination with sleeping pills.

I stared into space to absorb that parallel. I thought about my ignorance of both of them, the lethality of depression, the sad truth that I might never have read them right. They had both told me they were thinking of suicide. Both of them. And I still hadn't seen it coming. Two times. I had read both of them wrong.

I thought about the drinking, the sadness I had explained to Patrick, the warnings I thought would help him, the warnings I could not imagine would describe him. I thought about the similarities between him and my mother—their fragile sanity, their peaks and valleys, their flashes of energy, their catatonic lows. They bridged a gap too far between light and darkness. They struggled, unknown to each other, in their separate generations, and in their distant worlds.

Kitten, self-portrait, around 1962 when she was thirty-five.

Patrick, about three-years-old, with Libby behind him, 1985.

Resurrection

I once read somewhere that life is kind of like a bookshelf. Each of our friends are like a different book, and when they die, they don't completely leave us. The truth is that we will all keep part of Pat in us. While he may be gone, his essence will never die.

—Andrew Nielsen (MC Lars)
"Words for Patrick," 2006

I could travel back to all the family deaths I went through, sitting in my storeroom with boxes of albums and diaries. They would be precedents for death, but they would not be the resurrection I was really after. Only Jesus could do that. And even though I was not religious, the story of Jesus's mother came to me after Pat died. Death wasn't the end for her. It was a beginning, and I reread the crucifixion story to learn how she survived the death of her son.

I had taught the Bible to a ninth-grade reading class at Rectory School even though I rarely went to church. Rectory was a private school, where students went to chapel once a week and church on Sundays. Religion was part of their boarding school experience, and my department head wanted to expand that experience to the classroom. She wanted to connect biblical literature to education. She wanted to help students understand seventeenth-century language as well as biblical references, and she did. She re-opened memories of Sunday school and made me learn as much as I could about Genesis, Exodus, and the Gospel According to Mark.

My approach was not on religion so much as learning biblical stories and understanding the language of Shakespeare's era. I explained to my small class that we would read the King James Version because it was printed in 1611, toward the end of Shakespeare's career. It came out two years before his last play and five years before his death in 1616. The King James Bible and Shakespeare's plays were the most famous pieces of literature in the English language, and they were written at about the same time in history. Their similar language would help students gain proficiency with ancient pronouns like *thee* and *thine* and word endings like the *eth* in *creepeth*. I ended my pep talk to the class by saying that reading the Bible would help them read Shakespeare's language.

My pep talk failed. Students groaned that the class would be religious, and why couldn't we read something more modern? But I kept cheerleading. I told them they didn't have to be religious. They didn't have to believe in God. They could read the Bible like any other book of literature. They could read it as the story of three religions in which Abraham, his son Ishmael, and Jesus become the patriarchs of Judaism, Islam, and Christianity. Or they could read it as the Word of God. The choice was up to them. Our goal was to learn the vocabulary, the allegories, and a few literary devices—the imagery, for example, of the wells in the desert as sources of life.

The ninth graders breathed a sigh of relief. They read Genesis and were surprised by its simple words and short sentences. They chuckled at homework called "God's To-Do List":

- Monday, create light and darkness for the first day and night.
  - Tuesday, create heaven.
  - Wednesday, separate land from water.
  - Thursday, create the stars and the moon.
  - Friday, create birds and fish.
  - Saturday, create land animals and humans.
  - Sunday, stop working and rest.

Students wrote essays on Abraham's character and took quizzes on the Ten Commandments. They traced the preachings of Jesus, his arrival in Jerusalem, and his crucifixion in the Gospel According to Mark. They debated his disappearance from the sepulcher and his afterlife visions to his followers. They relearned stories they had known as children.

I returned to those stories after Patrick died. I saw them from a new perspective—as a mother who had lost a son. I saw the Gospels as a remembrance of the most famous son in history. They were a lament for the loss of Jesus. They were guidance on grieving death. I was not Mary, and Patrick was not Jesus, but I began to see parallels between Mary and me. Our sons strove for perfection. They tried for untrodden snow. They struggled for purity. Their struggle killed them, and they died before their time. Jesus may have also died by suicide. He may have gone to Jerusalem to be crucified to be with his father in heaven. He predicts his death many times in the Gospels. He knows he will be killed when he arrives. He enrages the chief priests and provokes his arrest by attacking commerce in a temple meant for prayer. He predicts his betrayal by one of the disciples at the last supper. He says in the Gospel According to John that he gives his own life. "No man taketh it from me, but I lay it down of myself. I have power to lay it down, and I have power to take it again."[139]

Mary is present at the crucifixion when Roman soldiers nail Jesus to the cross. They divide his meager clothing among themselves. Jesus tells Mary to "behold thy son!" He asks a disciple to take care of her. He dies "knowing that all things were now accomplished."[140] Weeks after the resurrection, Mary is with the disciples when they meet in Jerusalem. A wind fills them with the holy spirit, and the disciple Peter inspires them to become apostles. They transform from students of Christ to teachers of his life. Mary is present at the death of her son and the birth of his church.

Her story became my ideal—my rebirth. I wanted to do the same as Mary. I kept vigil after Pat's death. I met with his admirers. I told stories to anyone who would listen. I centered every conversation around him. I celebrated his life. I met with his disciples and urged them to become apostles. I wanted them to be teachers of Patrick. I spread the gospel about his beauty, his goodness, his purity, his brilliance, and finally, his sacrifice. I couldn't get over him. He was too good for this world. He was too perfect. He did not tolerate the imperfections, the rejections, the denials, the untruths, the fabrications, the disappointments. His standards were to reach the untrodden snow, to go where no footprints had been, where no one had climbed. And he almost succeeded.

When you lose someone you love so much, you cannot let him die. You won't let him die. And so you don't. You are like Mary Magdalene in the Gospels. You run from person to person, telling his story. New stories come out—visions, sightings. People just saw him. He was here. He was there. He was everywhere. Where is he now? His stories are not content to stay in your head. They must be told. They must be taught. People must know them. They must know him. You don't really understand him. He has, after all, suffered beyond anything you could imagine. He has suffered death of his own accord. You hope that his stories will keep him in your life, that if he cannot live, you will live for him. But it is a burden. You are living for him instead of yourself. You lose yourself. And so you enlist others to help you. You are driven to tell the gospel. You look for every opportunity to spread the word without turning people away. You are like a Jehovah's Witness. You have seen the ideal, and you must tell others about him. You must convert them. You want others to become believers so that they will help you spread the word because the more who do, the more alive he becomes, the more resurrected. You want him alive so much, you are willing to imagine that he is. Why not believe that the angel moved the rock from the cave and that the body is gone? Why not think of him sitting at the right hand of God in heaven? The alternative is so much more painful.

You think about becoming a nun so that you can pretend you are worshiping God when you are really worshiping your son. You could pray to him all day, and you would look as if you were doing your job—chanting, kneeling, bowing your head. No one would know that you had your own private god—a better one, a real one. You would seem dutiful, even noble, because you have seen him. You have known him. You gave birth to him.

You talk about the time that, as a child, he would sit in your lap as if he were part of you. You talk about how he learned to read soon after he learned to walk, how he would insist on "Lookit, Ma. Lookit this," and he would tell you the words in a small book. You talk about children who resented his ability and pounced on his awkwardness, how they made fun of him as he swung his foot and missed a giant rubber ball on the playground. He would drown them out with Brahms' second piano concerto. It channeled a force that lifted him above a rapturous audience. But when the concerto ended, the fear returned. Children frightened him. He felt "above or below them—he could not tell which."[141] You talk about his greatness, his perfection, his godhood. Who else could know Brahms in the eighth grade?

You talk about the taunting in high school that came from within, how he felt alone, scathed by laughter, "barred out of every closely locked circle," how conversations ended in awkward silences, how he flushed with embarrassment, avoided people, and drew inward, how his mind expanded and multiplied fear, how it smothered his attraction to boys.[142]

You talk about the thick shell and quiet smile which helped him soar in classrooms, how he ranked first in his class, how he struggled at sports, analyzing them as if they were math problems, rigidly tossing a lacrosse ball or swinging a tennis racket in slow motion. Rowing and cross-country were easier. They helped him try everything, do everything, be everything. His mind and strengthening body knew no limits. He was impatient with the commonplace. He found respect in the classroom and acceptance on the playing fields. His piano gleamed in front of audiences. He felt above them for brief moments but below them, unexplainably. Antidepressants and therapy smoothed the way to a National Merit

Scholarship, perfect SATs, acceptance at Stanford, and valedictorian of his class. He was invited to a graduation party. He had achieved an elusive goal: he was a social star.

You talk about how Stanford was harder, but his piano sang with Scriabin, and he met his first boyfriend. He would make friends with his German teacher and laugh with his math professors. He would stay up all night with his computer programming group so their software ran seamlessly. He would work at the *Stanford Daily* and hang out with his roommate. He would survive another roommate who dealt in marijuana. Drugs did not interest him. He wanted knowledge and laughter and love. He joked that life was intense, "like campers, in tents. Get it?" He called himself "man-orexic," but whatever, he was over it. He said that someone had "more chins than a Chinese phonebook," and "Ma, whaddaya dooin'" in his fake Boston accent. Want As on your papers? Throw *indeed* on the end of some paragraphs. Works every time.

You talk about how he tried to teach you to fly with him, how calculus was "elegant," how a simulation program was "easy. You just take the graphic interface thingy and plug in the code." How *Madame Bovary* deserved another try. And you should drop everything you're doing and read *The Once and Future King*, where the pure-hearted Wart pulls Excalibur out of the stone. He dreamed of his own Excalibur. He flew farther than you could see. He walked on untrodden snow.

You talk about how a boy in Berlin rejected him, how his fine senses, which sharpened his thoughts and electrified his gaze, beamed inward with deadly precision. He came to an inescapable conclusion, a mathematical proof. He would kill himself to end the love triangle. He was *The Sorrows of Young Werther*, *L'Étranger*, a boy—a man—lost to the world.

And afterward, as you watch his coffin lowered into the ground on a freezing February day, you don't know whether to admire his ideals or lament his short-sightedness. You are torn between his decision and your own existence. Is there a point to his death? You do not know. You only know that you are afraid of death and that somehow you must keep him alive. Somehow you must build a religion in his memory. There must be a center of worship. You make a shrine in his room. You unpack his books from Stanford and Berlin and store them in bookcases. You tape his Haus Mitteleuropa dorm room poster on his door. "General Hauspital," it says among pictures of soap operas. Pat's name is in the middle. He stars in the next episode about blackmailing Sonny. It's trivial college humor, but you are desperate for any shred of him.

You add his piles of music books. Mozart, Beethoven, Chopin, Schumann, Mendelssohn, Liszt, and Rachmaninoff lean heavily next to *Discrete Mathematics, Number Theory, The Moment of Proof: Mathematical Epiphanies*, and *The Deductive Foundations of Computer Programming*. His classical CDs tower next to them. His Pink Floyd, Blur, and Radiohead posters line a wall near prep school ties and literature books. Ancient stuffed animals pile on his bed. His grandmother Kitten's watercolor hangs over them. A Stanford banner, class of 2005, hangs nearby. A Wallace and Gromit alarm clock waits by his bed. Suitcases with clothes from Berlin sit behind Pat Wood t-shirts and hats and posters and CDs.

You do not understand how such a mind could see death as a solution. But you cannot desecrate his decision. You cannot think you know better. He was and always will be your perfect son, your very own Jesus, your Messiah. He will sit at the right hand of God if it is the last thing you do because you will not let him die. You will search for clues to his existence, his life, his dreams, and his death. And you will find nothing that explains him, nothing that replaces him. But you will find other lives and other stories, and that becomes the point—the story of life, life as story. You will remember that story is how we learn, how we cope. You will realize that Mary's story was the New Testament and that your story will be your memories. And, like Mary, you will have to be satisfied with story as resurrection.

Some of the quotes for this chapter came from the following story, which reveals Pat's sadness in the middle grades. He wrote it in his senior year of high school for an AP English class assignment to evoke meaning from a concrete image. In "Eighth Grader," Pat uses the wire of the headphones to lift him above the "claustrophobic sensations of the school day" and the "mindless jabbering of his classmates." He showed me the A+ at the top of his paper with a big smile on his face, but his joy hid the fact that his heart still "felt cold and small and sad."

"Eighth Grader"
By Patrick Wood

The bus came slowly to a halt with a loud hiss from the brakes, yet as always the boy was jolted a little against the back of his seat. He watched the flabby arm reach out from the driver's seat and pull the lever that folded the door against the wall. She smiled a fat smile at him as he passed, and he both pitied her for her ugliness and shuddered inside himself. Quickly, he dropped down the two large steps past the collapsed door. The long dirt driveway lay ahead of him and he barely heard the bus heave away down the road as he began to walk.

He was in his room at last, and he swung his book bag down onto the carpeted floor with a dull thud. He recalled the claustrophobic sensations of the school day—the mindless jabbering of his classmates, the stern faces of teachers, the sweaty feel of a pencil he had gripped too long. These sensations dropped from him in a slow exhalation.... Suddenly his mind cringed. He was again on the dusty kickball field during gym class. The ball was rolling toward him. He grossly misplaced his kick. The catcher behind him groaned, and worst of all, the pitcher screwed up his face in mock concentration as he rolled the next ball in exaggerated slow motion. Remembering, the boy clenched his fists and watched them turn white. Then he reminded himself that he was alone now, free; and thinking these thoughts, his body and mind relaxed. But he closed the door to make sure.

He kneeled and then lay on the floor and placed the headphones over his ears at first lying down, his nose dug awkwardly into the carpet. He turned his head to one side and lay down again, but now the headphone pinched his ear uncomfortably. Finally he rolled his whole body over, pointing his closed eyes toward the ceiling.

The strains of Brahms' second piano concerto reached his ears and enveloped them with warmth. The gentle current of the music lifted his heart and he let it carry him away. He succumbed to the pure and irresistible flow of emotion, rising and falling as it did. A connection seemed to grow then between the souls of listener and composer; Brahms' heart was speaking across the centuries in an utterly clear and perfect voice. The boy marveled at the mystery and magic of such a connection, electronic vibrations of air squeezed through a thin, tiny wire. He ran the wire through his fingers and pondered its thinness. Through that wire the vibrations flowed, and when they reached his ears they blossomed.

The boy realized with certainty that in that moment, borne as he was among the swells and waves and thrusts and threads of sound, in that moment he had been granted access to a source greater than words, than mankind. Perhaps it was like an invisible stream bubbling noiselessly through all time, from which composers' pens plucked out masterpieces. But it had to be something greater than mankind. How else could it strike him so purely, so directly? Brahms, too, and all other humans had been granted access to this medium; but the boy guarded jealously the emotions frothing in his own heart. He knew not everyone was given a soul like his, a soul which could be molded and shaped by a man centuries dead.

With religious zeal he envisioned his own hands performing the piece, recreating for others the sensations he felt. But "recreating" was not the word. No. He was taking part in a mystical experience, bathed in the glow of the concert hall, channeling a force which filled him with joy as it passed through his body. It inhabited him, it nourished him, it elevated him. And in a secret way he imagined that the audience worshipped him. He was above them operating a gleaming ebony instrument—yes, an instrument, a tool whereon he forged a dazzling array of emotions. He was above; he was the vessel for a shimmering outpouring; they sat below in silent, rapturous devotion.

The music in his ears climaxed in a long-held, grandiose chord; but soon it ended and there was nothing beyond. The boy felt drained, betrayed even, in the silence that followed. His laughable images of godhood were shoved aside by the realities of the soreness of his clamped ears and the hard, rough carpet under the back of his head.

The next morning the boy waited at the end of the long driveway. Brahms's second piano concerto suddenly seemed far away in the cold glare of the early morning.

I am a fool and a dreamer, the boy said aloud.

Walking onto the crowded bus he was frightened by how hostile and alien the children looked. He no longer felt one of them, but above or below them—he could not tell which. His mind counseled patience; his time would come, it told him. But he sat in an empty seat, and his heart felt cold and small and sad as the bus rolled away.

Berlinale bear with Patrick's grave, 2006.

Colin in Antoinette Eno Wood's mausoleum with my mother, Harriet, and their husbands' urns behind him, Simsbury Cemetery, 2013.

The Interment

He touched us not because we have lost his love of humanity and its questions—
but because he dared to ask them at all.

—Ryan Wirtz,
"The Essential Patrick," 2006

Seven years after Pat died, Colin, Libby, Bob, and I gathered at the top of the Simsbury Cemetery in Connecticut on a bright March day. Bob admired the mausoleums that looked like small mansions with gardens to themselves. The grass was edged, the bushes trimmed, the mulch plentiful. An open bronze door on one of the mausoleums revealed a center aisle with three levels of stone vaults on either side. Antoinette Eno Wood, my mother's namesake, was at eye level to the right. Her husband, Charles Boughton Wood, was to the left. Their names and dates were tinged with green mold from the dampness. Below were the vaults of my great-great-grandparents John and Hattie Eno. Harriet and Jack's gray marble urns sat on the windowsill of the back wall next to the brass urns of my mother and her husband, John McGinley. An arrangement of spring flowers beneath them defied the unseasonable cold. Libby wandered in the aisle, dressed in my great-grandmother Flo-Flo's raccoon coat. Colin wore a navy pea coat and dark suit with a tie snugged tight. He traced Antoinette's name with his finger on the stone.

Harriet's daughter Pam tiptoed toward the entrance of the aisle. Heads bowed at the sight of her tearful face. "We are gathered here today to celebrate the lives of Harriet Eno Goetz Andrews Holly and her husband Jack Hugh Holly, my mother and father. We are here to honor their final wishes, that they be placed with the remains of their family. Harriet Holly was a daughter, sister, mother of two, divorcée, aunt, wife again, mother of two more, cancer survivor, grandmother, and great-grandmother. She was an army brat, patriot, linguist, seamstress, knitter, lover of orchids, quilter, swimmer, ballet dancer, and comedian. She was loving, serious, witty, funny, and opinionated. She was my best friend."

Oldest daughter Heather followed with a French rendition of "Amazing Grace." Daughter-in-law Donna read a poem that likened death to a larger cycle. Don't worry, it tried to say. She's in the wind and the trees and the growing earth and the flowers, which she loved so dearly. Part of her is still here. She's not really gone. She's not in the urn. She didn't die. The poem gave karmic refuge from the stale smells of Harriet's nursing home the year before, but its vain attempt fell flatter than the thin logic after Patrick's death: He's still alive in you. Others will give him back to you. His struggle is over. He's at peace.

The small crowd began to disperse. I pulled some papers out of my pocket and walked toward the center of the group. There was one more poem, I said, one more indulgence in spite of the cold. The group came back into hearing distance and pulled their coats tightly around themselves. I began to read "The Horizon," which had been read at my great-grandmother's funeral, my mother's funeral, and then Grandmère's. It began with the line, "Death is only an horizon and an horizon is but the limit of our sight."[143] It, too, played on the theme that Harriet wasn't really dead, but somehow the images softened the reality. They gave kinder pictures than the stark gray urns in Antoinette's mausoleum.

"You are standing upon the seashore," I read. "A ship at your side spreads her white sails or steams out to the morning breeze and starts for the blue ocean. She is an object of beauty and strength, and you stand and watch her until at length she hangs like a speck of white cloud just where the sea and sky come down to mingle with each other." The crowd listened quietly. I went on about how the ship is gone, but then you realize that she is only gone from your sight. She still exists just as large as she was. "Her diminished size is in you, not in her."[144] The crowd kept their heads bowed, and I took strength from their patience and the vision of a large vessel sailing away from us. Harriet had left the shore, and we could barely see her, but she was still as large in mast and hull and spar as when she left. She was out there, somewhere, and something else was seeing her even if it wasn't us, even if it was the nothingness that we suspected, even if it was only the very fine company in the cemetery with whom she was resting.

I finished reading, and the group wandered amongst the small Grecian temples. William Phelps Eno, my great-great-uncle and author of the first traffic codes in New York and Paris, began the line. "Highway Traffic Control Pioneer" was written on his vault under the glowing reds and yellows of the Tiffany stained-glass window on the back wall. Next was Antoinette's columned pediment with Harriet and my mother. At the center was the largest parthenon, belonging to my great-great-great-grandfather, Amos Richards Eno, and his wife, Lucy Jane Phelps. Amos had owned the Flatiron property and built the Fifth Avenue Hotel in the mid-1800s. Beneath Amos's window, a dome-shaped urn held the combined ashes of my great-grandparents Flo-Flo and Popsy. Next to Amos, a rounded art deco building housed Flo-Flo's sister Tantine and her husband, *Titanic* survivor Hokan Steffanson. Amos's son Henry Clay Eno, a doctor in New York, completed the line. The Eno temples looked down on acres of tombstones and a wide grass lane with arborvitae standing like soldiers at attention. It sloped to the iron gate on Hopmeadow Street and then across to the Eno Memorial Hall donated by Antoinette. They looked to the older part of the cemetery where the stones were cracked and covered with lichen. Willow trees and skulls framed the tops.

Hands reached down from heaven with roses. Lambs marked the deaths of children.

And suddenly, the strength of generations guided by example. They guided by life that was actually lived and fought and knowable. They guided by greatness and then nothingness, by beginnings to endings, by meaning and then the great unknowing. They were a cycle of life but not a generic tree or a ship leaving shore. They were not a metaphor. They were real, and that made them better than any poem or figurative language that tried to conjure meaning. They *were* the end. They were the horizon to which Harriet was heading. She needed them as she drifted away from us standing on the shore. She needed the dead to bury her, not the living. She needed the parades of the past—the unliving, unseeable ghost—to convey her to the bottom of life. The graves in Simsbury Cemetery made the descent almost palatable.

Patrick had needed the dead as well. He needed Beethoven as a call to action. He needed Friedrich Rückert, who was lost to the world. He needed Kurt Tucholsky, who climbed trodden snow, and Goethe, who raised the curtain and stepped behind it. The musical and literary dead were Patrick's horizon. They were his guides to leaving the shore. They conveyed him to the bottom of life. They made his descent imaginable, doable. They were the other voices who would greet him. I needed Goethe, too. I needed to know why Patrick killed himself while reading an author centuries dead. He joined a stream of readers who had done the same since 1774 when *The Sorrows* was published. Some dressed in Werther's blue coat and yellow vest. Others held a copy of the novel when they died. Death was their liberation, Werther their Christ figure. He sacrifices himself for perfection.

I poured over an English translation to find its power. Werther moves to the country and revels in nature. He thrills in blades of grass near a brook in the woods. The sun's rays penetrate the darkness. A breeze becomes the presence of God, filling his soul. Life is paradise, fantasy, and suddenly epitomized in a motherly young girl named Lotte, who is engaged to another man. Werther is tormented. Lotte cannot be with him, but her lips are too charming, her music too sweet. They lure him like a siren call.

Werther weeps incessantly. He toys with an unloaded gun to his head. He must control himself, but his frustration erupts at Lotte and at himself. He cannot escape her. Dreams fuel his lust. He roars with anger—or withers with no feeling at all, exhausted from the struggle between passion and constraint. He is out of control until a failed embrace forces a decision. A calm comes over him. He sees his course—a fate that Lotte will someday share. He sees her in the constellations of the night sky. He sees her everywhere.

Werther borrows pistols, which Lotte hands to his servant. She gives him the means to the heaven he seeks. He writes her a final letter and wears the clothes she has touched. He puts the red ribbon she has given him in his pocket. The clock strikes midnight, and Werther shoots himself while sitting at his desk. The bullet hits above his right eye. He falls awkwardly around the base of his chair and convulses on the floor. He lies on his back, his brain protrudes, and blood flows from an open vein in his arm. His lungs rattle for breath until they give out the next day. He is buried that night, two days before Christmas, without a funeral, without clergy, without Lotte.

Goethe pleaded that his "poetry" was not reality, but he gives his poetry the power to influence. He argues for what can be, what should be. He soars to the failed embrace with Lotte and the flash of gunfire in the middle of the night. He fuses passion and danger, conflict and resolution. He makes them one and the same with the magic of words, and those words invited Patrick to become Werther. They convinced him to live in the ideal, demand purity, reject reality, and step behind the curtain.

Suicide became an obsession. It became the exhilaration of control, the warmth that Werther felt before the gunshot, his "giddiness of death."[145] Patrick imagined Werther lying on the floor, gasping for breath. But rather than pain, Patrick saw release. He felt envy for Werther's freedom. Relief became a fantasy more real than life. Patrick dwelt in Werther's mind more than his own. He craved his escape, which turned into habit, which turned into plan, which turned into action. He would do it at the same midnight hour, but he would do it better. He would find a faster, pain-free method. He would plan every detail, rehearse in secrecy—the time, the place, the tools. The plan would terrify but also empower and give greater relief. Death became a hypnotic overdose as lethal as drugs.

I underlined the sentences that Pat had underlined and dog-eared the pages he had folded over in his German version of *The Sorrows*. It had a cloth bookmark attached to the red leather binding like a small bible. The bookmark was placed on the passage where Werther decides to leave the world. "And I am finished! My mind is all confused, for a week I have had no power of consciousness, my eyes are filled with tears. I am happy nowhere and happy everywhere. I wish nothing, desire nothing. It would be better for me if I went away."[146] But I could not feel its despair. I could not transform poetry into reality. I was still on the shore, hoping that Patrick's diminished size was in me, not in him. I hoped that he was gone only from my sight and that he was just as large in mast and hull as when he left. I hoped he was among the dead poets in his quiet realm, in his love, and in his song.

White rose, Patrick's grave, 2006.

Libby, South Cemetery, Pomfret, 2017.

The Long Term

When we were twenty-three, everything stopped. It's like we both disappeared instead of just Pat.

—Libby Wood
The Pomfret Times, 2014

The years after Pat's death were a cycle of pain, confusion, acceptance, and regression. At first, I felt like a pinball machine being knocked from Pat's death to my father's. It seemed as if Pat's death began a pervasion of death, a pervasion of life with holes. But I had to fill them somehow. I needed Pat to come alive in some form, and that became this book.

Pat's death was a matter of lurching forward, of trying to understand, of making progress but never enough. A friend who lost her brother to suicide told me that maybe we weren't meant to know why. We could never know why. We could not know what that person was thinking or feeling to make them want to kill themselves.

I disagreed. I was going to learn why if it took the rest of my life, and so far, it has. Information about suicide and depression is endless, changing, and never enough. The hard part is balance. How much do I do for Patrick? How much do I do for the living? Balance is elusive and never achieved. After fifteen years of writing, after interminable remembering, researching, editing, re-remembering, proofreading, copyrighting, publishing, and just downright sobbing with guilt and sadness, I made a full circle and came back to where I started. I came back to the question: Why? Why am I living Patrick's life for him? I came back to the realization that resolution comes from exhaustion, not from comprehension. There aren't any answers. Only questions. And no matter how hard I try to answer them, Patrick will always be gone.

There is survival. Time passes. It does not stand still no matter how long I am standing still within it, and that passage of time changes perspective. It's as if I'm looking at a scene from a speeding car on a highway. The vantage point shifts, and the scene changes. The scene is still there, but it gets farther away. That's what happened after Pat. The pain of his death shifted as time passed. I wanted to stay close to the scene or back up before the scene, but instead, I traveled farther down the road. Other obligations came into view. Funeral expenses were exorbitant. One small example was bringing Pat's body home from Frankfurt. A ticket for his metal coffin in the baggage compartment was many times the cost of a ticket when he was alive. And then there were the expenses for the living. Colin needed help through college. I had to go back to work.

Rectory School was the best second home possible. Students and faculty let me ease back into teaching at my own pace, and that made me willing to try. Rectory was a model of embrace after tragedy. I continued tutoring and teaching there until there was a moment when my priorities shifted.

Seven years after Pat died, I was meeting with Head of School Fred Williams in his office at Rectory. We were discussing the spring term issue of the school newspaper when he came across the article about Amanda Todd's suicide. He read a line about the suicide rate being high in South Korea. He looked up at me piercingly. "Parents don't want to read about that," he said.

Fred was right. I had crossed a line between personal interest and appropriate subject matter. Suicide was maybe not a topic for a school newspaper read by students as young as fifth grade, and Rectory had a large population of South Koreans whose families might be offended. A story about a teenager killing herself was risky for a private school that depended on tuition payments. But we had covered suicide in the paper before. I had spoken about it in a school assembly, and I had always believed the paper should be student-centered. Students joined the paper so they could write about their own interests instead of class assignments. Suicide, gay rights, the Iraq War—it didn't matter as long as they wrote fairly and factually, which is why ninth-grader Jason Zhao had come to me about Amanda. He knew about Patrick, and he knew I would understand his concern about suicide. He and I wondered about the same question: Why would a high school student, about the same age as he, kill herself? We worked on the story together— researching, summarizing, and fine-tuning the wording.

The story was published with few changes. Fred was accepting, but I took his initial reaction personally. I took it as criticizing Patrick, as denigrating what happened to him. I thought, maybe stubbornly, that parents *did* want to read about suicide. It did, after all, affect middle-schoolers. In 2009, it had killed eleven-year-old Carl Walker-Hoover, who lived about an hour from Rectory. His mother found him hanging from an extension cord on the second floor of their apartment after another day of bullying at his Springfield, Massachusetts charter school. Suicide was a middle-school issue. But there was an understandable hesitation about covering it in a student publication How do you promote your school and at the same time talk about the danger that can happen there?

Not long after the meeting, Bob and I paid off a thirty-year mortgage along with college tuition for all three children. I was able to retire at age sixty-five, and I left the school to write about Patrick. I didn't want to be a writer. I never wanted to write a book, especially about suicide. But I wanted Pat to be remembered. I wanted him to live on in the best form I could manage, and I had to explore the question, as I had with my ninth-grade student: Why does an otherwise healthy person turn on himself? In the process, I learned what Pat might have been thinking in the moments before death. I felt a little of what he went through. I learned a lot about why.

The book helped me put the pieces together. As Kay Jamison says in *Night Falls Fast*, many factors are manageable on their own, but when they come together, "It is as with fire: dry grass and high winds may remain, in themselves, only dangerous possibilities, elements of combustion. But if lightning falls across the grass, the chance of fire increases blindingly fast: it leaps from slim to given."[147] The most dangerous catalyst in Pat's case was the disease of depression. It worsened in his college years when first episodes of depression are likely to strike. He had to navigate a complex mental health system when he could barely function. He had to advocate for himself without family to help. We were not there to have the conversations which might have encouraged him to reveal the depth of his illness.

Combined with the genetic background of grandparents on both sides of his family who killed themselves, depression may have started an unstoppable fire. It tortured him with disappointment over the boyfriends he wanted. It tempted him with the unobtainable goal of perfection. It savaged his motivation to get help. Pat wrote that he hated dealing with "this crap," meaning that he couldn't deal with it because he was too sick, that he couldn't take the initiative to seek therapy in Germany, and that he was not taking the medication that could have saved him. Jamison points out that psychotherapy increases the likelihood that patients will stay on medication. That probably translates to in-person visits rather than the phone calls Pat had with his therapist, who could not prescribe medication in Germany.

Jamison emphasizes that external events—heartbreak, in Pat's case—often occur before suicide, but that the real danger is internal with depression, mania, and schizophrenia. Suicide lurks unseen like the "giant Pat iceberg" of Andrew Nielsen's eulogy. It is the vastness below, but a glimpse does surface in a photo that Karen Kramer sent to me as I was writing this book. Pat is standing in a group of students in front of a stone wall at the Stanford Center in

Berlin. The students appear happy, smiling, and squinting in the sun, but Pat's eyes say otherwise. They are wide, defying the sun, and deep in their sockets with shadows above and below. They speak what he cannot say, that he should be happy, that he has loved Munich, that he has adopted Berlin, but he does not fit in. The man in Munich plagues him. He is tired of struggling. The medicine isn't working. He stares at the camera as if it makes no sense, as if he makes no sense.

I wish I could say that Pat's story might help others, but what I really wish is that we get beyond the ostensible reasons for suicide—the money problems, the rejection, the abuse. They are part of the reason but not the whole answer, and if we don't look deeper, we are misleading survivors who blame themselves instead of mental illness. I think the value of Pat's story is that there is no better example that most suicide is caused by disease. He is proof that you cannot just love and support someone out of severe depression. You cannot always talk someone out of killing themselves. You could be dealing with disease as much as the logic of your persuasion. In the moments before death, you are not as important as the relief they seek, and neither were we. Pat's suicide notes to people who didn't love him are proof that we were too distant. There is very little in Pat's life, other than disease, that can be identified as a cause. But what fostered that disease? What pushed his stress beyond recuperation? Perfectionism was a strong component. It set him up for failure and made him wobble on relationships when his mathematical mind craved certainty. Did he have the right boyfriend? Could he do better? Should he lower his standards? Perfectionism clouded those answers.

Being gay was the most obvious factor, even though all his friends with whom I've spoken say he was out. He was okay with it. He was better than okay. He had fun with it. He was comfortable with it. Friends had crushes on him. He was admired in the ways he wanted. He became so unselfconscious that he walked down the main street of Palo Alto holding hands with his partner. His identity had been achieved, but the struggle along the way probably fed his depression, and that fed the disease.

Dr. Rona Hu helped me understand those struggles through the many gay people she has known and treated. They face rejection within their families, within their schools, within society. They hide their identities to avoid the risk. They hide during their formative years when most of us are sharing our relationships openly. Most of us survive rejection. Young gay people just survive. Their development is delayed. They whisper junior-high gossip when they are in medical school. Some strive for perfection, for acceptance beyond reproach. They cannot take one more criticism, one more rejection. Fear forces them underground. They lead dual lives. The stress is incalculable. It damages the brain. No wonder gay people suffer depression more than the straight world. No wonder mental health is more than the formula I naively believed—the formula of good family life. That formula was actually code for a good straight life.

There have been many times of peace and joy since Pat died— Colin's marriage to his wife Jennifer, for example, his daughters Addison and Raegan, Libby's master's degree in psychology, her therapy with autistic children and suicidal patients. But the joys are overshadowed. There is always something Patrick to do— memorials in Berlin, tree plantings in Pomfret, scholarships to award, Libby's art shows, a concert with his piano teachers where Deborah Beers released the pain of Pat's loss in her composition, "Through Tears and Beyond." She began her solo performance with gentle turmoil that intensified and darkened until she slammed the palm of her hand on the lowest keys of the grand piano in the Pomfret School chapel. She sustained the crash and thinned it slowly until it decayed into a brief silence and the last movement emerged. "Meditation by Starlight" was Deborah's way of saying that her music would not end on Patrick's suicide but on her gratitude for having taught him for several years. It was her way of reflecting on Patrick's brilliance. He was the star by whose light she was meditating.

Composer Howard Frazin, Pat's music theory teacher at Longy School of Music, captured Patrick's shadow in a concerto for him and another musician, whose brother, Steven Woolweaver, had also died. He gave us a tidal wave of sound at Faneuil Hall in Boston in 2017. We were swept away with the power, the mind-opening force of an orchestral performance, as if we were listening to our misery, as if we were vindicated in constant sorrow. I could hear the opening storm, the thunderous descent, the rise and fall of confusion, the lull, the brooding, the decision to drown in a sea of darkness, the wistfulness, the long good-bye, changing his mind, rethinking, swimming for air, enjoying it briefly, basking in a half-life, indecision, going inward, finding nothing, an absence of feeling, of life, gasping for life, not finding it, and letting go, releasing his grip, sinking, sleeping, his breath slowing down, quieting, his heart straining, stopping, gone, still, weightless, floating, and suspended by the final movement—a rondo that lifted the agony. It restored the life force and then hung on to the last notes as Patrick drifted away and disappeared. How much should we be grieving eleven years after Pat died? This is how much. It's never enough. It's never over. But in the process, it can be transformed into something we embrace—a balance between sorrow and beauty in which grief is acceptable, even desirable.

Not long ago, I fed the horses on a moonless night and heard coyotes howling from the top of the hill behind the barn. They yipped and barked as if they had nabbed another calf from the neighbor's dairy farm, and they were celebrating an easy kill. I turned toward our house with the Christmas tree showing through the windows and the lights on the bushes. A warmth came over me, as if I was still okay, as if I was protected against the ravages of nature. The howls trailed behind me as I walked toward the house, hoping that someday, when I was safe no longer and joined Patrick in the cemetery, I would join him knowing that his story has been told.

"Libby with Hole," Stanford memorial, 2006.

Epilogue

If I really thought about the moments before and during his death, I felt that my heart might stop.

—Libby Wood
Pomfret Magazine, 2011

No book about Patrick and the journey from suicide should end without mentioning the one who suffered most. Libby was more than Pat's twin sister. She was his guide through all things social and athletic, especially the maze of adolescence when she would pick out his clothes for school and teach him how to throw a ball without looking like a robot. His death shredded her life. Half of her was gone—*is* gone, she corrected me. She found her own journey by moving to San Francisco, where she and Pat had planned to live when he returned from Berlin.

Two years after Pat died, she rode her bike across the country with her partner Linden Crawford. She shaved her head to look like Pat and named her bike Zwilling, meaning twin in German. Pat had shared the word with her when he was in Berlin, and he threw it into conversations whenever he could. She began the trip by dipping the tires of her bike into the Pacific Ocean in Anacortes, Washington and then headed into the country and into herself. Some days, she didn't know if she was riding away from Pat or toward him. But fifty-seven days and 3,643 miles later, along with mosquito bites from camping and one last flat tire, she pedaled into Hampton Beach, New Hampshire.

I told police parked on the beach that Lib and Linden were ending their cross-country trip. They set off congratulatory sirens and blinking lights as Lib and Linden hoisted their bikes down some stairs and rode on the sand past beachgoers, who stared at them from their towels. They rode through deep sand and then into small waves washing up on the beach. The August sun shone on their backs as they balanced on their bikes in the shallow surf and looked out at the Atlantic Ocean. They hopped off their bikes and let the waves wash over their sneakers. They stared at the expanse of water as if to absorb the accomplishment of pedaling an average of sixty-four miles a day for nearly two months, and then they turned around, smiled broadly, and held their bikes over their heads. Libby had spent two months riding her bike as when she and Patrick were children, and it felt good. It made her feel stronger, as if she could get beyond sadness, as if she could achieve whatever she wanted.

Lib returned to the West Coast and worked in graphic design, but the corporate world didn't feel right. She earned a master's degree in psychology at the California Institute of Integral Studies. She used art therapy to counsel elementary-school children in Hawaii. During COVID, she suited up in a face shield and an N95 mask at the locked unit of a Santa Cruz psychiatric hospital. But the locked unit was only a temporary fix. She wanted to delve deeper into the causes of breakdowns. She studied analysis with the Palo Alto Psychoanalytic Psychotherapy Training Program for three years. It was a turning point in her career. It helped her assess mentally ill and suicidal children at the UCSF Benioff Children's Hospital in Oakland. It helped her counsel young adults and their families at the Community Hospital of the Monterey Peninsula. It prompted her to open a private practice in psychotherapy and inspired her to begin a PhD in Clinical Psychology. She has dedicated her life to helping those, like Patrick, who find themselves in crisis. In her words:

> It's been a coming together of my life and Pat's so that both of us can go forward. But I'm still suffering. Daily. Grief is not something we go through in the past. It is today. It is yesterday. It is tomorrow. In truth, I often describe the center of my soul as a dark and heavy setting. My humor, my productivity, my connectivity surround this porous center. My twin brother, my soul mate, is no longer alive. It's a complex and evolving grief. It

feeds my creative impulse, my sensory system, and my spirituality. It informs my clinical practice. While it's been seventeen years since Pat's heart last beat, I continue to feel it in my blood flow. I am constantly reliving memories—smells, songs, drawings, jokes, magic tricks, drag queen dress-ups, travel, golf, sunbathing, clothing, objects, breath, touch. It's a visceral fantasy—a balance between a reality that was, the reality that is, and the imaginary realm that fills in the gaps. So much is unknown to me about his sadness with such a finite ending of his life. I am dedicated to learning more about depression, the suicidal mind, and the relationship to artistic genius. I want to know more about Pat's psyche, which I didn't fully explore while he was alive. I am reaching out now, Pat, to get to know you beyond my curiosities, beyond my memories. You have inspired me to confront truths I have not yet heard of. You have inspired me to be more honest and help others enduring your condition.

Linden and Libby, Hampton Beach, New Hampshire, 2008, after fifty-seven days biking across the northern United States.

Appreciation

Legions of Pat's friends came to my rescue with Pat stories and details. Stanford Center Director Karen Kramer and her assistant Jutta Ley in Berlin were the first to find Pat's body along with Steve Pryce and Ryan Wirtz. They sustained me with constant support and details for *Back from Suicide*. Ryan taught me about Patrick's life in Berlin through long emails and phone calls. He was my partner in grieving.

I lost Patrick all over again when Ryan passed away in 2018 at the age of thirty-eight. I lost the joy of sharing the completed book about the essential Patrick with the friend who coined the term. I found out about Ryan's death while I was driving home from errands on a late fall day not long after Ryan texted me that he was doing well. Joe Dröge sent a message that Ryan was now with Patrick. I had to pull the car over and sob on the side of the road. And then I sobbed all over again when Ryan's ex-husband Steve explained that Ryan died peacefully in a hospital in London. Ryan's mother, Judith Hennessey, and his sister, Jennifer Wirtz Bennett, were with him, and when they knew the end was near, they called Steve, who took the first flight out of Germany. He arrived early the morning of December 16, and was with them in Ryan's hospital room when Ryan died late that afternoon. Steve became a consoling source of details on Patrick and translations of German poetry after Ryan's passing. I owe much of the accuracy of Patrick's life and death in Berlin to Steve.

Patrick's piano teachers, Ann Warde and Deborah Beers, were devoted and stalwart guides to his musical achievements. They held my descriptions of his performances to their same high standards and made my recollections sound knowledgeable. Ann guided Patrick in his voracious appetite for repertoire when he was six years old and then guided me while I was writing this book. She helped me understand why that appetite may have isolated him from others with lesser cravings. Her best advice about teaching bright, young children: Make the learning fun. Make children feel good about themselves. The brilliance will always be there. Make sure the joy is there as well. And she did.

Ann was the first to see Patrick's potential for chamber music and found a coach at the University of Connecticut. Amanda Crane guided Patrick's "Wildwood Trio" to first place in the junior division of the Hartford Camerata Ensemble Young Artist Chamber Music Competition in 1992. Patrick was nine years old. Ann also supplemented Pat's musical education with theory lessons from Kim Bova, who prepared him for the rigor of the Longy School of Music.

Deborah made sure my writing was on par with her superb memory and expertise. She wrote long emails correcting my amateur descriptions of Pat's Schumann concerto at Longy and his Mendelssohn trio at Tanglewood. She made his art glisten high above his turmoil, as it should. Seventeen years after his death, we both lost sleep at night remembering how well he played.

Ann and Deborah made me realize the extent of Pat's accomplishments and the magnitude of his loss. They understood his musical language, which I did not speak. They composed pieces and performed in his honor in the 2015 concert "Playing for

Patrick" at Pomfret School, along with teachers Howard Frazin, Kathleen Stephenson Sadoff, and Margreet Francis. Kathleen persuaded Patrick to attend the Boston University Tanglewood Institute and prepared him for his successful audition. Margreet guided him through the Beethoven, Schumann, and Prokofiev that Patrick played on the Tanglewood Institute stage. She made his high school summers a creative peak in his life. I owe them all more than my appreciation. I owe them a strong promotion for their ability to draw out Patrick's reticent genius without more pressure than he could handle and then to compose and perform music in the wake of his suicide. The CD of their performances at the "Playing for Patrick" concert can be found at:

"Playing   for   Patrick,"   open.spotify.com/album/3c8rNbiRp2meWkuYXLYL1d.

More recent versions of their compositions can be found at:

Deborah   Yardley   Beers,   "Through   Tears   and Beyond":   www.deborahyardleybeers.com/compositions/throughTearsAndBeyond.html.

Howard Frazin, "Rondo": www.howardfrazin.com/music/chamber-music/rondo-for-clarinet-bassoon-and-piano/.

Ann Warde, "For Hands Vier Hände": zsonics.org/?page_id=801.

Information on **Kathleen Stephenson Sadoff** can be found at: www.facebook.com/kathleen.sadoff/about.

The same deep appreciation goes to the many fine teachers at the Boston University Tanglewood Institute, chiefly among them, **Maria Clodes Jaguaribe** (1928-2015), former Director of the Young Artists Piano Program, who loved Patrick and coached him to masterful solo performances. Patrick's Tanglewood performance of the first movement of the Mendelssohn Piano Trio in C Minor, op. 66 described in the chapter "Who Was He?" is available on his CD, "Patrick Wood: Piano Solo and Trio" at:

"Patrick Wood: Piano Solo and Trio": open.spotify.com/artist/2xuajWcJzX2h2vSk3GiyeI.

Neal Larrabee, a highly acclaimed pianist and Chopin expert, taught Patrick briefly during high school. He kindly understood when Patrick had to withdraw from lessons because of increasing pressure from school and worsening depression.

George Barth, professor emeritus of piano at Stanford, guided Patrick through his first Stanford recital in 2001, performing the fourth of Alexander Scriabin's Eight Études, op. 42. He knew Patrick was capable of high-level music and wisely encouraged him to play fearlessly with less emphasis on control. Information can be found at:

George Barth: music.stanford.edu/people/george-barth.

Bob, Colin, Libby, and I came to know Pat's Stanford friends through Sheena Chandran Ranade, who organized the Stanford memorial a month after Pat died in 2006. Sheena, Ryan Sands, Ankur Dalal, Heidrun Belzner, Lauren Schneider, Christian Krüger, Andrew Tompkins, Joe Dröge, Tibor Wolf, and Tobias Bader guided us through Stanford dormitories, clubs, museums, restaurants, parks, workplaces, and apartments from Germany to California. They adopted us as if we were the reincarnation of Patrick himself.

Andrew Nielsen, Pat's roommate from Stanford, wrote the song "Twenty-Three" with help from the American Foundation for Suicide Prevention and performed it throughout England and the States. He recorded a podcast with me while I was writing *Back from Suicide*. We shared Pat stories and the struggle to understand suicide through writing. It can be found at podcast.mclars.com, episode 31.

Mike Love was the first to collect Pat memories at patrickwood.blogspot.com/, many of which I used throughout *Back from Suicide*. I owe him for helping me in the depth of his own sadness.

My vet and neighbor Gene White, Director of Tufts Veterinary Field Service, patiently explained the euthanasia process described in the chapter "Other Deaths." He saved my horses many times and gave them a good death when he couldn't save them anymore.

Huge editorial relief was provided by dear friend Mike Pastore, founder of Zorba Editing, who shaped the initial jumble. Mike and his partner Ann came to my rescue by creating the ebook versions of *Back from Suicide*. I owe them for their constant guidance and their technological prowess. More information on Zorba Editing can be found at:

https://ZorbaEditing.com

Shirley Rapose, Marge Mosher, and Thelma Barker, colleagues at Rectory School, were pressed into proofreading. My English department head, Ruth Healy, nurtured me after Pat's death and throughout the manuscript. She read with a sharp pencil and a soft heart. Question marks in the margins by my aunt, Beverly Rimer, resulted in greater clarification. She gave me courage when she read it three times and called it a work of art.

My cousin and editor Fair Alice McCormick thrilled with me in the family history discoveries of early drafts—the ancestor who owned the Flatiron property and another who stole $4 million from his father's bank. But most editors wanted more on Patrick. Kenneth Wapner was the first to nudge me in that direction. I could not have progressed from unrelated anecdotes to story without him. My friend Susie Merry Sapp beat me over the head with the same concept. Debbie Danielpour Chapel nudged harder by schooling me on the "spine" of a story and connecting the jangling thoughts after suicide. She had a jeweler's eye and made me shine dull writing. My cousin Polly Rimer Duke dealt the final death blow to many family wanderings. She made me face the daunting question of why Patrick was depressed and make it central to the book. Former student Maddy Hutchins pounded that same perspective into my thick skull with several patient readings. Her Yale divinity background spurred the "Resurrection" chapter. My friend and editor Margie Huoppi knew how to brighten everything from em dashes to details. Her questions brought out a more complete story. Mary Murtha knew Patrick and Libby in high school and gave me insight into their relationship and their development as gay children. Long-time teacher and friend Jamie Johnson added her laser-beam vision and soft red pencil to tutor me in the fine art of copy editing. A sad footnote is that while she was editing, one of her high school students killed himself. She had to put down the manuscript for fear she would cry all over it. He was the second suicide from her school that year. Rona Hu added perspective on treating depression, LGBT patients, and Patrick himself at Stanford Hospital. I owe many hours of Zoom interviews and therapy to her detailed discussions of gay issues, suicide, and the dangers of perfectionism.

Margaret Diehl was the final overseer of everything from content to commas. Her own survival through the death of her fourteen-year-old brother, her father's suicide, and her depression made her an expert on grief. Her encouragement gave me confidence to handle the weaknesses in the story—the lack of emphasis on suicide in my family, for example. She was a therapist as well as an editor, revealing the layers of Pat's death.

Information on **Margaret Diehl** can be found at: www.reedsy.com/freelancers/margaret-d.

Louise Stahl proofread with an eagle eye, spotting italicized commas "from across the room," as one editor put it. Beyond her gentle corrections and explanations, she added a stunning endorsement for a first-time author

> This manuscript has left me speechless.... I found myself having trouble putting it down, pulling myself away from it, and when I did, I would have to take a moment to regain my bearings. I can honestly say that this is by far the best, the most professionally written, manuscript I have had.

Information on **Louise Stahl** can be found at: www.reedsy.com/louise-stahl.

When the writing was over and it was time to publish, friend Nora Robbins made my clunky, "horsey" cover come alive. She made it sing with her musical staffs and golden colors.

The support of many made this book happen, but the most surprising was a huge donation out of the blue by friends and Patrick admirers John and Jane Muir. They knew the sadness of dwelling on loss along with the financial investment that a book requires. They were the catalyst for completing Pat's story.

Devoted beta readers waved me toward the finish line. They include Ryan Wirtz, Jennifer Wirtz Bennett (Ryan's sister), Judith Hennessey (Ryan's mother), Brad Davis, Bibi Gaston, Stephen Pryce, Joe Dröge, Ann Warde, Margaret Smolack, Karen Kramer, and Lauren Schneider.

Crucial insights into depression and suicide were provided by authors who brought clarity to a barely understandable subject. They include: Kay Redfield Jamison (*Night Falls Fast: Understanding Suicide, An Unquiet Mind: A Memoir of Moods and Madness*, and *Touched with Fire: Manic-Depressive Illness and the Artistic Temperament*); Andrew Solomon (*The Noonday Demon: An Atlas of Depression*); William Styron (*Darkness Visible: A Memoir of Madness*); Leroy Aarons (*Prayers for Bobby: A Mother's Coming to Terms with the Suicide of Her Gay Son*); Derek Humphry (*Final Exit: The Practicalities of Self-Deliverance and Assisted Suicide for the Dying*); David Vann (*Legend of a Suicide*); Thomas Joiner (*Why People Die by Suicide*); Jesse Bering (*Suicidal: Why We Kill Ourselves*); Joan Wickersham (*The Suicide Index: Putting My Father's Death in Order*); Dorothy Tennov (*Love and Limerence: The Experience of Being in Love*); Jennifer Michael Hecht (*Stay: A History of Suicide and the Philosophies Against It*); Donald Antrim (*One Friday in April: A Story of Suicide and Survival*); Kate Fagan (*What Made Maddy Run: The Secret Struggles and Tragic Death of an All-American Teen*); Rory O'Connor (*When It Is Darkest: Why People Die by Suicide and What We Can Do to Prevent It*); Jennifer Ashton (*Life after Suicide: Finding Courage, Comfort & Community after Unthinkable Loss*); Carla Fine (*No Time to Say Goodbye: Surviving the Suicide of a Loved One*); Sherwin B. Nuland (*How We Die: Reflections on Life's Final Chapter*); Danielle Steel (*His Bright Light: The Story of Nick Traina*); and Clancy Martin (*How Not to Kill Yourself: A Portrait of the Suicidal Mind*).

The suicideanonymous.net website offered inside perspective on the lure of suicide as a misguided solution. Peter Kramer's *Against Depression* gave me scientific explanations of depression a year after Patrick died when I needed them most. He made me realize that depression can kill like a terminal disease. My therapist, Sandra Rigazio-DiGilio, helped me understand Pat's decision to die and adjust to life without him. She lifted the guilt when she stressed the point that I should not have known he was going to kill himself.

My husband Bob was the first, last, and most patient editor. His support through all phases—from Patrick's death, to life without him, and to the hours hidden away, writing his story—kept me intact. My surviving children, Colin and Libby, were constant cheerleaders. They listened patiently to my Patrick wanderings. Colin added his memories of Pat's apartment in Berlin, including the cigarette lighters to light the charcoal and the comforter where Pat's body had lain. His support through all the Pat trips, the reminiscing, and the silences about what went wrong steadied my confusion. He showed me that even if we couldn't know the truth, we would not know it together, and that would keep us going. Years after Pat died, Colin said, "I miss Pat every day, especially having two little girls, knowing how much they would've loved him and how much he would've loved being an uncle. From a professional perspective, working in technology, I think about how Pat would appreciate the tools we take for granted to stay connected like Facebook and Instagram. I wish he were still here to experience it all."

Libby guided the final editing with her therapist/artist eye. No vague pronoun or blurry description escaped her. She was my teammate and collaborator in understanding Patrick's suicide. Most importantly, she brought a clear eye to my vagaries of gay life. She helped me see Patrick more deeply through her gay twin lens.

By Andrew Nielsen (MC Lars), 2021.

Illustrations

Most of the photographs in *Back from Suicide* are from family collections. Some deserve special mention.

Page

xxxvi. Pat's window, Berlin, 2006, by Libby Wood.

12. The death notice, by Libby Wood.

19. Berlin postcard, Libby's reflection, 2006, by Libby Wood.

20. Libby, Berlin airport, a week after Pat's death, 2006, by Libby Wood.

25. Pat's profile on gayromeo.com, by Tobias Bader.

48. Libby, Pat's apartment, Berlin, 2006, by Libby Wood.

49. Colin, Potzdamer Platz, Berlin, 2006, by Libby Wood.

50. Libby, Stanford Center memorial, Ryan and Karen to the left, Berlin, 2006. Used by permission from the Bing Overseas Studies Program in Berlin, Stanford University.

51. Bob, Stanford Center memorial, Berlin, 2006. Used by permission from the Bing Overseas Studies Program in Berlin, Stanford University.

85. Below: Patrick and Libby, two years old, the *Norwich Bulletin*, 1985, by Randy Flaum. Used by permission from the *Norwich Bulletin*.

89. Libby and Patrick, sailing with my father and Anne off the coast of California near Santa Monica, early 2000s, by Anne Rimer.

91. A *Norwich Bulletin* article during Pat's senior year in high school, which talked of his awards, his "knack" for the piano, and his dreams of travel and independence, 2001, by Megan Bard. Used by permission from the *Norwich Bulletin*.

92. Above: My father, David Rimer, and Pat, Hotel Adlon, Berlin, 2004, by Anne Rimer.

92. Below: Pat, Neuschwanstein Castle, Schwangau, Germany, 2004, by Ryan Wirtz.

93. Above: Pat at Siemens when he was featured in a Stanford Overseas Studies Program newsletter, 2005, by Cathrin Bach of PKonzept und Bild/Fotografenbüro Berlin, Germany for the "Bing Overseas Studies at Stanford University Newsletter," Vol. 4 No. 2 Fall/Winter 2005-06. Used by permission from the Bing Overseas Studies Program in Berlin, Stanford University.

93. Below: Ryan and Patrick, Krupp Internship luncheon, Essen, Germany, 2004, by Lauren Schneider.

94. Pat's grave. Libby's shadow, Pomfret, Connecticut, 2006, by Libby Wood.

105. Bob, Stanford memorial, Palo Alto, California, 2006, by Libby Wood.

119. Patrick's balcony, second floor, Berlin, 2006, by Libby Wood.

120. Pat and my father, David Rimer, Stanford graduation, 2005, by Libby Wood.

128. "Recent grad dies in Berlin," front-page article in the *Stanford Daily* a few days after Pat's death, 2006, by Courtney Weaver, the *Stanford Daily*, February 8, 2006, ©2019 the *Stanford Daily*, Inc. All rights reserved. Reprinted with permission.

141. Colin, day one, Berlin, 2006, by Libby Wood.

162. Depression poster, Logan Airport on the way to Berlin, 2007. The poster was photographed by the author and lists supporting organizations including www.depressionisreal.org, the American Psychiatric Foundation, the Depression and Bipolar Support Alliance, the League of United Latin American Citizens, Mental Health America, the National Alliance on Mental Illness, the National Medical Association, and the National Urban League.

182. Patrick, Stanford graduation, 2005, by Myles Morrison.

196. Pat, Stanford, 2002, by Sheena Chandran Renade.

212. Pat with Shrek, Worldcon (comic book convention), San Francisco, 2005, by Ryan Sands.

231. Death and grief, 2006, by Libby Wood.

250. The author with Klaus Wowereit, the mayor of Berlin, Gay Pride Parade, 2009, by Tibor Wolf.

257. Above: Tibor and Pat, by Joe Dröge.

257. Below: Joe, Pat, and Tibor, Gay Pride Parade, Berlin, 2005, by Joe Dröge.

261. Patrick, while interning as a programmer at BMW, Munich, 2004, by Klaus Bogenberger.

295. Berlinale bear with Patrick's grave, 2006, by Libby Wood.

296. Colin in Antoinette Eno Wood's mausoleum with my mother, Harriet, and their husbands' urns behind him, Simsbury Cemetery, 2013, by Libby Wood.

303. White rose, Patrick's grave, 2006, by Libby Wood.

312. "Libby with Hole," Stanford memorial, 2006, by Libby Wood.

Notes

1. Excerpts from *Night* by Elie Wiesel, translated by Stella Rodway. Copyright 1960 by MacGibbon & Kee, pages 2-3. Copyright renewed 1988 by The Collins Publishing Group. Reprinted by permission of Hill and Wang, a division of Farrar, Straus and Giroux. All Rights Reserved.

2. Johann Wolfgang von Goethe, *The Sorrows of Young Werther*, trans. Burton Pike (New York: Random House, 2004), 52, 59.

3. The poster was issued by the Berlin city cleaning authority (Berliner Stadtreinigung) to encourage people to put their litter in bins. Trans. Ryan Wirtz and Stephen Pryce, 2019.

4. "Abroad: The Newsletter of the Bing Overseas Studies Program," Bing Overseas Studies at Stanford University, Vol. 4 No. 2 Fall/Winter 2005-06.

5. Klaus Bogenberger, "Zeugnis Patrick Wood," September 17, 2004 in which Dr. Bogenberger, Pat's supervisor at the "Traffic and Science" Department of BMW in Munich, evaluated Pat's performance as a programmer.

6. Kurt Tucholsky (aka Kaspar Hauser), "There Is No Untrodden Snow," trans. Stephen Pryce, 2006, *The World Stage* (Berlin, Rowohlt Publisher), Vol. 14, April 7, 1931, 515.

7. Friedrich Rückert, "I am Lost to the World," translation copyright © by Emily Ezust, from the LiederNet Archive, www.lieder.net.

8. Johann Wolfgang von Goethe, *The Sorrows of Young Werther*, trans. Burton Pike (New York: Random House, 2004), 122.

9. Patrick Wood, email to the author, January 26, 2006.

10. Karen Kramer, letter to Robert Wood and family, February 10, 2006.

11. *Visit of George W. Bush President of the United States of America* (Berlin, US Embassy, 2002), 1-2.

12. Kurt Tucholsky (aka Kaspar Hauser), "There Is No Untrodden Snow," trans. Stephen Pryce, 2006, *The World Stage* (Berlin, Rowohlt Publisher), Vol. 14, April 7, 1931, 515.

13. Johann Wolfgang von Goethe, *The Sorrows of Young Werther*, trans. Burton Pike (New York: Random House, 2004), 121.

14. Karen Kramer, "For Patrick," memorial service at Stanford-in-Berlin, February 15, 2006.

15. "Haus Cramer, Dahlem, Berlin, Germany Hermann Muthesius (1861–1927)," findingaids.library.columbia.edu/ead/nnc-a/ldpd_6909165, accessed April 18, 2024.

16. Karen Kramer, "For Patrick," memorial service at Stanford-in-Berlin, February 15, 2006.

17. Ryan Wirtz, "The Essential Patrick," memorial service at Stanford-in-Berlin, February 15, 2006.

18. Ibid.

19. Tobias Bader, "Patrick Wood Memorial, a place for your thoughts, photos, stories, or memories of Pat," March 6, 2006, patrickwood.blogspot.com/2006/, accessed December 7, 2020.

20. Sandra Ahola, "Patrick Wood, Current Performance," June 25, 1991.

21. Ann Warde, CD notes, *Patrick David Wood: Piano Solo and Trio*, remastered by Mark Thayer, Signature Sounds, 2011.

22. Ibid.

23. Ibid.

24. Deborah Beers, email to the author, May 3, 2019.

25. Ibid., April 27, 2019.

26. Patrick Wood, email to unknown recipient, January 17, 2003.

27. Howard Frazin, "Longy School of Music Preparatory Studies Theory Evaluation Form," June 5, 1997.

28. Howard Frazin, email to the author, March 14, 2022.

29. Deborah Beers, "Longy School of Music Student Progress Report," January 25, 1997, and "Longy School of Music Preparatory Studies Division Student Performance Evaluation Form," for the school year 1996-1997.

30. Mitch Pinkowski, "Pomfret School Progress Report," Spring 2001.

31. Edward J. Kelley, "Pomfret School Progress Report," Spring 2001.

32. Patrick David Wood, "An Analysis of Beethoven's Piano Sonata in C, op. 2, no. 3 (First Movement)," June 1, 2000.

33. Margreet Francis, "The Hartt School Community Division Semester Progress Report," Fall 2000.

34. Phillip Falk, CD notes, *Patrick David Wood: Piano Solo and Trio*, remastered by Mark Thayer, Signature Sounds, 2011.

35. Patrick David Wood, "Being Shy," October 18, 1999.

36. "What Hope for Dead Loved Ones?" copyright owned by the Watch Tower Bible and Tract Society of Pennsylvania, published by Jehovah's Witnesses, 1987, 3.

37. Brad Davis, "For Patrick," Clark Chapel, Pomfret School, February 20, 2006.

38. Kurt Tucholsky (aka Kaspar Hauser), "There Is No Untrodden Snow," trans. Stephen Pryce, 2006, *The World Stage* (Berlin, Rowohlt Publisher), Vol. 14, April 7, 1931, 515.

39. William Shakespeare, *Romeo and Juliet*, The Temple Shakespeare, which states, "by the kind permission of Messrs. Macmillan & Co. and W. Aldis Wright, Esq., the text here used is that of the 'Cambridge' Edition. First Edition of this issue of *Romeo and Juliet* printed 1896. Reprinted 1896; 1897; 1898; 1899; 1899; 1900; 1901;

1902; 1902; 1903; 1904; 1904; 1905; 1906; 1907; 1908; 1909; 1909; 1910; 1912; 1914," I:i, lines 146-147.

40. Andrew Nielsen, "Words for Pat's service," email to Sheena Chandran Renade, March 18, 2006.

41. Jerome Murphy, email to the author, March 2, 2020.

42. Ibid., March 3, 2020.

43. Ibid., March 2, 2020.

44. Ibid., March 4, 2020.

45. Ibid.

46. Ibid., March 2, 2020.

47. Ibid., March 4, 2020.

48. Ibid., March 4 and 10, 2020.

49. Ibid., March 2, 2020.

50. Jerry Cain, "Recommendation for Patrick Wood," February 18, 2004.

51. Patrick Wood, email to unknown recipient, January 17, 2003.

52. Ibid.

53. Unknown sender, "My Favorite Things about Pat," email to Patrick Wood, January 17, 2003.

54. William Shakespeare, *Romeo and Juliet*, The Temple Shakespeare, which states, "by the kind permission of Messrs. Macmillan & Co. and W. Aldis Wright, Esq., the text here used is that of the 'Cambridge' Edition. First Edition of this issue of *Romeo and Juliet* printed 1896. Reprinted 1896; 1897; 1898; 1899; 1899; 1900; 1901; 1902; 1902; 1903; 1904; 1904; 1905; 1906; 1907; 1908; 1909; 1909; 1910; 1912; 1914," III:v, lines 55-56.

55. Wanda Sykes, thinkb4youspeak campaign, Gay, Lesbian and Straight Education Network, www.youtube.com/watch?v=sWS0GVOQPs0, accessed April 18, 2024.

56. Sara M_____, "It's Time to Tolerate Your Equals So Think Before You Speak," the *DiRectory*, published by Rectory School, Pomfret, Connecticut, May 31, 2009.

57. Gary Smith, "Gareth Thomas," *Sports Illustrated*, May 3, 2010, 54-55.

58. Nadette De Visser, "15-Year-Old Amanda Todd's Alleged Sextortionist on Trial at Last," *Daily Beast*, published February 16, 2017, updated April 11, 2017, www.thedailybeast.com/15-year-old-amanda-todds-alleged-sextortionist-on-trial-at-last, accessed April 18, 2024.

59. Amanda Todd, "My Story: Struggling, Bullying, Suicide, Self Harm," September 7, 2012, www.youtube.com/watch?v=vOHXGNx-E7E, accessed April 18, 2024.

60. Jason Yingqing Zhao, "Amanda Todd and Newtown: What Do They Have in Common?" The *DiRectory*, published by Rectory School, Pomfret, Connecticut, March 1, 2013.

61. Nadette De Visser, "15-Year-Old Amanda Todd's Alleged Sextortionist on Trial at Last," *Daily Beast*, April 11, 2017, www.thedailybeast.com/15-year-old-amanda-todds-alleged-sextortionist-on-trial-at-last, accessed April 18, 2024.

62. Courtney Weaver, "Recent grad dies in Berlin," from the *Stanford Daily*, February 8, 2006, article by Courtney Weaver. ©2019 the Stanford Daily, Inc. All rights reserved. Reprinted with permission.

63. Friedrich Rückert, "I am Lost to the World," Translation copyright © by Emily Ezust, from the LiederNet Archive—www.lieder.net/in conjunction with Stephen Pryce.

64. Kay Redfield Jamison, *Night Falls Fast: Understanding Suicide* (New York: Vintage Books, A Division of Random House, Inc., 1999), 5.

65. Ibid., 181.

66. Patrick Wood, "Personal Statement for the Krupp Internship Program for Stanford Students in Germany," January 6, 2004.

67. Kay Redfield Jamison, *Night Falls Fast: Understanding Suicide* (New York: Vintage Books, A Division of Random House, Inc., 1999), 171.

68. Peter D. Kramer, *Against Depression* (New York, NY: Penguin Books, 2005), 150.

69. Ibid., 156-157.

70. Andrew Solomon, *The Noonday Demon: An Atlas of Depression* (New York, NY: Scribner, 2001), 442-443.

71. Peter D. Kramer, *Against Depression* (New York, NY: Penguin Books, 2005), 67.

72. Ibid., 53.

73. Ibid., 54.

74. Ibid., 55-56.

75. Ibid., 61-62.

76. Ibid., 118.

77. Ibid., 119.

78. Ibid., 152.

79. "Suicide Rising Across the US," CDC Vital Signs, www.cdc.gov/vitalsigns/pdf/vs-0618-suicide-H.pdf, June 7, 2018, accessed November 13, 2019.

80. Peter D. Kramer, *Against Depression* (New York, NY: Penguin Books, 2005), 142-143.

81. Kurt Tucholsky (aka Kaspar Hauser), "There Is No Untrodden Snow," trans. Stephen Pryce, 2006, *The World Stage* (Berlin, Rowohlt Publisher) Vol. 14, April 7, 1931, 515.

82. Andreas Sternweiler in cooperation with Karl-Heinz Steinle (translated by Maika Leffers, William Peacock, Keith Green, and Patrick Lanagan), *Self-Confidence and Persistence: Two Hundred Years of History: Schwules Museum* (Berlin, Germany: published by the Schwules Museum), 2004, 57.

83. Ibid., 107.

84. Ibid., 108.

85. Ibid., 117.

86. Ibid., 124.

87. Guenther Siegl, email to the author, December 24, 2006.

88. Peter D. Kramer, *Against Depression* (New York, NY: Penguin Books, 2005), 61.

89. Lisette Rimer, "Op-ed: An open letter to President Hennessy," the *Stanford Daily*, www.april16archive.org/items/show/514, May 14, 2007, accessed July 3, 2020.

90. Comments on Lisette Rimer, "Op-ed: An open letter to President Hennessy," the *Stanford Daily*, www.april16archive.org/items/show/514, May 14, 2007, accessed July 3, 2020.

91. Lisette Rimer, "Op-ed: An open letter to President Hennessy," the *Stanford Daily*, www.april16archive.org/items/show/514, May 14, 2007, accessed July 3, 2020.

92. Andrew Nielsen (MC Lars), vocal performance of "Twenty-Three," *This Gigantic Robot Kills*, by MC Lars, Amoeba Records, San Francisco, CA, March 12, 2009 (recorded by Horris Records, Redondo Beach, CA, The Oglio Entertainment Group, Inc. 2009), compact disk.

93. Mike Love, "Patrick Wood Memorial: a place for your thoughts, photos, stories, or memories of Pat," January 30, 2007, patrickwood.blogspot.com/2007/, accessed April 16, 2020.

94. Patrick Wood, email to the author, July 29, 2004.

95. Peter D. Kramer, *Against Depression* (New York, NY: Penguin Books, 2005), 25.

96. Patrick Wood, email to the author, May 22, 2005.

97. Frank Newport, "In U.S., Estimate of LGBT Population Rises to 4.5%," Gallup News, May 22, 2018. news.gallup.com/poll/234863/estimate-lgbt-population-rises.aspx, accessed April 18, 2024.

98. Dorothy Tennov, *Love and Limerence: The Experience of Being in Love* (Lanham, MD: Scarborough House, 1979, 1999. All rights reserved.), 41. I owe the discovery of Tennov to Jesse Bering, who footnoted her work in *Suicidal: Why We Kill Ourselves* (Chicago, IL: The University of Chicago Press, 2018) and who suffered from limerence to the point of suicidal thoughts.

99. Patrick Wood, email to the author, February 22, 2005.

100. Patrick Wood, email to the author, March 3, 2005.

101. Patrick Wood, emails to the author, February 22, 2005 and April 10, 2005.

102. Ibid.

103. Patrick Wood, email to the author, April 12, 2005.

104. Patrick Wood, email to the author, May 22, 2005.

105. The author, email to Patrick Wood, May 23, 2005.

106. Patrick Wood, email to the author, December 12, 2005.

107. Guenther Siegl, email to the author, December 24, 2006.

108. "Suicide Rising Across the US More than a Mental Health Concern," Centers for Disease Control and Prevention, June 7, 2018, stacks.cdc.gov/view/cdc/55609, accessed April 18, 2024.

109. "20 Leading Causes of Death, United States 2019, All Races, Both Sexes," National Center for Injury Prevention and Control, Centers for Disease Control and Prevention. Data Source: National Center for Health Statistics (NCHS), National Vital Statistics System.

110. Asha Z. Ivey-Stephenson, PhD; Zewditu Demissie, PhD; Alexander E. Crosby, MD; Deborah M. Stone, ScD; Elizabeth Gaylor, MPH; Natalie Wilkins, PhD; Richard Lowry, MD; Margaret Brown, DrPH, "Table 3. Percentage of high school students who seriously considered attempting suicide, had made a suicide plan, had attempted suicide, or had made a suicide attempt requiring medical treatment during the 12 months before the survey, by sex, sexual identity, and sex of sexual contacts—Youth Risk Behavior Survey, United States, 2019," "Suicidal Ideation and Behaviors Among High School Students—Youth Risk Behavior Survey, United States, 2019," Centers for Disease Control and Prevention, Morbidity and Mortality Weekly Report (MMWR) Supplement, Vol. 69. No. 1, August 21, 2020, 51.

111. C. W. Drapeau & J. L. McIntosh, "U.S.A. Suicide: 2019 Official final data," Washington, D.C.: American Association of Suicidology, December 23, 2020, downloaded from www.suicidology.org, accessed August 18, 2021.

112. Simon Parry, "Taking the easy way out?" *South China Morning Post*, January 9, 2005, www.scmp.com/article/484827/taking-easy-way-out, accessed May 28, 2019.

113. Ibid.

114. Ibid.

115. *Merriam-Webster*, www.merriam-webster.com/dictionary/commit, accessed November 26, 2019.

116. "Carbon Monoxide Poisoning: Frequently Asked Questions," Centers for Disease Control and Prevention, www.cdc.gov/co/faqs.htm, March 21, 2018, accessed November 29, 2019.

117. web.archive.org/web/20181122142800/https:/archive. ashspace.org/asm_guide/, 2010, used by permission as stated on the website, "ashspace is proud to host the OFFICIAL "alt.suicide. methods Reference—A Practical Guide to Suicide" as constructed by its various editors. All other sites and hostings are mere reflections. This document is copyright 2010 the sources quoted and its editors, and its new 2010 version is adopted as its working form. If you are interested in updating or correcting this guide, please contact the alt.suicide.method REF editors at asm.ref.editor@gmail. com. If you want to reproduce this document feel free to do so as long as its current form is reproduced and this copyright notice is left intact upon it. Thank you for your support and your cooperation," accessed May 3, 2020.

118. Ibid.

119. "Carbon Monoxide Poisoning: Frequently Asked Questions," Centers for Disease Control and Prevention, www.cdc.gov/co/faqs.htm, March 21, 2018, accessed May 28, 2019.

120. Derek Humphry, *Final Exit: The Practicalities of Self-Deliverance and Assisted Suicide for the Dying* (New York, NY: Dell Publishing, a division of Random House, Inc., 1991, 1996, 2002), front cover, XV, and 45. Digital Edition, 2011, location 141 of 3210.

121. Sherwin B. Nuland, *How We Die: Reflections on Life's Final Chapter* (New York: Vintage Books A Division of Random House, Inc., 1993), 151-152.

122. Dante Alighieri, *The Divine Comedy: The Inferno, The Purgatorio, and The Paradiso*, trans. John Ciardi (New York, NY: New American Library, a division of Penguin Group [USA], *The Inferno* copyright © John Ciardi, 1954, *The Purgatorio* copyright © John Ciardi, 1957, 1959, 1960, 1961, *The Paradiso* copyright © John Ciardi, 1961, 1965, 1967, 1970), Canto XIV (*The Inferno*), 112.

123. Alan L. Berman, "Estimating the Population of Survivors of Suicide: Seeking an Evidence Base," Suicide and Life-Threatening Behavior 41(1) February 2011, 110-116.

124. Julie Cerel, PhD; Myfanwy Maple, PhD; Judy van de Venne, PhD; Melinda Moore, PhD; Chris Flaherty, PhD; and Margaret Brown, MPH, "Exposure to Suicide in the Community: Prevalence and Correlates in One U.S. State," Public Health Reports, Jan-Feb 2016, v. 131(1), 100–107. www.ncbi.nlm.nih.gov/pmc/articles/PMC4716477/, accessed February 19, 2022.

125. "Release of *13 Reasons Why* Associated with Increase in Youth Suicide Rates NIH-Supported Study Highlights the Importance of Responsible Portrayal of Suicide by the Media," National Institute of Mental Health, April 29, 2019. www.nimh.nih.gov/news/science-news/2019/release-of-13-reasons-why-associated-with-increase-in-youth-suicide-rates, accessed November 10, 2020.

126. Steve Jobs, "'You've got to find what you love,' Jobs says," *Stanford News*, June 14, 2005, news.stanford.edu/2005/06/12/youve-got-find-love-jobs-says/, accessed October 30, 2021.

127. Gillian Brassil, "Where Do Stanford Students Go if They've Attempted Suicide? Between One and Three Students Are Admitted to Stanford Hospital's High-Security Inpatient Psychiatric Ward Each Week," the *Stanford Daily*, April 5, 2019, www.stanforddaily.com/2019/04/05/where-do-stanford-students-go-if-theyve-attempted-suicide/, accessed November 24, 2020.

128. Rona Hu, in discussion with the author, August 19, 2020; October 20, 2020; November 17, 2020; and February 9, 2021.

129. Rona Hu, "Health in High Ability Students Webinar," Center for Excellence in Education, November 16, 2017, www.youtube.com/watch?v=D3mAvT5hLG4, accessed November 18, 2020.

130. "Top 100 Lowest Acceptance Rates," *US News & World Report*, www.usnews.com/best-colleges/rankings/lowest-acceptance-rate, accessed May 5, 2021.

131. Tracie White, "Intense magnetic stimulation could reduce severe depression, new study shows," SCOPE, published

by Stanford Medicine, February 14, 2018. scopeblog.stanford.
edu/2018/02/14/intense-magnetic-stimulation-could-reduce-se-
vere-depression-new-study-shows/, accessed December 5, 2020.

132. German Resistance Memorial, n.d., www.berlinexperi-
ences.com/featured_experiences/visit-the-german-resistance-mu-
seum/, accessed July 20, 2015.

133. Leroy Aarons, *Prayers for Bobby: A Mother's Coming to Terms
with the Suicide of Her Gay Son* (New York, NY: HarperCollins,
1995), 206.

134. Antoinette Goetz Rimer to Florence Eno Graves, August
22, 1951.

135. Freeman Wate Bowley, "West Point Has Grown," *Assembly* Vol. II, No. 4 (Newburgh, NY: Association of Graduates,
United States Military Academy, January 1944), 10.

136. Mary Laveratt, "Parker Gallery," Parker Playhouse, February 25, 1974, 36.

137. Schubert Jonas, "Kitty Logan's Watercolors Project Spirit
of Time, Life," *Fort Lauderdale News*, March 17, 1974. © 1974 *Fort
Lauderdale News*. All rights reserved. Distributed by Tribune Content Agency, LLC.

138. Marie Graves Bullock to Antoinette Goetz Logan, 1979.

139. Scripture taken from the King James Study Bible® Copy-
right© 1988 by Thomas Nelson. Used by permission. All rights
reserved. John 10:18 KJV.

140. Ibid., John 19:26-28 KJV.

141. Patrick Wood, "Eighth Grader," October 1, 2000.

142. Patrick Wood, "Being Shy," October 18, 1999.

143. William Penn, "We give back to you, O God, those whom
you gave to us," *The Communion of Saints: Prayers of the Famous*, Hor-
ton Davies, ed. (Grand Rapids, MI: Wm. B. Eerdmans, 1990), 97.

144. "The Horizon," adapted from "What is Dying?" which
has been attributed to several authors, most notably Henry van
Dyke (1852-1933) and Luther F. Beecher (1819-1903). Beecher is
credited in the *Northwestern Christian Advocate*, July 13, 1904, page 14
and is probably the reason "The Horizon" was preferred by many

in Harriet's family. He was a cousin of Harriet Beecher Stowe whose son, Charles Edward Stowe, performed the marriage ceremony for my great-grandmother Flo-Flo and her husband William Léon Graves in Simsbury in 1899. He also baptized Grandmère in Paris in 1900. "The Horizon" was read at the funerals for Flo-Flo, her daughter Grandmère, and her descendants, my mother, her sister Harriet, and Harriet's daughter Heather Holly.

145. Johann Wolfgang von Goethe, *The Sorrows of Young Werther*, trans. Burton Pike (New York: Random House, 2004), 147.

146. Ibid., 121.

147. Kay Redfield Jamison, *Night Falls Fast: Understanding Suicide* (New York: Vintage Books A Division of Random House, Inc, 1999), 200.

148. Charles Stoddard, "Dedication of a Memorial Beech Tree for Patrick Wood," October 30, 2018.

149. Ibid.

Patrick Wood Scholars

Thousands of dollars from family and friends poured in after Patrick died in 2006. We asked that the money be given to Pomfret School, where Patrick had won a full-tuition, merit scholarship in 1997. The funds quickly reached $20,000, thanks in large part to a contribution from my father six months before he died. Pomfret School Development Director Geoff Liggett asked how we would like the money to be allocated. He knew students like Patrick could raise the level of a class, and he wanted to attract more of them. Bob suggested a scholarship in Pat's name, and Geoff quickly agreed. We all felt strongly that hard-working students should be recognized, and that was because of Patrick. All throughout his school years, he ran past the TV set to play the piano or read or do his homework. He was driven to learn everything, absorb everything, to climb untrodden snow.

Hannah Leo was the first winner in 2007. She went on to receive her medical degree at the University of California, Los Angeles and become a psychiatry resident at the University of California, San Francisco. In 2022, she received a fellowship in child and

Patrick D. Wood '01 Memorial Prize logo by Libby Wood

adolescent psychiatry at the New York Presbyterian/Weill Cornell Medical Center and then became a Columbia Public Psychiatry fellow to study public-sector health care. She has dedicated her life to the wellbeing of young people in crisis.

Every year since the scholarship began, Bob, Colin, Libby, and I have recognized one or two Wood Scholars entering Pomfret School. We have gone to their middle school graduations and praised their achievements. We have put a face on Pat's life and death so they can see what kind of family a suicide victim comes from, so they can see we are an ordinary family—a lucky family, actually, with two magnificent surviving children and two granddaughters.

At times it feels wrong. When I sit in school auditoriums waiting to present Pat's scholarship, I remember that we used to be in the audience of parents watching Patrick on stage accepting awards. Now we are the ones on stage giving awards to other families in the audience. But when we meet each Wood Scholar after the ceremony, we know it is the right thing to do. They are surprised and grateful. They are lost for words but smiling with humility while we take pictures and congratulate them, much like Pat used to do while we took pictures and congratulated him.

Twenty students have become Wood Scholars. They have learned about Patrick's musical talent, his brilliance, and his irreproachable character—qualities best described by former Pomfret resident Charles Stoddard, who felt a connection to Patrick even though he never met him. Charles and Patrick both spoke German and loved the *Sorrows of Young Werther*. That was reason enough for Charles to donate two European beech trees to Patrick's elementary and high schools in Pomfret. At the dedication near the chapel of Pomfret School, Charles' hands shook as he read from a short speech. He said the *Sorrows of Young Werther* is the story of unrequited love. But not only that, "it is the story of a man, who must die because he cannot endure the limitations of mankind."[148]

Like Werther, Patrick died because he could not endure the limitations of mankind. We were dedicating Pat's tree to celebrate the expanse of his life, the qualities beyond the accomplishments.

We were there to memorialize what Charles called Patrick's *überpersönlich*, a German word meaning "beyond the experience of a gifted and talented life."[149] We were there to celebrate his unrestrained heart, his boundless passion, and we were there to support those qualities in others.

Each year, thousands of dollars are awarded to students at Pomfret School on the basis of academics and character through Pat's scholarship. By purchasing *Back from Suicide*, you are supporting those qualities. All proceeds will be donated to the Patrick D. Wood '01 Memorial Scholarship at Pomfret School. Thank you for considering a review to support the book and grow the scholarship.

For more information, please visit: www.patrickwoodprize.org/

The author and Patrick, Tanglewood, Lenox, Massachusetts, 2001.

Marie Lisette Rimer grew up in Fort Lauderdale, Florida and gravitated to New England for a BA in sociology and an MA in secondary education at the University of Connecticut. She was a publicist in the Connecticut legislature and an award-winning English teacher at Rectory School in Pomfret, Connecticut. The joy of three children and country living with her husband Robert Wood were shattered by the suicide death of her youngest son, Patrick Wood. She began a search to learn why—at first through Patrick's life and then through the ravages of depression and her mother's similar death. *Back from Suicide* is the story of life after tragedy. It is the fall from grace and the search for respite through understanding.

www.lisetterimer.com